D0711866

A Great Big Adventure
on a
Good Little Boat

To Donald,
Silmaril 1067
Happy Sailing on a
Great Boat

A Great Big Adventure
on a
Good Little Boat

Linda Petrat

Linda Petrat

Published by FirstPersonPublications.com
liz@firstpersonpublications.com

Dedication:

To my parents Jessie and Bill Petrat, who inspired me by their courage and strength.

Acknowledgments.
My friends and family made my hard times survivable and my good times great. I'd also like to thank the many boaters and marina dock hands for their kindness, their big smiles, and enthusiastic welcomes. I want to thank my talented niece, Jessica Petrat, for the wonderful cover she created for my book. I am grateful for the diligent work and support of my editor Liz Coursen. She kept me on track.

Photo credits.
Front cover photos by Don Lafreniere.
Back cover photo by Jessie Petrat.

Table of Contents

Foreword

    This book started as just a log of my voyage on my little boat the *Summer Wind,* from Maine to Florida. I had moved to Florida and my boat was in New Hampshire. Simple: I needed to get her to Florida. I had contacted a boat hauler and I tried to buy a trailer. After much calling around without results, I gave up with these ideas and decided to sail my little boat to Florida. I had worked in Maine through the summer and by the middle of September my job was completed, so I was able to start preparing my boat for her astonishing trip.

    As with everything I've ever done in my life, I readied my boat and myself for this adventure with a huge passion. I believe that whatever you do, if you plan to do a great job (there can be no other way), it has to be done with a passion. The ancient philosopher Patanjali wrote:

A Great Big Adventure on a Good Little Boat

When you are inspired by some great purpose, some extraordinary project, all your thoughts break their bonds: Your mind transcends limitations; your consciousness expands in every direction. And you find yourself in a new, great, and wonderful world. Dormant forces, facilities, and talents become alive, and you discover yourself to be a greater person by far than you ever dreamed yourself to be.

After the initial legs of my adventure and when I had been sailing alone for a while, I realized that this was more than a sailing trip. This was becoming an epic emotional journey for me. I was experiencing an awakening of some kind. I was becoming free. I was seeing a new me. I knew I was strong and capable enough to meet the challenges of the trip, but I was finding a happier and a more contented person inside of me. I was breaking my bonds. I was finding a new peace and confidence. I have always been goal driven: needing to create and accomplish amazing feats. On this journey I was content to accomplish nothing more than getting my little boat from one place to the next.

A brother of mine has been afraid to go cruising, fearing that he would become fat and lazy and complacent. I discovered that his fear is unfounded. At least for me. I didn't become fat and not a soul would consider me lazy or complacent. Because of this experience, I have a new excitement for life and the adventures that await me.

There is nothing mundane about the expectations that I have for the rest of my life. Six years ago, I thought that my life was over and actually, my life, as I knew it, *was* over. I had to create a new me. I buried myself in my work and I was lucky enough to find a project that I could totally immerse myself in and become passionate about. It was a great project with great timing, but all good things end and this one did. Now what? With winter coming and no work lined up, a two- to three-month sailing trip, heading south, looked like a good idea. So I ran with it and I had the adventure of a lifetime.

I hope you read this record of my journey and that it may inspire you to create your own voyage of discovery, whatever it may be. Enjoy Life and its Journey!

A Great Big Adventure on a Good Little Boat

List of characters

Family:

Jessie Albina Hall Petrat (Mom). Born April 3, 1922; died July 12, 2009.

Willard "Bill" Fredrick Petrat (Dad). Born October 30, 1922; died December 22, 2007.

Linda Elaine Petrat (me). Born 1947 in Honolulu, Hawaii, where both my parents were stationed when I was born—lucky me. Divorced in 2006 from Don; two daughters, Angela and Ericka.

Carl Spencer Petrat (brother). Born 1948 in Brooklyn, New York. Carl is married to Bonnie; they have a daughter Jessica and a son Taylor. Carl also has a daughter Jenny from a previous marriage.

A Great Big Adventure on a Good Little Boat

Deborah Petrat (sister). Born 1949 in Norfolk, Virginia; died in 1995. "Debbie" never married.

Gregory John Petrat (brother). Born 1952 on Long Island. "Greg" is married to Alice, and they have a daughter Meagan and a son Matthew. Alice has a daughter Stephanie from a previous marriage.

Willard Grant Petrat (brother). Born 1955 in New York. "Willy" is divorced and has one daughter, Aubrey. Willy's girlfriend is Leona.

Cindy Louise Petrat Hayden (sister). Born 1959 in Bayshore, New York. Cindy is married to Tim, and they have a daughter Samantha and a son Marshal.

Joyce Petrat (sister). Born 1960 in New York; died 2011. "Joie" never married.

Angela and Ericka are my beautiful grown daughters; I miss the close relationship we shared before Don left. Yes, we had our differences on occasion, while they were growing up, but as they matured and became the remarkable women that they are, we shared many wonderful times together. Their father's decision to leave me has been difficult for them and somehow I became the "bad guy" in the deal. I miss my fantastic daughters the most of all that I miss, and I hope that someday we can enjoy each other's company, laugh together, and hug each other and mean it. Someday.

Don was my husband for 37 years. We met when I had come to Portsmouth to live with one of my aunts to attend high school. (I was the oldest student in my class.) We'd known each other for over 40 years when he decided to leave me. Through the years he was always there for me and we were good partners. I was totally unprepared when he told me that I wasn't happy, so he was leaving. To this day I still don't understand how he could walk away from our long relationship. We have not said one word to each other since the divorce became final. The person I married is dead. The relationship is dead. Don killed it.

My Aunt Martha (my Mom's sister) and Uncle Ansel Braseth have been very helpful and supportive during the trauma of my divorce, and we have become comfortable friends. Ansel isn't a lawyer, but he is a retired, successful, and educated businessman, and his help was instrumental in my negotiations during the beginning of my divorce. Martha and Ansel had sailed many times with my parents aboard the *Sea Fox,* and my conversations with them have given me a better picture of my parents' love for sailing when I was too young to remember. I'm looking forward to my next visit with them and listening to their stories.

Each of my family members is a great friend, and they were always there for me during my long and painful divorce.

The *Sea Fox* and the *Sunbeam* were the beautiful sailing yachts my parents owned when I was young. These boats played a big part in my love of sailing and my appreciation of the sea.

Friends (in no particular order):

I met Marty and Steven Carpenter many years ago at the scuba diving shop that Don (my former husband) and I started well over 40 years ago. The Carpenters' grown son was a young boy when we taught him to scuba dive, and we became friends over the years. Marty is an outgoing, gregarious, and a free-spoken woman, totally dedicated to her husband, and quite accomplished in her own right. She is one of the best painters I've ever known. Steven is the very quiet type who doesn't waste his time with people he doesn't like. He is an able navigator

List of characters

and sailor, and he and Marty took a six-year sail around the world aboard their beautiful wooden sloop. They were shocked to hear about Don leaving me, and Marty was very caring during my most difficult times of the divorce. She was a kind and sympathetic listener. Marty fed my dog and fed me and tucked us into a comfy bed on many nights.

Mary and Bob Flannery are another couple of fabulous friends. I met Mary many years ago when I was a member of the Portsmouth Garden Club. Mary is a sociable and caring person. She and I worked together on different committees during the Festival of Trees, the club's only annual fundraiser. The festival turned into a semiannual affair and was cosponsored by the New Hampshire Division of Forests and Lands—Urban Forestry Department. All of the funds earned were earmarked for scholarships and grants to assist conservation education and to support historic gardens in the seacoast area. We also provided money for schools, groups, and individuals who submitted plans to plant green spaces in local communities. I became the chairman of this fundraiser, a position I held for three or four festivals. I reluctantly quit the garden club and my position during the trauma of my divorce. Bob, an ex-submariner (as was my Dad), was very helpful with the wiring and the other preparations aboard the *Summer Wind.* He was always there to give me a hand.

Vivian and Paul Pelletier are fantastic, longtime friends. My ex-husband Don and I have known them since our collective kids were very young. (They had two boys and we had two girls.) Don and Paul worked together at a bioenvironmental company studying the possible environmental effects of the proposed nuclear plant in Seabrook, New Hampshire. Vivian and Paul gave us a car when we were too poor to buy one. Paul worked for me as a scuba instructor when I was running the dive shop. I loved it when he called me "boss lady." Vivian and Paul have given me so much during the years, not just during the divorce time but always. I love them dearly. They were flabbergasted when they heard that Don had left me. Vivian's meals and friendship more than helped me on the road to recovery through the divorce, and I think that they are still upset about Don's actions. Paul was very instrumental in helping me outfit my boat for this voyage, and I greatly appreciate his expert knowledge of boats and seamanship, and his kind patience.
Nita Libby and I have known each other for a few years. I met her at a Farmer's Market in

List of characters

Portsmouth, New Hampshire. Nita was there with a booth, trying to drum up interest and memberships for the Piscataqua Maritime Commission. Of course I was interested because the PMC hosts Sail Portsmouth, which brings tall ships into the port of Portsmouth. I joined the group and soon worked on the board with Nita. Nita was the treasurer and I was the liaison officer. I enjoyed my position on the board, and my relationship with the skippers and crews of the stately tall ships led me to a few adventures at sea aboard some of these magnificent vessels. Nita and her husband Gene have been good friends over the years.

Tom Moulton and I became fast friends after we met during my yard sale at my marital home, the home I spent years designing and building, the one the court ordered me to vacate. He owns the beautiful cottage that I restored on Monhegan Island off the coast of Maine. Tom loved my work and I loved working with him. He is generous and he has a heart of gold. He has become a helpful and true friend over the years.

Karen and John Oliver were acquaintances of mine for many years. I think I met them when they visited my cut-your-own Christmas tree farm in Rye, and they became repeat customers.

A Great Big Adventure on a Good Little Boat

Their beautiful eight-year-old daughter was a newborn then. I didn't really get to know them until after Don walked out of our marriage. Karen, John, and I became close friends. I spent many a night drinking away my sorrows with them. The Olivers included me in many of their family outings, including very special Christmas mornings. I had to come wearing my nightgown and robe. I'd sit, sipping coffee, watching their lively daughter Lily open her mountain of gifts from Santa. Karen, John, and Lily are important people in my life. Lily nicknamed me "Lindy," so in the Oliver house I am known as Lindy. I enjoy their hospitality every time I return to New Hampshire.

Sue Reynolds and Leo Axton have become good friends over the last few years. I've known them for many years, but it wasn't until during and after my divorce that we grew close. I actually renovated the house where they live now. Leo is the harbormaster of Rye Harbor and a professional boat captain. Sue is a retired schoolteacher and owns and captains the *Uncle Oscar*, a tour boat running out of Rye Harbor. She runs cruises to the Isles of Shoals, which are 12 miles off the New Hampshire coast. I spent many evenings at Sue and Leo's home in

List of characters

Rye, enjoying Sue's good cooking and Leo's stories. We spent many an evening talking about what is really important in life and how to cope with loss. Sue and Leo were very kind and giving to me and I miss them. This couple was good enough to store my *Summer Wind* while she was on the hard, waiting to be rescued and put to sea. Sue and Leo were a huge help to me during the preparations for my sea trip and I hope to visit them when they return to Boynton Beach this winter.

I have many more friends who have supported me through the years. They know who they are, and I thank them.

Finally, my very special friend, Meg. Meg was my Australian Shepard. She was my best friend and companion. Meg was and will always be my hero. She never rescued me from a burning building or pulled me from a raging river, but she stayed by my side and gave me the support I needed to survive a massive crisis in my life. Meg needed me; she protected my well-being and kept me from falling too deep into the darkness. I will always thank her and miss her. Meg, my best friend, my hero.

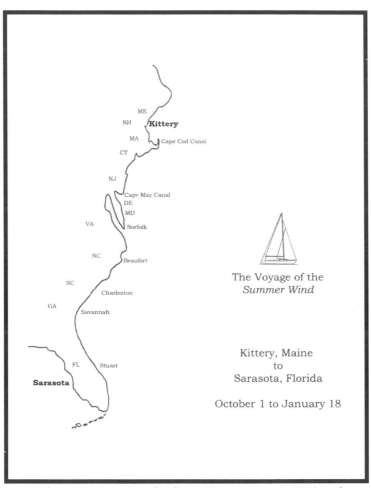

The Voyage of the
Summer Wind

Kittery, Maine
to
Sarasota, Florida

October 1 to January 18

ME
NH Kittery
MA
Cape Cod Canal
CT
NJ
Cape May Canal
DE
MD
VA Norfolk
NC Beaufort
SC
Charleston
GA
Savannah
FL Stuart
Sarasota

The Route of the *Summer Wind*

Preparation

September 21
Rye Harbor, New Hampshire
42° 59.41' / 70° 44.03'

My anxiety grew as I followed my little boat to the harbor. My friend Leo and I had hitched my boat trailer, which is old and rusting away to nothing, to his truck. I traveled behind him in my van through the tree-lined back roads of the small town of Rye, New Hampshire. The yellow, the red, and the gold leaves were spectacular this fall. I so love fall in New England. I love the cool crisp air and the smell of wood-burning fireplaces on chilly evenings. The beautiful homes along the road looked spectacular draped in the colors of fall.

I'd just spent a hectic week of working on my *Summer Wind,* preparing her for launching into the water. Fortunately, when I had put her on her trailer about four years ago, I covered her well and I had put her to bed ready to sail, so my work consisted mainly of cleaning and removing mice and their droppings. However, there is always something to do aboard a boat! I inspected the sails and changed her New Hampshire registration to her new Florida numbers. I had to repair and change a few rigging issues and replace some old and missing turnbuckles. Since she's a fiberglass boat, her hull was still water-tight after such a long time of sitting. After sanding and painting her bottom, she was ready to finally return to the water.

If all goes well, today will be the start of a challenging new chapter in my life. Today we are launching my 22-foot sailboat, the *Summer Wind*, and I am itching with excitement. I was so nervous that I didn't sleep all night. Now, with every bounce of the trailer ahead of me, my heart seems to stop. When Leo finally pulled into the harbor parking lot, I pried my white knuckles from the steering wheel and started to breathe again. Thankfully, for the first time since I've owned the *Summer Wind*, I have hired professional boat haulers to accomplish the launch. All I had to do was get her to the harbor, so I really have no reason to be uptight. My

A Great Big Adventure on a Good Little Boat

friends at Independent Boat Haulers are trusted experts in the fine art of safely putting boats in the water and taking them out.

But today is special for me. Today we are launching my boat, and I am launching the beginning of a voyage from Maine to Florida, a voyage that will take me over 2000 miles and probably about three months. After the initial week or so, I'll be by myself, on my very small boat. Today, we are launching the beginning of an epic journey.

The *Summer Wind* is a Pearson Ensign racing sloop. She is a fun little racing boat and not a boat built for cruising. She's got a very low freeboard, a tiny cutty (when the cabin is too small to be called a cabin, it is called a cutty), and she sports a large cockpit that is not "self-bailing," which means it can fill with water and cause the boat to founder.

For the past eight years I'd sailed her out of Rye Harbor, New Hampshire; pleasant sails in the Atlantic for a few hours or an afternoon of relaxing. I usually sailed with my dog Meg. Though I never got around to teaching Meg to steer, she rarely complained and she was a good sailing buddy. She's been gone for only a short time; I miss my constant companion. On occasion, my friend Marty sailed with me. After

Preparation

sailing around the world for six years with her husband, Marty has quite a few stories to tell about her many adventures at sea. I always enjoyed sailing with her and listening to her interesting tales. Marty was a fun sailing companion and she never failed to bring food.

Because of all the changes in my life, my poor boat has been "on the hard" for over four years. This past winter I moved from New Hampshire to the west coast of Florida. I had work scheduled in New Hampshire, so I returned to New England this summer to work, visit friends, and figure out what to do with my little boat. I spent a warm winter in Florida without my boat and I really missed sailing the *Summer Wind*. I also missed my friends in New England. I'd lived in New England for over 40 years, and there are a few friends who are very special to me. I was looking forward to visiting them when I returned this summer.

While in Florida, I tried to quench my need to be on the water by buying a kayak. I enjoyed paddling around, but it wasn't sailing! I ached to enjoy the freedom of feeling the wind filling my sails and almost magically propelling my boat forward. I love to hear the gentle and hypnotic sound of the waves caressing the bow of the *Summer Wind* as she cut her way through the water. Sailing always recharged my batteries and made the stresses of everyday life disappear.

There is a compelling simplicity about making headway under sail; no moving parts, no lubrication or fuel, no noise—just the wind in the sails and the boat in harmony with nature.

~John Beattie, *The Breath of Angels*

I considered buying a sailboat in my new locale, but I already owned a sailboat in New Hampshire, and I found it hard to justify buying another boat.

Now that I live in Florida, I needed to bring my boat to my new home. I thought: she's a *sail*boat; I should do what I love to do. I will *sail* the *Summer Wind* to Florida! I realized that it was rather late in the season to consider the voyage, but I had no choice. I had no immediate jobs lined up, so why not spend my time on a fun adventure? Most of my friends thought that I was crazy to sail *that boat that distance*. I was reminded over and over that she is a little day sailer. "You can't sail to Florida in *that* boat!" Experienced sailors took pains to tell me that my boat was not seaworthy enough to sail in the open waters that I would encounter on this trek.

Preparation

When someone tells you that you can't do something, perhaps you should consider that they are only telling you what they can't do.

~Sheldon Cahoon

My *Summer Wind* has a large, open cockpit, which is a big safety issue. She's got no amcnitics and a very small and uncomfortable cabin. These were the arguments that I heard. I appreciated the fact that people were concerned for my safety, but I am not foolhardy; I believed that my boat was capable of withstanding the rigors of the trip, as was I. I know where my strengths lie. One must rely on one's insistence. And you know what? She was the boat I had, so she was the boat I was going to sail to Florida.

I *did* have concerns though, and I had some doubts about this undertaking. It had been a while since I'd done any long-distance sailing, and never alone. Most of the sailing I'd done recently had been day sails and racing, both in Key West and here in New England. My boat and I were going to start a long voyage and we were both unproven.

Thoughts of my Mom and Dad came into my head every time these doubts and fears invaded my excitement. Years ago, Mom and Dad bought a large schooner, the *Sunbeam*, and

21

embarked on a voyage to Australia with their seven very young kids as crew. Two of their "crew" were in diapers! Mom and Dad had the fortitude to set out on an ambitious adventure like that, so what am I worried about? I plan to travel down the coast of the United States, not cross an ocean! I have no one to be responsible for except myself. My husband left, my two daughters are grown, and my dog died. There is just *me*.

My doubts faded as my excitement built. I remember one of Dad's favorite expressions was: "The only thing to fear is fear itself." Just do it. I remember reading somewhere that in any moment of decision, the best thing you can do is the right thing, the next best thing you can do is the wrong thing, but the worst thing you can do is nothing. I don't know who said it, but I believe it's true. I am definitely an action person—"doing nothing" never enters my mind. This attitude doesn't always work to my advantage but it is who I am.

Fortunately, right now I don't have too much time to think about missing my old way of life. I have to focus on my new life and this adventure. I need to be active. The planning and preparing for this trip keeps me excited enough

Preparation

that I have little time to fret and be sad about leaving my home and my many friends.

Action may not always bring happiness, but there is no happiness without action.

~Anonymous

Leo and I had successfully brought the *Summer Wind* to the harbor via her unreliable trailer. Leo drove carefully and we arrived at the harbor on a prayer and a heartbeat. Thank goodness we didn't have far to go. Leo and his friend Sue are a couple of really special friends who I will miss. Every once in a while, I realize how monumental this move is. So many people here in New England have been such an important part of my life for many years. I plan to walk (sail) away from everything I've known and loved for the last 40 some-odd years. Right or wrong, I've made my decision: I am leaving my business, my home, and the people I know and love and moving my life to Florida.

A Great Big Adventure on a Good Little Boat

To reach the port of heaven, we must sail sometimes with the wind and sometimes against it, but we must sail, and not drift, nor lie at anchor.

~Oliver Wendell Homes

The actual launch went off without a hitch. The professional Independent Boat Haulers team, also long-time friends, simply launched my little boat between two of the boats they were hauling out. It is fall in New England and boats are coming *out* of the water, not going *in*. Except for my boat, a fact which did not go unnoticed by any of the yachtsmen at the harbor, many who I've known for years. I got lots of odd looks and some unwelcome advice and comments. I tried to ignore everybody and everything except the task at hand. Carl and Rick backed the *Summer Wind* into the water and I checked below for leaks. Then I tried to start the outboard while they waited to release me from their rig. I found no leaks, but the outboard wouldn't start. I finally got it going and told the guys that I was fine and they could set me free, and thanks, I was all set.

When I put the engine into reverse to back out of their trailer, the engine kicked up. The

Preparation

outboard's prop sprayed harbor water everywhere and roared as it sucked air, alerting every boater in the harbor that something interesting and worth a look was going on. I could feel all eyes on me as I tried to lower the engine. I couldn't get it back down right away and then I had a problem shifting the damned thing into gear. The result was a very embarrassing dock landing with a large, attentive audience. Where are all these people when you come into the dock, under sail, with the precision of a skilled yachtsman? No one is around then! Oh well, someone has to give the crowds a chuckle. It was my turn today, and I had a full audience!

Red faced, I tied up to the dock and worked on finishing the rigging and bending on the sails, all the while trying to look like I knew what I was doing in front of the peanut gallery of sailors, many who had nothing else to do while waiting their turn to be hauled out of the water. My every move was to be their entertainment for the afternoon.

I poked my head below and saw water gushing in! There was a leak in an old through-hull fitting. I slowed down the leak so that the boat wasn't in danger of sinking. My good friend Karen happened by, so I calmly asked her to get the parts needed to make a permanent repair to

25

my leak. I went back to trying to remember how to rig the boat. It had been four long years since I'd dealt with all the halyards and sheets and other lines on the *Summer Wind*. Sad, but I have forgotten so much. Finally I got everything fixed, resolved, and situated, except for the outboard. It still wouldn't start. My friend Bob, who had been helping me all day, tried, I tried, and a few of the curious onlookers tried—without luck. It was getting late and I had to leave this dock and get to my temporary dock in Kittery, Maine. It's not a long run to Kittery, but I wanted to make sure to get docked before dark. My friend Bob offered to sail with me, so we raised the sails and headed out of Rye Harbor under sail. After all, she *is* a sailboat! This may be the last time I sail out of this harbor. I will regret leaving it and the fantastic people I've known here. I love this quaint New England harbor with its mixture of working boats and yachts. The fishing boats return from sea and back to the fishing pier to unload their heavy crates of fish. There are a few charter boats that tie up to the floating docks and it is always fun to watch the sunburned tourists and fishermen happily clamber down the ramp after a day on the water. The small snack bar has good coffee and the breakfast is tasty. I will miss being one of the local characters in this colorful place. I'll never forget the true friends I've made here through the years. They have helped me, they have worked with me, they have fed me, and they have always cared for me. They will forever hold a special place in my heart.

I enjoy Bob's company. I've known Bob and his wife Mary for many years, and ours is a relaxed and easy friendship. I have always felt comfortable just stopping by their home for a drink and conversation. I'm so glad that I am totally involved with the preparations of my voyage; otherwise, I might feel unbelievably sad to leave the people and the place I love.

Bob and I had a calm and pleasant sail to Kittery until we got into the Piscataqua River, where the wind quit on us. The Piscataqua is known for its swift currents, and here we were aboard a sailboat with no wind, no working outboard, and a current that was pulling us out of the river and back into the Atlantic. After drifting for a bit, we finally got the outboard going and almost made it to the dock before the engine died again. We paddled to the dock. Another great docking job! Fortunately we had no audience this time. I hope this doesn't become a habit. We reached the dock and that's what *really* mattered.

A Great Big Adventure on a Good Little Boat

I am rafted up to the *Razmataz*, another Ensign. I've crewed aboard the *Razmataz*, which is owned by my friend John McNair, in the summertime evening races off Kittery. I am thankful to have a safe place to dock where I can finalize the preparations for my trip. This dock is owned by Peter Bowman, retired commander of the Portsmouth Naval Shipyard and former state representative of District 1 in Maine, and I'm glad to be here. In the divorce I lost my mooring in Rye Harbor, which actually was a good thing because it would have been difficult to finish loading gear aboard the boat while she was at a mooring. I would have had to row back and forth in a small dingy, hauling gear and people from shore to boat and back again. Being at a dock will make life so much easier.

It has been a long and stressful day, but the *Summer Wind* is in the water and safe at a dock. Time to enjoy dinner and drinks with friends. Bob's wife Mary picked us up at the dock and we retired to their home for a celebratory dinner. Bob has been helping Paul with the wiring aboard the *Summer Wind*. Mary and I served on many nonprofit boards together. Bob joined me on occasion while I was building a house on speculation. He is retired and he would volunteer his time to work with me while I was roofing or working on whatever. Mary often came by at lunchtime with a hearty meal for us. Mary and Bob and I have had many memorable experiences together. During my divorce, I would show up at their house during cocktail hour and we'd talk and laugh while sipping wine. They never failed to lift my spirits.

September 22
At the dock in Kittery, Maine
43° 5.35' / 70° 43.41'

It rained all night, and I worried about my little *Summer Wind*. This was her first night back in the water after sitting on her trailer in the woods these last four years. Had I done everything necessary to keep her safe and afloat? What if the bilge pump stopped working? Maybe I hadn't fixed that through-hull fitting well enough and water was leaking in. I imagined that in the morning I would find my poor boat on the bottom of the harbor and my adventure would be over before it started! I missed being able to ask Don if he remembered seeing me fix this or do that. I realized how often

Preparation

I had relied on my partner to put my mind at ease with my many problems, ideas, and worries. Those days are over; it's just me now. Needless to say, I didn't sleep well and I drove to my boat at first light. It was a relief to find her afloat and seemingly happy to be in the water! Boats have a soul that must be appeased and cared for.

It drizzled all day, so I spent my time organizing the huge amount of gear that I had bought for the voyage, and then I went out to get some more. The outboard problem has me concerned. I need a reliable engine for this trip. An acquaintance who is a good outboard mechanic had offered to help me, so I called him. He can meet me here tomorrow night and we'll see if he can figure out what's wrong with my frustrating engine. Paul will be here tomorrow to do more wiring for me. He and Bob are helping me install a solar panel to power the two 12-volt batteries onboard. These batteries will supply power to my automatic bilge pump, my GPS, and the chargers for my VHF radio and cell phone. I hope the solar panel is large enough to charge the batteries and keep these important pieces of equipment operating throughout my trip. I don't want any more systems onboard. I don't have the space and I need to be able to understand everything and be

31

able to do my own troubleshooting and repairs, so everything must be kept simple. I've opted to use the new battery-operated LED navigation lights and reading lights. The navigation lights are Coast Guard-approved and portable, making them perfect for my small boat.

I have had so much help and support from my friends! The true friends have stepped up when I needed them. I am blessed, they are special, and I hope they know how much I really appreciate their concern and help.

It is 1800 and I am sitting in my cockpit writing my log, sipping a glass of wine, and feeling extremely lucky. I am thankful to have such great friends and I am fortunate to have the ability to make this proposed voyage happen.

There is no wind tonight and a thick fog shrouds the boats in the harbor. It is very eerie and peaceful here and I will miss it. I plan to spend the night on board. It will be the first of many.

Life certainly has its ups and downs. I guess one can never be too complacent. People die, relationships end, but life goes on and we have to continue. We have to paint a smile on and work to put all the horribles behind us. My Dad did teach me that each time you get knocked off your feet, you just have to forge ahead and start again. There are much worse things in the world than failure. Doing nothing is much worse than failing.

Sept. 23, through Sept 29

I am stuck in Kittery! I'm still having issues with the outboard. We've replaced parts, ordered and installed repair kits, and the damned thing still isn't running right. I am getting pretty frustrated with my engine. Maybe I should just buy a new outboard. A simple solution, but a simply too expensive one.

At the recommendation of my cautious friend Paul, I installed a bellows hand-bilge pump for extra safety. I didn't know this kind of pump was available but when Paul told me about it, I purchased one. Good idea, Paul! A bellows pump is a hand-operated pump that has the ability to move a lot of water quickly. My cockpit is large and not self-bailing, so if a huge wave pooped my little *Summer Wind*, my small-volume auto-bilge pump would not be able to move the water out fast enough and I would be in big trouble. This hand-bilge pump might save my boat and me. Thank you, Paul.

I have been running around like a crazy woman trying to get everything that I'll need for this trip. I make lists and more lists. I need navigation equipment. This boat has none. Remember, she is just a day racing sloop. I asked Paul to help me with this. Paul has been a professional boat captain for many years and his knowledge has been invaluable to me. Paul has just retired; for years he was the captain of the University of New Hampshire's research vessel. I am very fortunate to have been friends with Paul and his wife Vivian for more years than we would like to count.

Paul has a small pleasure boat now and uses a laptop loaded with all of the charts of the entire United States waterways. His laptop is connected to his GPS and this is what he uses for navigating aboard his pretty powerboat, the *Abby Rose*. I considered using this method of navigation. I liked the large-screen format of the laptop, but price was an issue and moisture was another. Paul uses his laptop in a protected cabin; I would be using mine in my open cockpit, where it would be constantly exposed to salt water. The saltwater exposure would be disastrous to the laptop. I ended up buying a Garmin GPS Map 640, with an idiot-proof touch screen and I hope it will suit my needs. (The idiot-proof part appealed to me!) The 5x7-inch screen on the Garmin is smaller than that of Paul's laptop and although it's not waterproof it should stand the rigors of my watery environment better than a laptop. Paul and I wired it into my battery system. A VHF radio was next on the list. I needed a VHF to communicate with the Coast Guard, other boats, bridge tenders, and lockmasters. I bought a mid-priced, hand-held model.

Next on the list were charts, charts, and more charts. I like reading charts and I believe that one cannot have too many charts. The chart books I needed were large and expensive. I had to buy five of these chart books to get me down the coast. I ended up storing the books that I wasn't using at a specific time under my bunk pad. Thank goodness that they came in a plastic sleeve, because there was always a puddle under my sleeping pad. (A cabin-top leak, not a Linda leak!)

At Paul's recommendation, I also purchased three editions of *Dozier's Waterway Guide*: the

Preparation

Northern Guide covered the New England waters from Maine to New Jersey and the Long Island Sound, the *Chesapeake Bay Guide* brought me from the Chesapeake to Florida, and the *Southern Guide* included Florida and the Bahamas. These I stowed at the foot of my bunk. I found the books extremely useful and I used them daily. Another kudo to Paul. The books listed anchorages and marinas along the inland waterway, including navigation into these places. The marina listings included details like available dock space; whether or not they had floating docks (floating docks are nice for small, low freeboard boats like mine); whether or not the marina sold fuel; if it had showers, laundry and the like. The availability and the use of a courtesy car was a great bit of knowledge to have, too.

A compass was the next navigation tool I needed. I found one at a yard sale and set it to my GPS. It worked fine. Since I had the availability of a compass on my GPS and also my hand-held GPS, there was no need to buy a more expensive compass. I already own a good set of binoculars and a personal floatation device. I bought two extra life jackets and a fire extinguisher. I added a large, battery-operated spotlight to the safety gear. A small medical kit, and a flare gun and flares rounded out the safety equipment. The LED navigation lights I bought proved to be perfect. The batteries in all but the anchor light lasted throughout the entire trip; I had to change the anchor light batteries only once. I also bought extra batteries, bulbs, sail repair tape, lubricant, electrical tape, and (of course) that old standby—duct tape.

Repair and maintenance tools were very important and I chose them carefully. Fortunately I didn't have to buy tools since I have a van full of just about everything I would need for my boat trip. I did buy a battery charger and a meter to check the voltage in the batteries; I have always had a few sharp knives on board, ready and handy at all times. I bought replacement rigging parts and spare lines at the local West Marine supply store. While cruising the aisles of a sporting goods store I found an inflatable two-man kayak to use as a tender.

These are a few of the little pieces and parts I thought I would like to have at my fingertips on the trip. Inevitably, this list grew as my date to leave got closer. Every time I ticked one thing off my list, two more items were added. It will never end! Where was everything going to fit?

Because I am going to have companions for the first week of my journey, I decided that I should get some bedding. The *Summer Wind*

Preparation

sports two narrow but long bunks. The bunks are hard and made of plywood; there are no mattresses. I found two blow-up camp sleeping pads. They would do. We would each bring our own sleeping bag. Clothes and personal gear would be stowed at the bottom of each person's bunk. I'll need a crew with short legs! Sleeping accommodations—done. For cooking food and making coffee, I bought a two-burner Coleman camp stove and fuel. (In retrospect, a single-burner stove would have been fine.)

A small saucepan, a frying pan, and a coffee pot rounded out the cooking gear. I also purchased two plastic plates, two sets of forks, knives, and spoons. Two mugs would serve as coffee cups and rum cups.

For my food items I figured that I needed at least a week's worth of food. I found the necessary foods in the local grocery store and the camping section of the local big box store. I bought soups and canned green vegetables like spinach and green beans, because I need to eat green things. I'm not a fan of canned veggies or any canned goods. My normal diet consists mostly of fresh vegetables, beans and legumes; I eat a minimum of wheat products and very little meat or dairy. Since I have no refrigeration onboard, canned and processed foods will be my staples for the trip; they will have to do. I added the old mainstay—peanut butter and grape jelly —to my growing mountain of food. I didn't forget to add the important bottle (or two) of Sailor Jerry rum and a few bottles of tonic water.

A seaman in general would as soon part with his life as his grog.

~Some sailor

I don't remember where I read this, but in the old days of sailing on the high seas, this was a true statement! When Captain Cook sailed on his voyages aboard the *Endeavour* in the late 1700s, his crew was rationed a gallon of beer, or two pints of grog a day! Old-time sailors liked their grog. Modern-day sailors like their spirits as well! A couple bottles of wine found their way into the grocery cart. I planned to stow the wine and rum in the bilge. Water, orange juice, tonic water, and any other plastic bottles will have to be stowed there also.

I need to find bins to keep my supplies dry and in order. The *Summer Wind* has a very large cockpit and a very small cabin. There is no room in the cabin except at the ends of the two long and narrow bunks. All personal items will be stowed there. There is no other space below. I

Preparation

was lucky to find plastic bins that are waterproof and will fit under the long bench seats in the cockpit—perfect for my needs. All this new gear has to somehow fit in these bins. I sorted, packed, and labeled the containers, and then made a system to secure all my newly packed gear.

I think I have everything and I am anxious to get going. The preparation for this trip has been its own adventure. I've enjoyed the challenge of trying to think of everything I might need for my voyage. On my shopping trips, I found great pleasure talking to salespeople about my upcoming adventure. They shared my excitement and were very helpful. On occasion, I could feel their envy. It was hard work to be thorough and careful in my purchasing. My funds were not without limits, but I couldn't skimp on important navigation gear and safety items. I want to be prepared and smart about my voyage and I don't want to fail. I also want to enjoy every minute.

Everything is ready. I am ready, the *Summer Wind* is ready, but the outboard is not ready! I picked up yet more parts today and we will work on the engine again tomorrow. There has been a problem getting some replacement parts because the factory in Japan was shut down by the tsunami. If we can't get this thing

A Great Big Adventure on a Good Little Boat

going with these new parts, I don't know what to
do. I can't stay here too much longer.

Preparation

Sept 30

This is the day that I had planned to leave and my boat is still sitting at the dock in Kittery. It is getting colder and windier every day! I'm afraid that if I don't leave soon I may get weathered in for the winter! I am so frustrated.

The outboard repair shop called and my parts have finally come in! They said that if I could get the engine to them within the next hour they could work on it and I could have it back by the end of the day. I couldn't wait for help, so I lugged the engine off my boat, across the other Ensign, up the 150-foot dock, up the hill, and to the back of my van. Try as I might, I just couldn't lift that outboard high enough to put it into the back of the van. I commandeered the help of a telephone repairman. He lifted the outboard into the back of the vehicle and I drove to the repair shop. I picked up the outboard a few hours later and Paul met me at the dock with a handcart. What a marvelous invention! We got the engine onboard and...it runs! I want to leave in the morning. I am *so* ready! Paul offered to sail with me to Rockport or Gloucester, Massachusetts. I think he is concerned about my safety and maybe about my ability. Regardless, I will be grateful to have his company.

The weather isn't supposed to be very pleasant tomorrow, and it will be nice to have another hand on board. Paul and I debated waiting another day, but I argued that the weather window is going to slam shut any day now, so I think that it is necessary that we sail tomorrow. Paul agreed. I met Paul and Vivian at their house for dinner, where I spent the night. I want to get an early start. There will be no shake-down cruise for the little *Summer Wind*.

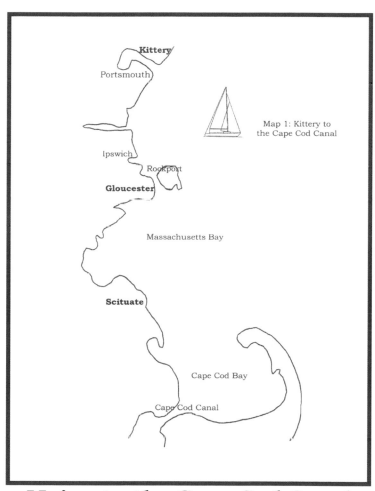

Map 1: Kittery to
the Cape Cod Canal

Kittery

Portsmouth

Ipswich

Rockport

Gloucester

Massachusetts Bay

Scituate

Cape Cod Bay

Cape Cod Canal

Maine to the Cape Cod Canal

A Great Big Adventure on a Good Little Boat

October 1
Kittery to Gloucester, Massachusetts
40° 36.56' / 70° 39.46'

Paul and I are off! We finally left the dock this morning. After all the preparations and purchases and frustrations, I cast off the *Summer Wind*'s lines and began my great big adventure. I didn't sleep at all last night; I was too excited, too nervous, and too scared.

Sailing is in my blood. When I was very young Mom and Dad owned a beautiful 58-foot schooner and we kids were seldom left behind on their sailing weekends. We sailed the *Sea Fox* in Long Island Sound, making trips to New London, Connecticut, with occasional sailing journeys up the New England coast. After I earned my Coast Guard 100-Ton Captain's License, my Mom gave me a gift-wrapped present. She told me that it was my "first ship command." I opened it to find an old, faded photo of me sitting behind the wheel of the *Sea Fox*. I was probably about five years old with curly blond hair. I was wearing one of those bulky orange life jackets and a big smile.

About ten years ago I bought the little *Summer Wind*. Actually, my then-husband bought her for me. He surprised me on my birthday early one June. She had belonged to a friend who raced her until she was damaged in a storm. As I fixed her "stove in" gunwales, I remembered how much I hated working with fiberglass, but she was a pretty little boat and I couldn't wait to sail her. We launched the *Summer Wind* by early July and every chance I had I would be sailing my little boat off the coast of New England. I've always been happy at sea. I felt reunited with my heritage.

Over the years, I've been able to involve myself with quite a few sailing vessels. I became a board member of the Piscataqua Maritime Commission. The PMC sponsors tall ship visits to the port of Portsmouth. My work on the board led to my meeting the owner of the 78-foot square topsail schooner, the *Lynx,* when she was being built at Rockport Marine. I was fortunate to view the *Lynx* many times as she was being built in this yard in Maine. A few of the board members were invited to join in the gala launching celebration.

The *Lynx* is an interpretation of a "Letter of Marque" Baltimore Clipper. A Letter of Marque was a license given by the government that authorized an armed vessel, her captain, and crew—known as privateers—to attack and capture enemy vessels. Cruising for prizes with a Letter of Marque was considered an honorable calling, combining patriotism and profit. I read a description of a privateer in *Under The Black Flag* by David Cordingly. In essence, he wrote that a privateer was an armed vessel that was licensed to attack the vessels of a hostile nation. By the sixteenth century, the system was used by maritime nations as an inexpensive method of attacking enemy shipping in a time of war. The licensed privateer was recognized by law and could not be hanged as a pirate. The system was open to abuse and privateers were often no more than licensed pirates.

The Baltimore Clippers were often considered to be among the finest privateer schooners ever built. They were swift and maneuverable, making them effective blockade runners. Before she was captured by the British, the original *Lynx* was of one of the first ships to defend American freedom during the War of 1812. The new *Lynx* planned to make Portsmouth her home port, and the PMC was proud to welcome the *Lynx* to our city for her first "ship visit."

The designer of the new *Lynx* is the noted marine architect Melbourne Smith of Annapolis, Maryland. I met Melbourne during my family's stay in Annapolis while we lived aboard the *Sunbeam*. He and Dad became good friends. Melbourne personally painted the *Sunbeam*'s name on her transom.

I was lucky enough to crew on the gorgeous *Lynx* twice: once on her voyage from Portsmouth to Baltimore, and the second time when she sailed from the British Virgin Islands, through the Panama Canal, and up to Costa Rica. That was a trip to remember. We experienced everything from calm seas to huge following seas and an early pre-dawn jibe while sailing wing-by-wing. The huge main boom broke its preventer and violently whipped across the deck with what sounded like a cannon shot. (We were lucky not to have more broken gear.) All of us not on watch jumped to the deck in a heartbeat to help secure the boat from further damage. The wind was strong and the following seas were enormous! Our voyage through the Panama Canal was fantastic; I will always remember it, and thank her owner, Woody Woodson, for giving me the opportunity to sail on his gorgeous yacht.

For many years I had the distinct pleasure to crew aboard my brother Greg's beautiful 48-foot sloop *Constellation*, sailing during the Key West Race Week. The race week is an intense five days of hard racing, hard drinking, and parties. Once I crewed on Greg's boat in the Miami-to-Nassau race. It was one of my favorite races. It was an overnight race in heavy weather. Realizing we were being overpowered by the strong wind, in the dark hours during the race the crew contemplated a headsail change. No one moved, so I made my way to the bow to get the job done. A crewmate joined me and we raised one jib and then peeled the larger, original jib down. This way we lost no speed due to a sail change. There was green water crashing over us during our work on the bow—what a thrilling ride!

While our navigator Ken was sleeping below, we decided to take a shortcut through a reef-laden area. It saved us time and we made it through the reefs and later through a mooring field. Our navigator came topside and marveled at the bright stars. We told him, "Those aren't stars, those are anchor lights!" He couldn't believe we would risk running up on the rocks just to win a race. I guess Ken shouldn't have gone below! I believe we placed first in our class and we were all glad to finally reach port after a grueling race.

Our visit in Nassau was like old home week. We docked at the unbelievable Atlantis Resort. I loved the gigantic aquarium. The massive numbers of fish swam among the ruins of what looked like the lost city of Atlantis. After walking through the casino and around the resort with my mouth open, we retired to "over the hill," the native area on the island of New Providence. We met great people and ate delicious native food. Many thanks to Alice and Greg for inviting me aboard their gorgeous *Constellation.*

I've also helped transport boats quite a few times, and I enjoy the quiet of sailing in a nonracing mode. As kids, my brothers and sisters and I spent most of our lives on the water, messing around with boats. I am content and experienced on the water.

My proposed trip from Maine to Florida is a bit different. My little *Summer Wind* is a day-sailing boat. She is not designed for the rigors of such a long and potentially rough voyage. I plan to escape out of the North Atlantic Ocean at the first opportunity, but many of the open bays and rivers can pose as much, if not more, of a threat and danger as the ocean.

Unlike crossing the ocean, I can stop and rest every evening. I can take a respite at any time and wait out foul weather. I don't want to make this adventure out to be more than it is. There are many braver and more adventurous sailors than I who have accomplished greater feats than I am willing to face. I'm not starting my quest to prove anything to anyone but myself. I am at the point in my life when I do not need to impress anyone. I want this voyage to allow me to break the ties of the small New England town of Rye, where everyone knows what you are doing before you do. I will prove to myself that I am a capable and whole person without my husband. I want to prove to myself that I didn't fail, I am not a failure, and I have value. My life is just beginning. It sounds like a lot to ask of a boat trip! This voyage seems like a good thing to do. Act now, think later! Just Do It! Theodore Roosevelt once said: Get action, do things, be smart, don't fritter away your time, create, act, take a place wherever you are and be somebody.

Maine to the Cape Cod Canal

I figure that I will be en route for about three months, and after the first week of travel, when my different crew members leave me, I plan to sail solo. I am not afraid to be by myself. I have been on my own for over five years now and I am quite comfortable. I usually work alone and I enjoy it that way. My trip will take me into mostly unfamiliar waters every minute that I am moving. Each harbor and bay will be new to me as skipper of my own boat. They may be challenging and exciting. I am sure that at times it would be comforting to be able to ask a mate: What do you think that boat is doing? Can you see our next marker yet? Can you check the chart? Can you steer while I reduce sail? Can you get me a beer? However, while sailing alone there will be no relief from steering while I'm underway. There will be no one to take a turn at the tiller. I have no auto-pilot. Regardless of all these things, I know I will be happier by myself.

I am so excited to start this challenge. I need it at this stage of my life. I need to be challenged, thrilled, and scared. I need to test myself. I don't know, maybe I just want to escape. Whatever it is, the adventure has begun and I am ready for this undiluted experience. I blame my desire to sail on this adventure to the "Ulysses Factor." The Ulysses Factor is a powerful drive made up of imagination, self-discipline, selfishness, endurance, fear, courage, and, perhaps most of all, social instability. It is a genetic instinct in all of us, but dormant in most. J. R. L. Anderson, a British journalist, succumbed to the call of adventure and, after several risky boating expeditions, he gave the will-to-adventure the name the "Ulysses Factor," in honor of the mythical Greek hero and Mediterranean wander.

After yet another engine issue, Paul and I finally left the Kittery dock at 0800. I will miss the quiet and quaint waterfront town of Kittery, home of the Portsmouth Naval Shipyard. The shipyard is locally referred to as the Portsmouth Navy Yard, or simply as the Yard. It is located on Seavey's Island in Kittery, just across the river from Portsmouth. Many years ago my Dad was stationed here while his sub was being readied for duty. I was a year old and my brother Carl was an infant when we lived here. We rented an apartment in the old Jones Estate. I remember hearing a story about an altercation my Dad had with a truck driver on the old Memorial Bridge between Portsmouth and Kittery. The truck driver almost ended up in the river. Dad was feisty at times! The Portsmouth Shipyard still repairs and remodels our Navy's ships.

Maine to the Cape Cod Canal

There is so much history here. Kittery was settled in 1622. It is one of Maine's oldest towns, and is the first port on the Piscataqua River. The *Ranger*, the first vessel to fly the Stars and Stripes, was launched here in 1777. The blockhouse and parapets of old Fort McClary, which is now a memorial park, are landmarks on Kittery Point. Fort Foster on Garish Island, Kittery Point, offers an excellent view of Portsmouth Harbor, including Whaleback Light, Portsmouth Harbor Light, and Fort Constitution.

Fort Constitution, located on the island of New Castle in New Hampshire, was originally the British Fort William and Mary. On December 13, 1774, Paul Revere rode from Boston with the message that the fort at Rhode Island had been attacked and the British troops were headed to take over Fort William and Mary. The next day, the Sons of Liberty and 400 local men raided the fort and captured the small group of British who were defending it. The Americans escaped with about five tons of gunpowder, hiding it from the British. One day, my father-in-law was volunteering at the fort, which is now a tourist destination. As he was locking up, he was attacked by a rampant moose! He wasn't hurt, but I always wondered if it was a *British* moose! I will miss living in a community so steeped in history.

A Great Big Adventure on a Good Little Boat

Paul and I sailed past Rye Harbor and then Boars Head, and then past the popular Hampton Beach. On the Sunday of Labor Day weekend back in 1964, the infamous Hampton Beach riots erupted and thousands of teenage rioters turned the beach into a battleground, forcing the governor to call in the National Guard. Today, Hampton Beach is a peaceful and popular summer resort area.

Leaving the New Hampshire coastline behind us, we entered the waters off Massachusetts, passing Salisbury Beach and Plum Island. I was able to see the old Crane Estate above Ipswich Beach. I thought of the heartbreak my parents must have felt to witness the wreaking of their *Sea Fox* during a horrific hurricane that hit the New England coast. It made me sad.

The *Sea Fox* was lost during Hurricane Carol in 1954. It was the first time Mom and Dad had gone sailing without us kids. They put out from Boothbay, Maine, with a friend and two other couples, and were headed for Port Washington, Long Island, aboard our 58-foot schooner. Hurricane Carol had been predicted to veer off the coast and head out to sea, presenting no threat to my parents and their friends. The prediction was wrong. The *Sea Fox*

56

was caught in the 100-mile-an-hour winds off the Massachusetts coast. The first of the hurricane gusts ripped off all her sails. Moments later the heavy seas snapped her propeller shaft. The helpless *Sea Fox* was thrown about in the angry seas until dawn, when the winds and waves drove the yacht onto a sand bar about three miles from shore off Ipswich Beach. The *Sea Fox* bounded over the bar in 20 bone shattering bounces. Dad said that with each bounce they were tossed 15 feet into the air; my parents' passengers must have been terrified! It was dark, and their vessel was being tossed like a cork in the violent winds and waves. The sounds and the motions must have been overwhelming. It had to have taken all their strength not to panic. They had no control. The main mast split and came crashing down onto the deck. Then the *Sea Fox* capsized and began to founder. Dad called to abandon ship. Dad believed, as all seamen do, that you do not leave your ship until you have to climb *up* into the rescue boat; in other words, your vessel is the safest place to be until she is sinking. As his boat was sinking, he helped his frightened guests into the dingy. My Mom remembered that my parakeet Salty was still on board the foundering *Sea Fox*. She insisted that Dad return back to save my bird. Dad rescued Salty, and he and Mom swam toward shore, towing their cold and petrified guests in the small dingy. Dad held Salty's cage above the breaking waves until they safely landed on the beach. My parents dragged themselves ashore and watched in despair as their beloved yacht was tumbled by the violent waves. Mom and Dad had to have been heartbroken! The good news was that Mom and Dad, their friends, and their schooner landed on one of the very few sandy, rock-free areas on the New England coast. Evidently, King Neptune was not ready for my parents or the *Sea Fox*. Mom and Dad stayed on the beach under a tent made of the remnants of their yacht's mast and sail for as long as it took to salvage the hull and tow her home.

I remember Dad telling me about the shipwreck. One of the things he said was that after they landed on the beach, he saw the lights of the Crane Estate on the hill. He figured that they had all died and gone to Valhalla. As Dad explained it, according to Norse legend Valhalla was the "hall of the chosen dead." It seemed to Dad that the castle-like mansion was the "majestic and enormous hall," and Dad was one of the "chosen dead."

My Uncle Ansel, who was a fellow Annapolis graduate with my Dad, sailed with us many times aboard the *Sea Fox,* and he still calls her a "hard luck boat, as vindictive as a jealous mistress." As all sailors know, there are quite a few superstitions surrounding the sea. Many boat builders believe that each boat has a personality and a soul. A boat can be docile and obedient to her crew; another boat might fight her crew and need taming. Sailors believe there are many reasons that a boat may be ornery. My parents' yacht may not have liked her name and showed her rejection by creating misfortune at their every attempt to sail her. Perhaps the *Sea Fox*'s keel was not laid along a north-south meridian as some beliefs demand, and of course a keel must never be laid on a Friday. Who knows why the *Sea Fox* was so difficult. Ansel also said that she was hard to tame; every sailing outing seemed to be fraught with mishaps.

After the demise of the *Sea Fox,* my parents bought the *Sunbeam,* a 65-foot wooden schooner. We were older and my siblings and I learned a lot about sailing and seamanship aboard that grand lady. Mom and Dad loved the adventure of sailing. I don't ever remember a time when we didn't have a sailboat. When I was young, most of my parents' sailing was in the Long Island Sound and the North Atlantic. They sailed off the coasts of Maine, New Hampshire, and Massachusetts. Every weekend was devoted to sailing, and we kids were always a part of their cruises. It's no wonder that most of us have multiple boats, all my siblings live in Florida, and I couldn't live there without owning a boat.

At 1320, Paul suggested that we go through the Annisquam River and head for Gloucester, rather than sailing around Cape Ann to Rockport. The seas had been building all day and this shortcut to Gloucester seemed like a good idea. We were experiencing four- to five-foot seas and a 15- to 18-knot easterly wind, making for a rolly—but not-too-wet—ride. Paul mentioned that he wouldn't want to be out in this boat in seas rougher than we had today. He wasn't, but I would be. *Way* rougher! It was a cool but sunny day and a very enjoyable beginning of my voyage. Paul's support and presence was important to me on my first day of cruising down the coast. His knowledge of the area was comforting. It was a lovely day for a sail.

As we entered Gloucester Harbor, we passed Woe Rock, site of the famous, tragic Longfellow poem, *The Wreck of the Hesperus*. Gloucester is also one of the land-based settings of *The Perfect Storm*, a book and later a movie about a violent storm that lashed the East Coast of the United States with high waves and coastal flooding. The storm attacked on October 30th and is also known as the Halloween Nor'easter of 1991. During the height of the storm, the *Andrea Gail*, a swordfishing boat out of Gloucester, was caught in the deadly seas off the coast as she headed back to port. She sank with a crew of six aboard. All were lost. A buoy off the coast off Nova Scotia reported a wave height of more than 100 feet!

For centuries the name Gloucester has been synonymous with fishermen and fishing boats. There is still a fishing fleet here, but Gloucester is now an important recreational boat harbor.

Paul and I docked at the Studio Restaurant at 1500. We ordered beers and congratulated each other for a great day of sailing while we waited for Karen, my next crewmate. Karen had been planning to meet us somewhere in Massachusetts, so we called her as soon as we knew where we were going to stop.

Before marriage and motherhood, Karen did a lot of sailing in the waters off the Massachusetts coast. Her knowledge of the area will be invaluable. Karen and her husband John are long-time acquaintances of mine, and since my divorce we have become very close friends.

61

A Great Big Adventure on a Good Little Boat

They live in Rye, as I had, and we three spent many an evening together during my divorce trauma. Besides being a good friend, Karen is a lawyer. Her support was priceless as she helped me muddle through all of the legal aspects of a complicated and nasty divorce. Karen and John have a beautiful and precocious daughter who has given me the nickname Lindy. Karen will sail with me for a few days, and I'm looking forward to our time together. Karen's life is so full and her time is divided between family, work, and friends. Onboard the *Summer Wind* I hope she can relax and lose herself in the sea and the task of sailing. We will have a fantastic time together!

I was so happy to have had Paul aboard for the initial leg of my trip. Paul is a calm and experienced sailor. He has cruised the waters off the New England coast for years and I am grateful that he took the time to sail with me. Paul helped me over the initial scary hump of my trip, and I felt more secure with him onboard. Paul and I passed under the first bridge that I had to call to open for the *Summer Wind*, and I was glad to have his company. We sailed and had a good voyage. I hope he enjoyed the sail as much as I did.

Maine to the Cape Cod Canal

Karen arrived and Paul drove her car back to the Portsmouth area. Wow! What an exciting trip Karen and I were about to have. Karen and I got her gear and coolers aboard, and, after a nice meal at the restaurant, we sipped drinks in the cockpit and hit the sack early. It will be an early start tomorrow. We had ice in our drinks, compliments of Karen! I had been wondering what was in those coolers. Before Karen joined on I promised her that she and I wouldn't sail in nasty weather. We would sail out of the harbor and if it was snotty on the open water, we'd head back to port. We would be fair weather sailors. Well, I meant it when I said it.

October 2
Gloucester to Scituate,
Massachusetts
44° 11.44' / 70° 43.35'

After a good night's sleep, Karen and I left the dock at 0700. It was still dark and the weather looked to be OK. As I said, I had promised Karen that we would turn back if we experienced rough seas. We had high winds overnight but the morning was calm, so we headed out to sea. We sipped our coffee as we rode out of the quiet, dark harbor. Karen suggested that Scituate Harbor might be a good refuge for tonight and that she remembered it to be a protected harbor. We raised sails and headed for Scituate. During the morning the wind and seas picked up quite a bit and we considered going into the closer harbor of Marblehead, but decided that since we were so cold and wet already (we were constantly doused with buckets of water in our faces), we should just tough it out and continue on to Scituate.

The seas were high and the wind was getting stronger. The strong winds were overpowering us and we needed to reduce sail. Without a word, Karen took the helm and steered us into the wind as I fought my way to the bow to get the jib down. The cold ocean water washed over the bow with every wave and threatened to take me with it as I worked to secure the sail. It was all I could do to hold on, as every sailor knows: "One hand for the boat and one hand for yourself." My body left the bow with every breaking curl of freezing water. Wow, what an exciting ride that was! I should have rigged jack lines and worn a harness, but I didn't. I secured the jib and returned to the cockpit. Karen said we needed to start the outboard and drop the main. She was right, but I wasn't ready to hang off the pitching stern to start the engine so soon after bouncing around on the bow. I needed a bit of a breather! We were still rocking and rolling so much! After my very short breather, Karen held the boat steady as I went aft to start the outboard. I wrapped one arm around the backstay, hung off the stern, tilted the outboard into the water, and pulled the starter cord. The engine purred to life and I put it in gear. Karen pointed us into the wind so that I could lower the mainsail. Thank God Karen can steer and keep us into the wind! She is a cool and calm and competent sailor! We worked well as a team. During this whole procedure, there was no need for words; we each knew what had to be done and we did it.

Scituate Harbor was easy to find on the chart. Not the case today in these rough seas of the North Atlantic. My boat is so low in the water and the waves were so high that the buoys disappeared in the high waves. We were maneuvering in eight- to ten-foot seas. One second we could see where the channel was and then it was out of sight, lost to the high waves! We had to enter the channel with following, breaking seas. We zigzagged as best we could to keep the seas from breaking on our stern and swamping us. We were racing at 7.5 knots down the waves, trying to stay in the marked channel. It was thrilling and scary; what a ride! With a collective sigh of relief we passed the breakwater that protects Scituate Harbor. Once we were inside the breakwater we found the harbor quiet and well marked. It was 1300. This is another boat-filled and lobster pot-filled basin. We weaved our way through the boats and pot buoys and headed to the fuel dock. It had been a short but exhausting day, with ten-foot seas and strong winds. We were cold, wet, and tired, and ready to stop.

We landed at the fuel dock and got some gas. We were told that the final sailboat races of the season had just been canceled because of high winds and unsafe seas. We heard more than once, "You came in here in *that*?" We were the talk of the harbor! The outboard died as we came into the dock and we had to be towed to our mooring. Wow, this engine just doesn't like to idle. We secured the boat to the mooring and hung out our wet bedding and foul-weather gear to dry in the stiff breeze.

After eating another delicious Karen-prepared lunch onboard, we took the launch to shore to indulge in hot showers. Feeling human again, we walked around Scituate for a while and returned to the boat to finish drying and organizing. We enjoyed a nice dinner and drinks on board. Besides being a good friend and a steady sailor, Karen is a fantastic cook. Karen brought on board delicious meals that she had prepared at home, then froze and put in her cooler. We not only reveled in her great meals but we also had, compliments of Karen, hors d'oeuvres before dinner and ice in our rum-and-tonic drinks. How civilized can you get? It was a real treat to eat such delicious, home-cooked meals aboard such a tiny boat.

October 3
Situate to Onset, Massachusetts
41° 74.64' / 70° 66.51'
27 miles plus seven miles through the Cod Canal

When we left our mooring at 0730 it was another overcast, gray morning, with 15- to 18-knot winds out of the south—on our nose. The water was choppy and it definitely was not a warm and sunny day in paradise. The North Atlantic just doesn't want to give us a break. We've been wearing our heavy foul-weather gear and the waves spit at us as we headed south. I don't know about Karen, but I shivered all day. We raised sail and lowered sail, the wind was on our nose, then it wasn't, then it was. We worked hard at trimming, raising, and lowering sail. At least all this work helped to warm us. The seas were not friendly; we were chilled and soaked, and I was glad that we had the option of taking advantage of the Cape Cod Canal.

The canal is a shortcut that allows boaters to eliminate having to navigate around the scorpion tail of Cape Cod, thus saving 135 miles of potentially hazardous seas. The canal opened in 1914, and because it was only 15 feet deep and 100 feet wide, there were a lot of accidents. The canal was heavily used during both World Wars because of possible German U-boat attacks in the offshore waters. In 1942, a steamship ran aground and sank in the shallow canal, blocking passage of other shipping. Traffic had to be rerouted into the dangerous waters off Cape Cod. As a result, another ship steaming off Cape Cod was torpedoed and sunk, with a loss of ten lives, promoting quick action to clear the canal. Over 17 tons of dynamite solved the problem. Today, the canal is the world's widest sea-level canal, with a channel width of 480 feet and an average depth of 32 feet.

Karen and I reached the canal breakwater at about 1320 and anchored in the quiet waters just inside the breakwater to wait for a friendly current. I had read the warnings about the strong currents through this canal. To quote my *Waterway Guide:* "The passage south [our direction] from Cedar Point headed into Buzzards Bay can be brutal, particularly when the ebb tide bound for Buzzards Bay is fueled by a strong southwesterly wind [which was today's wind direction]. That combination can challenge even adequately powered boats and moderately strong stomachs." Wow, talk about intimidating. The currents in the canal can range from over three knots to well over four knots. My outboard is just a slow four horsepower. I need to make sure that the current will be slack and then with us throughout our passage.

I studied the tide and current tables, and then I called my captain friend Paul to confirm my calculations. Over the phone he and I studied the tides together and agreed on the proper timing of our transit. Karen and I had a bit of time to kill before our entrance into the canal. We laughed at the "strong stomach" warnings and ate a nice lunch while at anchor and waiting. I was fairly confident that our passage would be pleasant. Usually we haven't had lunches because it has been too cold and wet in the cockpit to even think about eating. I have to admit that we always indulged in a mid-morning Corinita, a small Corona beer. Karen introduced me to Corinitas and she keeps a supply of these cold beers on hand. Karen is a gem!

By 1420 I was too antsy to wait for the tide any longer, so we decided to enter the canal early. Just after raising anchor, I saw the marine patrol headed our way. My boat meets all the safety regulations, but I don't want to test it. I'd rather they just go on their way and harass someone else. The patrol cruised close; we smiled and waved, and then they headed away. I was happy to see the stern of their boat.

Our transit through the canal was easy. We either timed our passage right or we were lucky. There was very little traffic and we caught the tide at almost slack water at the entrance, and then we benefited from a light, following current toward the end of the canal. We passed under two tall bridges and one open railroad bridge. There was no wind in the canal and the sun had broken through the clouds. It was fun to wave to the people along the shores of the canal and see them return our waves wearing envious smiles. Many were fishing, but most were just walking and soaking up the sun on a balmy fall day. It had been a long time since I'd been through this area and I found it beautiful and very peaceful. It was a nice passage.

Maine to the Cape Cod Canal

Karen used to do a lot of sailing off this coast, so she is very familiar with the area and she remembered a protected anchorage just outside of the canal in the Onset inlet. We found a mooring there and settled in for the night. We proceeded to hang out our clothes and bedding to dry. Even in a light chop during the day, we get wet, so hanging out our clothes to dry seems to be the routine each afternoon. I checked my charts and worked on tomorrow's navigating, while Karen produced her superb hors d'oeuvres and iced rum drinks. Today was a wet but not horrible day of travel.

As another one of Karen's prepared dinners heated, wc toasted each other and reminded ourselves that a day at sea doesn't court toward getting older.

A Great Big Adventure on a Good Little Boat

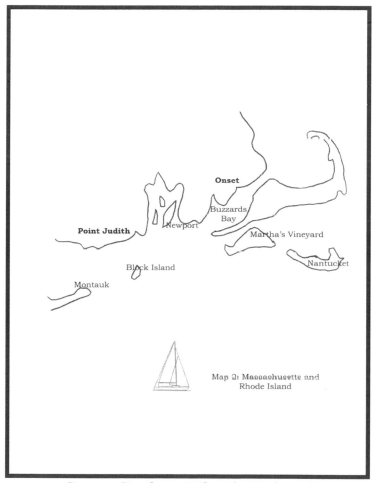

Onset

Buzzards
Bay

Point Judith   Newport

Martha's Vineyard

Block Island   Nantucket

Montauk

Map 2: Massachusetts and
Rhode Island

Cape Cod to Rhode Island

October 4
Onset to South Dartmouth, Massachusetts
41° 44' / 70° 39'

All night, strong winds and heavy rain buffeted the *Summer Wind* and howled through her rigging. Our sleep was not peaceful! I didn't sleep well because I worried that the mooring we had tied to would break free and we would drift with the wind and current until we hit something. I know that this scenario is not probable because whenever I am aboard a boat I am aware of how she reacts to the wind and waves and, like any seaman, I am aware of changes in my boat. In conditions like we had last night, I sleep with one ear open. Thankfully, the mooring we had tied to was a secure one. Karen and I woke early to a rainy morning, so making coffee wasn't an option. We gulped some orange juice and made quick peanut butter-and-jelly sandwiches, dropped the mooring, and headed into the dismal Buzzards Bay.

I found an interesting piece of information about the bay. It was named when the colonists saw lots of large birds near its shores. They called these birds "buzzards," hence the name of the bay. Actually, the birds they saw were ospreys, so this should be "Osprey Bay"!

Whatever the bay is named, it was nasty! We bucked short steep seas on the nose. The *Summer Wind's* bow rose and fell in the high waves. Each wave broke over the bow, soaking us with frigid water. We were dripping wet and so miserably cold. It was another day of buckets of water in our faces. After about an hour of this torture we were able to change direction enough to raise the jib and reduce the buckets of water in our faces to just spray in our faces. We didn't bother to raise the mainsail; the winds were just too strong and gusty.

The wind and waves started to calm down somewhat as we sailed toward the Padamaram Harbor in South Dartmouth. Once inside the harbor, the water was quiet and we found ourselves in a pretty and peaceful harbor. We sailed past seven or eight skillfully restored Concordia yawls. My jaw dropped. These boats were spectacular! I was in awe. After a meandering sail through the crowded harbor, we started our outboard, dropped sail, and headed into the dock. We paid for a mooring for the night and made arrangements to have the launch pick us up later. By the time we got our wet gear out and drying, the launch came alongside to take us ashore. I asked the launch driver about all the Concordia boats here and, because I was interested, he took us for a tour of the harbor. As we cruised past each boat he told us its history! He was proud of the special boats in his harbor, and told us that Padamaram is the home of the New Bedford Yacht Club and the big Concordia Boat Yard is close by.

I've always admired the sleek lines of the Concordia yawls, and it was a thrill to see so many of them up close and in one area. All of these yachts were in different phases of restoration. Most restorations were complete, but a few were still in the process. All were gorgeous. The Concordia Company was established in 1926, and it began building small boats through the 1930s, until it was commissioned to build a larger boat in 1938. Commissions for larger boats continued. The

Cape Cod to Rhode Island

Concordia Boat Yard is just a mile from the Padamaram Harbor. It's too bad we can't take the time to tour the yard, but it was a real treat to be able to cruise around these spectacular yachts. My brother Greg is a sailboat aficionado, and he would have loved to be here, seeing what I was seeing. Greg and I had a falling out a while back and I miss him. He loves wooden boats and, since I've lived in wooden boat country for 40 years, I'd always call him and send him pictures of the pretty yachts that I'd seen on the water and at marinas I'd visited. After telling Greg the name of the yacht or sending him a picture, many times he could tell me the whole history of the boat. Greg loves his boats. I hope that our mutual love of sailing yachts will someday bring us together again.

After our tour of the harbor, our friendly launch driver took us by car to the hardware store (I wanted to get another five-gallon gas can) and to the liquor store because we were getting low on rum. What a nice guy he was. Everyone we've met on this trip has been so friendly and helpful.

While ashore we showered and walked around the town to exercise our legs before we returned to the boat for cocktail hour. It was a beautiful night. The harbor was quiet, the stars were bright, and Karen's food was delicious. As

A Great Big Adventure on a Good Little Boat

usual, we hit the bunks pretty early. We enjoyed
a restful night in this snug and safe harbor.

October 5
South Dartmouth to Point Judith, Rhode Island
41° 36.53' / 71° 48.07'

We left our mooring at 0630 and powered the *Summer Wind* for yet another tour of the harbor on our way out so that we could enjoy viewing the classic Concordia yachts once more. There was a Concordia with the name *Summer Wind*, and we did a 360° so that we could admire her from all angles.

We reentered Buzzards Bay with the wind on our tail and not on our nose for a change! What a pleasant way to start the day. Oh-my-gosh—maybe we are going the wrong way! We set the main and the jib and enjoyed a great sail. The wind shifted to our beam at about 10- to 12-

knots out of the northwest. At around 0845 the wind increased and we reefed the main. The winds steadily escalated and the seas built to eight to ten feet. Water was breaking over the boat constantly. Everything was wet and we were drenched with the cold waves of the bay! We had to get the sails down. I went forward to lower the jib and I was underwater much of the time. It was really hard to stay onboard. It's a good thing that I have sticky feet! After securing the jib, Karen held us steady and I managed to start the outboard. While Karen pointed the boat into the wind, I took down the main and secured it. This was quite a workout.

We motored into a small, man-made cove called Point Judith Harbor of Refuge, planning to anchor and get some relief from the wind and waves. We entered the cove with high hopes of finding a restful anchorage where we could finally get dry and warm. We were so frozen and wet and we needed a refuge.

The cove was horrible. It was choppy with whitecaps and we were still getting wet. This is not the calm and idyllic anchorage we were hoping for. We were so tired of getting beat up that we opted to continue to the Point Judith Marina, where we would be protected and we could retreat out of the cold wind and rough seas.

Point Judith is the home of one of the largest commercial fishing fleets in North America, and there are lots of lobster pots, fish traps, and big boats to avoid while entering the harbor. To add to these obstacles, the terminal for the fast Block Island Ferry is here. Respect tonnage! We entered this harbor with caution. Karen and I checked in at the fuel dock and gratefully settled at our assigned dock space. We showered and finally began to warm up.

I am really pleased at how well my sturdy little boat has handled the miserable seas we've experienced these last few days. Even in those 10- and 12-foot seas I had no fears for our safety. My engine has run like a champ and starts with one pull. It seems like maybe we solved all of its earlier problems.

Karen has decided to leave me here and head for home. She has been making noises about missing her six-year-old daughter. Gee whiz, Karen, what about *me*? I have had so much fun sailing with Karen, enjoying her creative cooking, cold beers, and iced drinks. I will miss her! She is a very competent sailor and the best of friends.

I've called my last crewmate for this voyage: Nita. Nita enjoys sailing and we sailed together

A Great Big Adventure on a Good Little Boat

aboard the *Gazela*. The *Gazela* is an original 177-foot Barkentine, built in Portugal in 1901. She was built to carry fishermen to the fishing grounds of the Grand Banks off Newfoundland. The *Gazela* would leave Lisbon in the spring with 90 tons of salt in her hold, 35 fishermen, and 35 fishing dories, and would return to Portugal when her hold was filled with cod. Today the *Gazela* is Philadelphia's Tall Ship and belongs to the Philadelphia Ship Preservation Guild.

Nita will join me for a few days. I hope she enjoys sailing aboard the *Summer Wind*. My little boat is a far cry from the very large *Gazela*! Nita plans to drive from New Hampshire to meet us here tomorrow, and I've asked her to restock our supply of Corinitas and rum. Karen will drive Nita's car back to New Hampshire. These crew transfers have worked out well. Of course, the *Summer Wind* hasn't traveled down the coast very far and the drive from New Hampshire to Point Judith is an easy one. A very easy drive and a very difficult sail! Mark Twain once said: "Traveling by boat is the best way to travel, unless one can stay at home."

October 6
At the dock in Point Judith

I spent part of the day at the dock, virtual sailing. I was working on my GPS, planning the next few days of travel. I am still learning how to use this fantastic navigation tool to its full extent. So, I keep practicing, and I love learning everything that I can about it. Karen and I spent much of the day cleaning the boat, reorganizing, and drying everything. Not one piece of clothing or bedding or sails was dry. We pulled everything out from below. We laid the extra sails on the dock; the sleeping bags were draped over the boom. We tied our foul-weather gear to the mast; clothing hung everywhere. We looked like refugees! The book of charts I used for this area was soaking wet too. I laid it open on the cockpit bench and turned the pages as they dried. While underway, I mount my GPS to the bench in the cockpit and I keep it dry by covering it with a zip-lock baggie secured with a rubber band. This method isn't great but it works, although I find it hard to read through the wet and salty bag, so I keep paper towels handy. Of course, there is no place to keep paper towels *dry*! Karen has been reading the chart and the GPS while I'm steering and we're cruising. She'd mark our progress on the chart during the day. We do this by recording our position on the chart each hour with a dot and circle and the time. While on the water, it is important to always know your position. Most of my sailing on this voyage will be in sight of land and maybe this chart marking is a bit over the top, but I think it is important and a good habit; although, when I sailed alone, I was too busy steering and navigating to be faithful in continuing this practice.

While our gear dried in the breeze, we took a walk down the dock to check out a motor-sailboat. We heard that she had collided with a large fishing boat. The fishing boat won! Tonnage won! The motor-sailboat had both masts broken and lashed to her deck. It was sad to see. She was a pretty 40-plus-foot motor sail and a couple's home. I felt bad for them.

Karen and I walked to the Matunuck Oyster Bar and devoured a couple of dozen fresh, farmed oysters. We sat outside, basking in the warm sun as we watched the oystermen harvesting a new batch of oysters. We ate some of the most delicious oysters on the half shell. We also shared a fresh-caught fried cod dinner. I guess we were really hungry! When we returned to the boat, Karen packed her newly dried gear and we got the boat shipshape again. Nita arrived and we stowed her gear onboard, including our new supply of beer and rum. We loaded Nita's car with Karen's gear, and Karen headed home to her family. Before Karen left, I asked her to write in my log. This is what she wrote:

My last day on the boat. What a wild, fun ride it's been! From surfing down ten-foot waves in Scituate; to sailing with reefed main and baby jib off Newport in gale-force winds; to our quiet anchorage at Onset, just outside the Cape Cod Canal. I could not have asked for a better captain other than the fact that she lies like a rug. For example, Lindy would say that we wouldn't go sailing if the weather is bad, we will just go see what's happening out there and if it's rough out we will head back in. We never turned back! Lindy is intrepid, as is the Summer Wind. *Plus, she's fun and a prodigious rum drinker. Oh, and a sailing stalwart. Fair winds and following seas my friend.*

~Karen O.

In my defense, I knew that I wouldn't have Karen long and she is so familiar with the waters in this area. I wanted to get as far down this coast as I could with her onboard. Karen is an able and a courageous sailor; she just left because we were running low on rum and ice!

Nita got settled in and we readied the boat for another day of traveling. Nita and I have known each other for quite a while, and she and her husband are good and caring people. We've shared many a drink and dinner together, and I hope the passage aboard the *Summer Wind* will be exciting for her. After a drink and toast to my new crew, Nita and I hit the bunks and were able to sleep well because we were safe and sound.

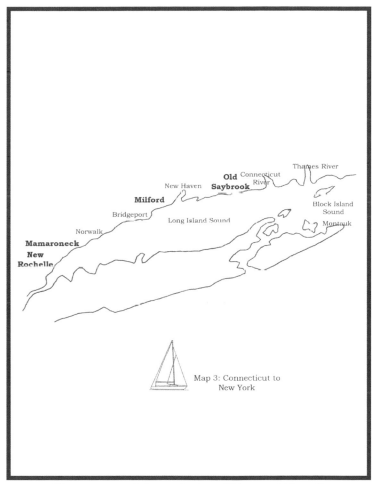

Map 3: Connecticut to New York

Connecticut to New York

October 7
Point Judith to Old Saybrook, Connecticut
41° 18' / 72° 21'

When Nita and I left the dock at 0730 the sea was flat and the sun was shining. What a change from the last few days! It was a pretty day to be on the water. The temperature was cool, but the sun was bright and the sea was quiet. There were no waves threatening to bathe us in salt water! We enjoyed a west-southwest wind and raised the big jib and shook out the reef in the main. What a marvelous feeling to be sailing again and to stand at the tiller dry and warm! There was a favorable breeze and the water was peaceful; we were comfortable and at ease. Unfortunately, the wind died to nothing about mid-day, so we had to start the outboard and lower sail. At least we got to sail for a while and it was a pleasant sail while it lasted.

After eight hours of cruising, we found a mooring in Old Saybrook on the Connecticut River. We've made it to another state! What a great day for Nita. She didn't have to deal with a headwind, there was no spray in our faces, there were no wet clothes and no wet bunks! We had nothing to hang out to dry tonight! Karen will be envious when she hears this!

We got settled at the mooring. I did my navigating for the next day as we heated a can of soup for dinner. We sat in the cockpit, enjoying a drink, watching a beautiful sunset.

I toasted Nita and her first day on the water. We were in a safe mooring field so we were able to enjoy a quiet evening in a protected harbor. Life is good! Besides spending an easy and almost perfect day on the water, I have reached the fourth state in my travels. It feels like an accomplishment every time I cross a state line.

A Great Big Adventure on a Good Little Boat

October 8
Old Saybrook to Milford
41° 13' / 73° 03.25'

I woke up well rested, knowing we were on a secure mooring. After making coffee, Nita and I dropped our tether at 0730. We faced a gray morning with the wind on our nose. We were forced to run the outboard the entire day, making for a noisy eight or nine hours. It was another cold, wet, water-and-spray-in-your-face voyage. I guess that old King Neptune thought that it was time that Nita was indoctrinated into a typical sailing day on the *Summer Wind,* and I know she was very uncomfortable. I have to give Nita credit, she never even groaned! We were suffering from the cold and I think that I shivered every minute of today's trip! My butt cheeks hurt from shivering. When will it get warm? Reaching a quiet port is so very nice after standing at the tiller all day, and getting wet with spray and water. My charts get wet, and the GPS is hard to read with salty and wet glasses. During days like this it is just too wet to eat much. Nita did make us each a peanut butter-and-jelly sandwich. It tasted salty! The sandwich and a warm Corinita rounded out the breakfast and lunch for today. (Since Karen left, I haven't bothered with keeping ice aboard). Nita and I gratefully powered out of the rough and cold waters of Long Island Sound into the calm Milford Harbor, but the harbor was full! There was not one dock space to be had. This is Columbus Day weekend and every boat in Connecticut must be here. There are sailboats everywhere. It looks like sailboat city.

The harbor is more like a narrow and crowded passageway, with lots of boats coming and going, than the broad open harbors that I am used to. The docks were full; boats were tied at the dock and people were barbequing, partying, and enjoying themselves. Without luck we tried our best to squeeze into a dock space and to meld into this fun group of sailors.

We stopped at the fuel dock to ask about dockage and were told to go to the end of what they call a harbor and we should be able to find someplace to tie up. We got to the end of the harbor without finding even a tiny spot for my boat. The harbor dead-ended at a low walking bridge and at that point the waterway was too skinny for even my boat to turn around in. All this time we were teased by the mouth-watering smells of food cooking on the barbeques along the way! It was getting late, and we were wet and tired and very hungry. We just wanted to tie up and get warm and dry and eat! At this point, I was beginning to think that we would have to leave the harbor and find ourselves another place to spend the night.

I was ready to give up when we finally found a tiny bit of dock space behind a big old commercial boat. We motored close to the dock and ran aground. That's why this dock space was empty. It was low tide and the bottom was mud, so we threw a line to a kid fishing off the dock. We had him tie it to a cleat on the dock and we pulled ourselves to the dock and tied up. Nita and I found ourselves at a public dock with people fishing and walking, so there will be no privacy tonight! Oh well, we are safely tied up and we will be secure here. We tidied up the boat and hung out our wet gear. I worked on tomorrow's navigating, trying to figure how far we will be able to get and where we might be able to anchor or find dockage before the next nightfall.

Nita and I were tired and hungry and we didn't feel like preparing our food and eating in front of an audience, so we decided to find a restaurant, to sit down and eat a real meal. (All cooking aboard the *Summer Wind* is done in the open cockpit.) We walked across the walking bridge and stopped at the first restaurant we came to. The place was warm and the food was good, and Nita and I got a chance to catch up with each other's lives. Nita is very involved in the Piscataqua Maritime Commission and I wanted to know what had happened at the board meetings of the PMC since I resigned my position as a board member. I miss being a part of the tall ship visits to Portsmouth and Nita filled me in about the commission's work and what ships the group is trying to entice to Portsmouth.

My ex-husband and I both served on the PMC board and we had fun working together until he became infatuated with his redhead. He quit his duties on the board before I did, but volunteered to help during a boat visit. He asked Nita where I was stationed because he didn't want to "upset me." Nita didn't believe him. He was putting on his alluring face, and it didn't impress her. Don thinks he can charm the rattle off a snake; he isn't fooling too many people anymore. In spite of the Don talk, we had a relaxing meal and returned to the boat, fat and happy.

Nita went up the dock ramp to see if she could find a spigot to refill a couple of water jugs. As she went up the steep ramp she lost her footing and fell on her knee. She returned and complained of the pain. This could become an issue. We had no ice, but she assured me that she was fine, so we had a medicinal drink and hit the bunks. I find that I have slept very lightly during this voyage, but I usually wake up rested and ready to start a new day.

Milford is located at the mouth of the Wepawaug River. It is easy to enter, and well protected. But, as we had found, it is a crowded harbor. Captain Kidd and other pirates roamed these waters and buried treasure is rumored to be lost here. My gosh, Captain Kidd has treasure buried everywhere, just like Washington slept everywhere! Interesting!

October 9
Milford, Connecticut to Mamaroneck, New York
40° 54.28' / 73° 45.70'

To me, nothing made by man is more beautiful than a sailboat under way in fine weather, and to be on that sailboat is to be as close to heaven as I expect to get.

~Robert Manty, *Tinkerbelle*

Nita and I slipped our lines and left the dock at 0600 and entered Long Island Sound. The wind was light and out of the southwest, and the seas were quiet. We raised the sails and were treated to a dry, warm, and sunny day of sailing. Maybe Nita is a good luck crewmate. I could get used to this! What a treat after the wet and cold day we experienced yesterday. Sailing like this makes me want this trip to never end.

After a lovely day of sailing, we lowered sail as we entered the outer Mamaroneck Harbor heading toward the west basin. We planned to tie up at the town-run marina there. As we got closer to the entrance of the west basin we could see lots and lots of little white sails in the outer harbor. It was a fleet of at least 100 small sailboats racing. It was really cool to see! It was a minefield of sails darting every which way. I didn't want to interfere with them, but I needed to stay in the channel, so it was a challenge to avoid the few boats darting about inside the channel. I felt guilty because my sailboat was motoring and not sailing.

There was no room at the inn again. This place is crazy, loaded with boats and more boats! We pulled into the fuel dock and were told that we might be able to pick up a mooring at the American Yacht Club located on the point. The directions to the yacht club were a little confusing but, after a while, we found the channel markers and we motored the *Summer Wind* up to the dock. This is a pretty place: definitely a yacht club and not a marina. There are fancy and expensive yachts in the harbor, the clubhouse is professionally landscaped, and the dock master's building fit the motif of a well-appointed yacht club.

No one was on the dock, so I walked up to the dock master's building as if I owned the joint and asked about getting a mooring for the night. From reading the cruising guidebook, I knew that this is a yacht club that welcomes only members and other affiliated yacht club members. Since I don't belong to any yacht club this might be a problem. (However, I am a *Petrat*; my brother Greg Petrat belongs and my parents Jessie and Bill Petrat belonged to the Sarasota Yacht Club. Should be no problem, I hope.)

I introduced myself and told the young man in charge that I was sailing from Maine to Florida in my little boat, and we needed a mooring for the night. He looked out the window and asked where my boat was. I told him that it was the blue Ensign right there at the dock. "You're sailing to Florida in *that?*" I told him yes, that is my boat, I am sailing it to Florida, and I plan to be out of here by 0600. He told me to take any mooring that I wanted, no charge. I wonder if I could get away with that again! (I didn't even have to invoke the Petrat name.)

After settling at our mooring, Nita showed me her sore leg. It looked painful, but she insisted that she was OK. Wow, this isn't something I'd planned on. I hope it's just a bad bruise. She took the launch ashore to shower and came back feeling a little better. She also told me how elaborate the clubhouse was and that the members were having a big fancy party there with huge amounts of luscious-looking food. Maybe we could crash it. We would stick out like sore thumbs in our boat garb! I considered it, but it was getting late and I needed to work on my charts and tide tables for tomorrow's trip through Hell Gate in the East River.

I was not looking forward to this next leg of the voyage. I had traveled through the East River and Hell Gate once before. It was many years ago aboard our family schooner, the *Sunbeam*. I was a kid, but I remember that it was scary. Hell Gate was *hell*! I remember the swift currents and the big wakes from the huge commercial ships. Our 65-foot schooner was tossed around like a tiny toy boat, and now I'm planning to bring my 22-foot sailboat, with a four-horsepower outboard, through these same waters. Whose idea is this? I must be nuts!

The cruising guide emphasizes the need for careful planning because of the strong currents. It also warns of the unpredictable eddies, uncertain winds, and lots and lots of commercial traffic making huge wakes. Wow, this sounds like fun! I need to plan our transit carefully and correctly to take advantage of a slack tide and a following current. I am nervous and a bit concerned. I realize though, that I can only do my best. I have studied my charts and tide tables, and it will be what it will be. It's not like I am going unprepared or without knowledge.

It is not the strongest of a species that survives, nor the most intelligent, but the ones most responsive to change.

~Charles Darwin

Nita had been planning to leave today, but, in spite of her hurting leg, she realized how nervous I was about Hell Gate and she offered to stay one more day to help me get through this difficult area. I am thankful to have a hand aboard. Thank you, Nita.

As I lay on my bunk that evening, I wondered and worried about our passage through Hell Gate. I realized that we all experience many "hell gates" throughout our lives. There are many times we doubt and fear the intelligence of our decisions. Sometimes decisions are made for us. I find those instances the most difficult to deal with.

I feel that I was forced to sell my home and change my life. Don's inability to pay the mortgage on our marital home placed my little house in jeopardy. I wasn't going to let the bank take my house from me, so I sold it before there was a chance of me losing it to the bank. I resent Don for putting me in that situation. I have no esteem for him at all. He acted like a weasel. He uses people to his advantage. The bank ended up buying back the mortgage on the big house and, as a result, the sale of my house wasn't necessary. I was aware of that possibility, but I had made my decision and I wasn't going to fret about it. I made the right decision. In the end, it will be right.

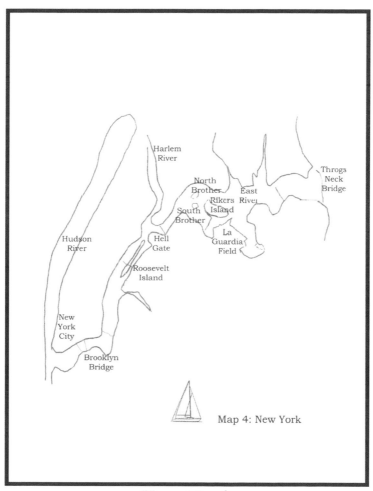

Map 4: New York

New York

October 10
Mamaroneck to Great Kills Harbor
(Staten Island)
40° 32' / 74° 08.'

After a night of fitful rest I was up early. I guess more than one Hell Gate was on my mind. I wanted to leave plenty of time to get to the entrance of the East River at the Throgs Neck Bridge, so we left our mooring at the yacht club at 0530. It was a beautiful day on the Long Island Sound. We set sail and made the straight run from the buoy off the yacht club to the bell buoy at the Throgs Neck Bridge and the entrance of the East River, arriving at 0740.

What an easy trip it was. Nita must be my light wind good luck charm! This was our last day sailing in the sound and we were so pleased that the water was flat and the winds were light. Our quiet sail gave me time to revisit the tide tables and recheck my calculations for timing our entrance into the East River. I need to have the tide with me through the transit and I really want to have the tide at slack water as I enter Hell Gate. Hell Gate is at about the midpoint of the 14-mile-long East River, between the Throgs Neck Bridge and the Battery, on the southwestern tip of Manhattan, and should be about a two-and-a-half-hour run. Our passage in Hell Gate won't be treacherous if I have my calculations right. Here's hoping!

We passed under the huge Throgs Neck Bridge and started our journey up the East River. It was easy to see and follow the buoys. I had entered the buoys into my GPS so we were able to follow the chart, the GPS, and the actual buoys, making our transit straightforward. We experienced little commercial traffic in this end of the river and I started to relax. We left Flushing Bay to the south and knew we were passing LaGuardia Field because of the many planes coming in and taking off, seemingly just over our heads. We felt like ducking and the noise was deafening! We left Rikers Island to our port and passed between the North Brother and the South Brother islands.

A Great Big Adventure on a Good Little Boat

After our cruise past the brother islands, I remembered that in 1904, North Brother was the scene of the worst maritime disaster in New York history. The *General Slocum*, an excursion steamer, exploded and caught fire, with over 1,200 people on board. The skipper ran the ship aground on the island, which at the time was a quarantine facility. The fire was so fierce and the currents so strong that more than 1,000 people died.

We started to pick up more traffic in the river, but the *Summer Wind*, Nita, and I were not being upset or getting wet from the wakes—yet. We passed under two bridges and entered the dreaded Hell Gate. This scary area is just a bend in the river. On the chart it looked like half of an S-curve to me. The Harlem River joins the East River here, and I'm guessing that the combination of the bend, the two rivers merging, and the big wakes from huge ships is the reason that this is a hell of a place to travel through! I think that I was lucky and all my planning paid off because our voyage through Hell Gate was fairly easy and not too nerve racking. We had to pay attention and had to anticipate the movements and wakes of the other boats, but we stayed dry and kept a forward motion. Nita was a great lookout and she allowed me to avoid the traffic as best as I could.

We took the west route along Roosevelt Island, where we started to pick up more commercial traffic. There were lots of small commuter ferries dashing across the river. Seaplanes were landing and taking off. Helicopters were flying overhead everywhere! There were cars and people and tall buildings on the east side of the river. Wow, what an overwhelming place to be. This was way too intense for me! It was hard to focus. Noise and movement were bombarding me from every direction, and I found it to be a massive overload.

As we neared the southwestern tip of Manhattan and the Battery, we passed under the beautiful Brooklyn Bridge. The Gothic-design bridge was completed in 1883 and spans the East River, connecting the boroughs of Manhattan and Brooklyn. The bridge was the longest suspension bridge in the world until 1903 and the first steel-wire suspension bridge. Since its opening, it has been an icon of New York City and was designated a National Historic Landmark in 1964. We were lucky to be able to admire this handsome bridge from below and aboard a small boat. The bridge looked so beautiful from this perspective. I thought that it was a sensational sight. It was a shame that I couldn't take pictures in this area, but both of us were too occupied keeping my boat moving and safe to use a camera.

We entered the busy Hudson River and encountered a deluge of big boat traffic. This place was bursting with more confusion and motion than anyplace I have ever experienced. I had to pay attention. Nita was a big help, keeping an eye open for traffic and listening to the VHF radio. I was so glad to have her aboard. The channel brought us very close to Liberty Island and the spectacular Statue of Liberty. It was unbelievable to be so close to her. She is so big! Words can't describe how awesome she was to see from my small boat! I can't imagine how the immigrants felt when they saw her after a long and hard Atlantic crossing. The Statue of Liberty is a symbol of freedom from oppression and hunger and she represented a new beginning to so many people. The sight of her gave me goosebumps. Nita and I were speechless.

A gigantic Staten Island Ferry almost swamped us because I couldn't take my eyes off that fantastic Lady and Nita was busy taking pictures! What a sight! What a big wake that ferry made. I needed to get back to driving my little boat. We spent the rest of our trip through the Hudson playing dodgeball with the big guys; we were the ball! Respect tonnage! We passed under the Verrazano-Narrows Bridge and made our way toward Great Kills Harbor.

What an exciting and nerve-racking experience the East and the Hudson rivers were. Planning for and understanding the tides made all the difference in the world. The trip through the East River is amazing; I would like to take that trip on an excursion boat and get to see the sights instead of avoiding other boats. That would be a fun trip to plan for. I will travel as a guest aboard a boat, not as the skipper.

We left the Narrows Bridge and headed a straight course to the buoy off Great Kills Harbor on Staten Island. *Kills* is an Old Dutch word meaning channel, stream, creek or river. The New York Harbor separates Staten Island from New York. Arthur Kill Straight and the Kill Van Kull Straight separate the island from New Jersey. In the 1600s, New Jersey and New York each claimed Staten Island as its own. The dispute was settled with a sailboat race. A New York captain and his sloop *Bently* won the race and the island became part of New York. A sailboat race! How interesting.

Nita and I planned to pull into the Great Kills Harbor because it would be an easy place for her to catch a ride home. Nita stayed the extra day to help me through Hell Gate, but now she has to get back to work. According to my *Waterway Guide*, there is easy transportation to New York via the Staten Island Ferry and the New York subway. Today had been a short traveling day, but we were tired and I was ecstatic that I had passed one of the major obstacles of my trip, imagined or not. Nita and I had done very well and we were pleased with ourselves.

We found the harbor easily, picked up a mooring, and hailed the launch. After a hot shower, I walked four miles to a drugstore to replace my broken reading glasses; the electrical tape holding my only pair together wasn't working too well. I can't read my charts or the GPS without my glasses. I bought three pair. Nita didn't join me on my walk because her leg is still very sore and painful. Nita and I met after my little jaunt and we enjoyed a much-needed dinner and drinks. We toasted our safe and exciting voyage through my dreaded gate of hell, and then we returned to the boat so she could pack for her voyage home. At the bar we found out that the bus stop was just around the corner and Nita could catch a bus running straight to the airport from there. Nita caught the last launch ashore at 1800. I'll miss Nita and her quiet, stoic presence. Safe travels, my friend.

I am alone and it feels good. I feel good. I am ready to continue this journey on my own. I was happy to have friends share the beginning of my adventure with me, and I am glad that I could share it with them. My many thanks to Paul, Karen, and Nita; they were wonderful and we had fun. Now it is time to make this adventure truly mine. My little boat and I will become one and sail into the future together, whatever that may be. Tomorrow is the day! Tomorrow is the beginning of my new adventure and I am ready.

> *The joy of life comes from our encounters with new experiences, and hence there is no greater joy than to have an endlessly changing horizon, for each day to have a new and different sun.*

> ~Chris McCandless

Today, I have no home, no job, no ties, and no plans. I have a long and colorful past, but my future is foggy with no definition. This isn't a familiar condition for me. I have always been a planner and a schemer, not a dreamer. I like to set goals and work to accomplish them. Today I am aimless. Yes, I have the goal of sailing to Florida, but I have no plans when I arrive there. I have no work lined up. My God, I have no plans at all. Mostly this feels liberating, but at times I feel guilty and useless. I should be productive and a viable member of society. Today I feel mostly content to accomplish my voyage from Point A to Point B. What has happened to me? Should I be enjoying this newfound freedom or should I feel guilty as hell? I am confused. I love this little adventure and I love my life at the moment, but there is an annoying bug in the back of my head, buzzing around and disturbing my sense of contentment. Next stop, I'll buy some bug spray!

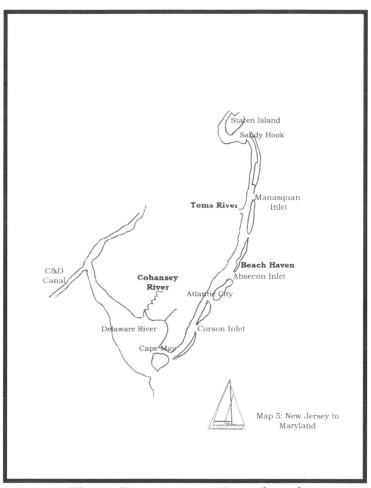

Map 5: New Jersey to
Maryland

New Jersey to Maryland

October 11
Great Kills, New York to Toms River, New Jersey (off Money Island)
ICW mile 5 NJ
39°57' / 74° 09.25'

I hadn't slept well because I was excited about the first solo leg of my trip. For much of the night I lay awake visualizing the next part of my voyage. I tried to "see" a quiet sail around Sandy Hook into the Atlantic Ocean. Wishful thinking? After listening to the marine weather reports I considered staying in the Great Kills Harbor because the weather is supposed to build and continue to be stormy until Saturday or Sunday; today is only Tuesday. The next section of the voyage takes me back out into the

New Jersey to Maryland

North Atlantic and it would be nice if the seas were calm. Upon leaving Great Kills Harbor my course will take me around the tip of Sandy Hook, New Jersey, and out into the ocean again.

I don't mind sailing in the Atlantic. I sailed in the Atlantic every time I sailed out of Rye Harbor. As I always say, I can deal with bad weather if it comes while I am sailing, but I think it's crazy to go out in bad weather. This voyage hasn't given me much choice. I'd still be in New England waters if I only sailed in pleasant weather!

Since I've started the voyage, I have had my butt handed to me by this ocean. I have experienced nothing but bad weather and high seas in the North Atlantic since I left Kittery, and I am not looking forward to sailing in the Atlantic again with a forecast of strong winds and rough seas. I think the winter storms are early this year. They certainly are chasing me, and I want to get as far south as fast as I can.

Since I had no desire to visit New York City, the thought of being stuck at this mooring for four or five days isn't appealing to me either, so when I woke up at 0200 I decided, over coffee, that today was the day that I would brave the big bad North Atlantic again. Why not? The weather was predicted to deteriorate and this might be the best day for three or four days; I might as well sail today.

After Nita left last night, I did my navigating for the next portion of my trip. I figured that once I rounded Sandy Hook, I would enter the Intracoastal Waterway (ICW) via the Manasquan Inlet on the New Jersey coast, which would put me sailing in the Atlantic for about five hours. Maybe the bad weather will hold off until I get into the inlet and the ICW. After today's sail, my ocean sailing for this trip will be behind me, unless I head to the Keys after getting to Miami. I'll think about that later. Now is now and tonight I will be in the Intracoastal Waterway. Hooray! Another milestone in my great big adventure.

The ICW officially runs from the Annisquam River in Massachusetts all the way down the United States' east coast to Miami. When most people refer to the waterway they are referring to the section that stretches from Norfolk, Virginia, to Miami. There are many miles of the waterway that offer no real protection whatsoever, since it includes much open water like Buzzards Bay, Block Island Sound, Long Island Sound, the Delaware and Chesapeake bays, and, of course, the Atlantic Ocean off the New Jersey coast. As I found, the bays and sounds can be as rough and nasty as any ocean.

The ICW can be narrow waterways with shallow water on either side. It can be water in wide sounds where the shore can't be seen, like in parts of the Long Island Sound. It can be water in canals and land-cuts, like the Cape Cod Canal and the Dismal Swamp Canal. Sometimes, the ICW is water in rivers and large bays. It can be deep water, shallow water, blue, green, and brown water. There are tidal waters with swift currents and calm, non-tidal waters. There are parts that are tranquil and other areas that are choppy and uncomfortable and downright miserable.

The land along the waterway is beautiful and fascinating. From Virginia to Florida I'll pass from a temperate climatic zone into a subtropical zone. The variety of vegetation is amazing and the numbers and variety of wildlife can make you wish you had brought along a better camera. I hope to see an incredible amount of birds. There are a great number of historic towns and cities along the ICW. Many Revolutionary and Civil War battles were fought along what is now the ICW. Wow, who wouldn't want to make this trip!

There will be lots of bridges and a few locks to navigate. I've never been through a lock alone and as skipper of my boat. Many of the low bridges are being replaced with high bridges, hooray. I expect that boat traffic may be extremely disruptive to my low and little boat. The huge wakes of the big commercial ships will definitely be a concern. There will be many areas of the ICW where I won't be able to avoid the soaking wakes of the large cruisers and the devastating wakes created by huge ships. The *Summer Wind* and I will deal with these problems as we encounter them. I might be really pleased with the addition of my bellows bilge pump.

I am looking forward to entering the ICW, even though there are many open and potentially rough bodies of water ahead of me. By the end of today I will be done with sailing in the North Atlantic on this voyage. I will be in the ICW and there I will be relatively safe and comfortable. Maybe the hardest part of the trip is behind me. It wasn't too hard at all! The *Summer Wind* and I sail south toward sunshine and warmth!

After rigging my lines for solo sailing, I dropped the mooring at 0345. My solo trip has begun! I was very happy and content. Well, for a while anyway. I soon realized that I had left a safe haven to sail into a very busy commercial traffic area. It was still dark and my course directed me into one of the busiest navigation routes on the East Coast. There were big ships everywhere. Two massive cruise ships were waiting for the tide to pass under the Verrazano Narrows Bridge. There were four other huge ships entering and exiting the busy New York Harbor.

What was I thinking? My little boat is out here with the big guys and I am sure that I am invisible to them. I haven't put up my radar reflector! Since small sailboats don't have much mass, they are very hard for other boats' radar to see. A reflector reflects the radar waves back to the source, allowing the small vessel to be seen on the radar screen of the larger boat. Without a reflector, I am pretty much invisible.

So there I was, in the dark, in rough seas, with huge ships all around me, and they were leaving big, very big wakes! I saw two cruise ships heading toward the Narrows Bridge and the city. Their wakes were enormous. What a ride I had! I wasn't worried about them; they were headed away from me. There was a tug with a tow. He worried me. The tug seemed to keep coming right at me. I knew that he didn't see me on his radar. I radioed the tug and got no answer, so I turned tail and headed back into the lower bay until he finally turned out to sea.

A Great Big Adventure on a Good Little Boat

Respect tonnage! It is amazing how much one can sweat even when you are cold to the bone!

There were no other ships that looked threatening, so I resumed my voyage and pointed my bow toward Sandy Hook. I rounded the tip of New Jersey, and there the wind and the waves hit me with a vengeance! Wow, it was rough. I was in the thick of it again. I just can't seem to catch a break. Again, I had about eight- to ten-foot seas on the beam. At least it's not raining!

I raised my small jib and sailed in this rock-and-roll ocean for about five hours (about 25 miles) until I got to the Manasquan Inlet. I was really concerned about the waves swamping my boat when I had to go forward to lower the jib. The waves were so high and I had no one to steer the boat into the wind. I watched the waves for a while so I could time my dash to the bow during the minimum wave height cycle. When I thought the time was right, I tethered the tiller and made my race to the bow. I managed to lower the jib, secure it, and return to the cockpit. I hadn't swamped the *Summer Wind* and I hadn't been washed overboard!

Entering the inlet was another challenge. The wind and the current were battling each other and I was entering into the middle of it. In narrow inlets the current can be quite strong and if there are strong winds blowing in the opposite direction, the wave action can be very nasty. We call this condition "confused seas." This is what I was facing in the inlet today. It was rough! Again, I was really afraid of swamping my boat! I might have a chance to try out that hand-operated bellows pump that I installed while I was in Kittery. The North Atlantic just doesn't want to let me go.

Once I was able to see the buoys marking the inlet, it was a matter of hanging on and steering. Finally I got past the pitching and rolling of the ocean and into the protected waters inside the inlet. I have entered the Intracoastal Waterway. Hooray! At this point, all I wanted to do was anchor at the closest place and crash. I was so tired. It had been a stressful day. In my first solo day, I have been chased by a tug, beat up by hefty seas in the North Atlantic, and conquered a difficult inlet. Now—at last—I'm in the ICW and all I want to do is go to sleep! Once past the confused waters of the inlet, I was no longer being bombarded with salt water.

The extreme motions and struggle to hold my footing in the ocean and the inlet were behind me, and I entered the relatively calm Manasquan River, and then into the Point

A Great Big Adventure on a Good Little Boat

Pleasant Canal. The Point Pleasant Canal is a narrow canal joining the Manasquan River and the Barnegat Bay. After exiting the tranquil canal, I entered the exposed and open waters of the bay, and I was back into the wind and waves. It was just choppy here, nothing like the ocean, but again I was getting wet.

After about three hours of uncomfortable, cold, and wet travel I entered the more protected Toms River. I finally chose a place to anchor near Money Island and I set my anchor in a tiny cove. All around my little anchorage there were beautiful homes with green manicured lawns reaching down to the water. Each home boasted its own private dock and boat. I have definitely encroached into the privileged world. Only dynamite would get me out of here. I was so tired! I was exhausted, cold, and soaked to the skin. After setting my anchor light, I crawled into my saturated and chilly bunk and fell asleep. My rest didn't last long.

October 13
At anchor in Toms River

Those who would go to sea for pleasure would go to hell for pastime.

~Eighteenth-century aphorism

My sleep was interrupted by the wind and waves. I had to get up often to check my anchor and make sure my boat wasn't dragging. The constant jerking of the *Summer Wind* against her anchor rode and the noise of the wind whistling in her rigging kept me awake. I've always been sensitive to the wind. I think it comes from the years of living with my parents and siblings aboard the *Sunbeam*. Being aboard a boat makes you aware of your environment at all times. You can't afford to be caught unaware; you have to be able to act at any moment, so you anticipate and keep alert. The wind was so strong that my little *Summer Wind* shuddered in its gusts. I shuddered right along with my boat. It was impossible to rest. I was happy when daylight finally came. Thankfully, my anchor held well in spite of the strong winds.

I woke up still cold and still wet and the day brought nothing but more cold, rain, and wind. It would be another gray and dismal day. I spent the day organizing the boat, trying to get warm, and listening to the weather on the VHF radio. The gale that has me in its grip is supposed to be here for a few days! Holy moley, this bad weather is following me like a hungry python! I just can't shake it.

During the day I slept and read and shivered; I checked the anchor and worried about dragging. I always worried about my anchor dragging because my anchor was the one piece of equipment that I didn't investigate for my trip. I just used the anchor that I always had onboard, never thinking whether or not it was big enough for my boat. I had an anchor. That was it. Now I worry and I keep checking.

New Jersey to Maryland

At 1500 I realized that I hadn't eaten since yesterday. I hadn't even made coffee. No wonder I had such a headache. The strong wind whipping across the cockpit and the wild movement of the *Summer Wind* made cooking difficult. It was hard to keep the gas flame from blowing out and it was a chore to maintain the pot of soup on the burner. I was finally able to heat a can of soup. The hot soup warmed my insides and I ate the whole can! It's amazing how good anything warm tastes aboard a boat in foul weather! I felt much better after filling my stomach. In retrospect, I should have found a dock to tie up to, but I was tired that I just wanted to anchor and be alone and have privacy. I have no privacy at a dock and I like my privacy. I enjoy being by myself and need to be by myself. After warming my tummy, I lay on my bunk in my tiny cabin and listened to the wind and waves buffeting my poor little boat. As small as the *Summer Wind's* cabin is, it is my home and I feel secure.

A Great Big Adventure on a Good Little Boat

The cabin of a small yacht is truly a wonderful thing; not only will it shelter you from the tempest, but in the other troubles of life, which may be even more disturbing, it is a safe retreat.

~L. Francis Herreshoff

Waiting out the newest batch of brutal weather and listening to the wind attack my poor little boat, I started to think about the great life that Don and I shared. We worked hard all our married lives. Our daughters were grown and had become productive and happy women. Our businesses were successful and we had a comfortable home. We were in the process of restoring our beautiful old Crocker Cutter sailboat. We envisioned sailing her and participating in the many wooden boat sail gams (a gathering of sailboats) held in the Northeast. We had plans. We were forging ahead with our lives. I thought we wanted to sail and start a new chapter of our lives together. I don't know what happened. Well, actually I do.

What was Don thinking when he fell for that redhead? That she would fulfill his every need? That she would make his world magic? That she would work alongside him to continue a prosperous life? Don's redhead must have stroked his titanic ego.

What a foolish thing that so many men fall prey to! It is such a fleeting thing. Don't they realize this? That's not what Don found. He and his redhead are no longer together. Maybe his enormous ego has been deflated somewhat. I remember reading somewhere something like: A fit of passion is a thing that has no foresight in it, and so we often rue the day when we gave way to it.

The trauma of my divorce, the end of a 37-year marriage, and my lost relationship with my daughters has taken its toll. None of these horrible events figure into the equation here and now. I am on a small boat battling the threatening seas and the numbing cold. My battle is here and now—not back there in the fantasy world of—if I had done this or that, if I'd said this or that, then maybe he would still love me. This voyage is allowing me to leave that world and begin my new and thrilling life where *I* am captain. *I* am master of my life. *I* am living *now*. The past is fading and its memory is becoming less painful with every mile of this voyage. My damaged relationship with my two daughters will always nag at my consciousness and will keep total happiness at bay.

A Great Big Adventure on a Good Little Boat

I miss what we had together, but it is gone. The Don I knew is dead and the relationship is gone. I can leave it in the past. It will no longer influence my every day. I am a 64-year-old woman who, for the first time in her life, has *no* responsibilities to anyone except herself. I own my boat, a van, and my tools. I owe nothing. I am finding this a really good thing. And it's funny; I don't wish Don ill will or good will; there is nothing there. Oh yes, there was a time when I wanted to kill him! Really kill him. Once, when I found out that he was making charges on our mutual credit card, the one the court had ordered me to pay, if I had seen him at that moment, I would have shot him. Right then and there. I had the gun and I knew how to use it.

All my feelings for Don are dead now; I feel that he is a foolish and shallow person. Except for having two beautiful daughters with him, I am sorry that I ever met him. Actually, I take that back. He gave me a lot and I gave him a lot. We had a full and adventurous life together. So many years ago, I made a choice. Right or wrong, I was committed to my decision to be married to Don. Obviously, his sense of commitment was different. Don is a user. His agenda suits his needs, and changes with his desires.

New Jersey to Maryland

Back to sailing. The weather has been worse than terrible during most of my voyage. I am challenged every day, the skies are gray and the winds are fierce, but I am happy and I am thriving. I am tired, I am cold, I am wet, I am challenged, and in spite of all of this, I am alive, really alive! Maybe I am just a whack case and thrive on adversity, but there would be nothing to remember or write about if every day was a sunny day in paradise!

Under better conditions, Toms River might be a nice place to visit. The houses along the river are pretty and well landscaped. Every night as the wind calms a bit at dusk, I can see about a dozen little "class" sailboats racing in the lee of the land. "Class" boats are organized into groups with identical specifications to fit a formula that is designed to equal the boat's performance, thus putting a premium on each sailor's skill and tactics.

As the wind starts to diminish, it is great to be able to hear the sounds of the ducks and geese landing on the water to rest for the night before continuing their flight south. This river would be fun to explore, but right now I can't wait to get out of here. Storms keep plaguing me; I am in a race with the winds and the winds are winning! I just can't seem to escape these weather systems. I need to get farther south and

A Great Big Adventure on a Good Little Boat

my little boat can't sail fast enough; there aren't enough hours in the day, but I will keep trying, and the sun will shine, and the calm, blue waters will sparkle, and I will be warm. Soon!

October 14
Toms River, New Jersey to Beach Haven, New Jersey
ICW mile 45
39° 34. '/ 74° 15.85'

Last night as I was lying in my bunk, I realized that the wind was no longer humming through my rigging and my boat wasn't shuddering with the strong gusts. The storm has passed. I will finally be free to raise anchor and continue my journey south. I'd like to return to Toms River when the weather is nice and the seas are calm.

Actually, I would like to return in August, when the Ensign National Championship is hosted by Ensign Fleet 63, which meets at the Toms River Yacht Club. It would be fun to be there for their regatta. The Ensign boats race in five regions in the United States. Region 1 is here in Toms River. Other fleets race in Massachusetts, Ohio, Michigan, and Texas. The "Ensign" evolved from a Carl Alberg-designed Electra Class of pocket-keel cruising sloops. The boats were introduced at the New York Boat Show in 1960. The Electra was modified from a cruiser to more of a day-sailing boat and the name was changed to Ensign in 1962, when the Ensign Association was formed. The association is quite active and members race throughout the season.

The Ensign sailboat is the largest class of full-keel boats in North America. Pearson Yachts of Portsmouth, Rhode Island, built the Ensigns from 1962 to 1983. Pearson manufactured 1,775 boats during that time. The original molds were sold to the Ensign Class Association when Pearson Yachts went bankrupt. The Ensign was inducted into the American Sailboat Hall of Fame in 2002. My *Summer Wind* has a hull number of 544 and she was built in 1964. She's done well for an old lady.

It will be good to be moving again. I've been here so long that I feel like I'm getting moldy. There has been so much rain and so little sun these last few days that things are starting to look somewhat green. I hope the nice weather will last long enough to dry everything, including my brain. I do feel a bit waterlogged.

I weighed anchor early and enjoyed a beautiful trip out of the river and back into Barnegat Bay, where I rejoined the ICW at mile 15. The river had been tranquil, but this open bay greeted me with a one-foot chop and gusty winds. I knew that I was traveling in the right direction because the wind was on my nose again. I had hoped to be able to raise sail in the open part of the bay, but the headwinds made that impossible. At about ICW mile 25 the chop was just off the bow and I was getting wet again. This would be another spray-in-your-face day. At about mile 30 the wind died, and drizzle and soupy fog took its place. The fog was so thick that you could cut it and serve it on a plate! Of course the fog enveloped me as I was entering a very narrow and twisty channel. I could see nothing beyond the bow of my boat. I pulled out my horn and blew a long blast every two minutes or so, to let other boats know I was traveling in the area. What fool would be out in this weather?

Thank goodness that I had my GPS. Although I couldn't see the channel markers on the water, I could see the markers on the 5x7-inch GPS screen, and I was able to stay in the channel by following this helpful navigating tool. Outside of the restricted channel the depth was only one- to two-feet deep, so I needed to pay attention and stay in the marked channel—the GPS helped me to do that.

I traveled in the rain and fog for the rest of the day. At least the choppy seas were gone and my hair was getting a freshwater rinse. The fog lifted a bit as I entered Little Egg Harbor and motored toward Morrison's Marina on Beach Haven. It was early, but there was no way I could make it to Atlantic City before dark, and navigating in the fog had been tiring. As I got into the marina, the fog lifted totally and the rain diminished to a drizzle. I made arrangements with the dock master and moved the *Summer Wind* to my assigned dock space. By this time the drizzle had ended and the wind was increasing, so I started hauling everything out of the cabin to dry in the wind. Karen had left me her small pillow and after putting it on the cabin-top to dry, the wind took it away! I never even saw it go. Darn, I was getting used to the luxury of putting my head on a soft pillow. I will miss it. Oh well, I enjoyed its comfort for a little while.

The wind was starting to really build and I'm glad that I stopped here. It looks like I might be in for yet another storm. The cruising guide mentioned that the area that I had just traveled through provides miles of scenic cruising and that it is one of the most popular boating areas on the East Coast. Barnegat Bay is a very busy body of water and one should keep a careful watch at all times! Wow, I will have to return to see the bay that I just traveled through. I am glad that I met up with no other boaters in the fog in the narrow part of the channel. I am sure that during the summer the bay is busy, but not today, a foul and foggy day in October!

It would have been nice to take a walk tonight and eat some real food, but I was so tired and there was a lot of cleanup to do onboard. I made a rum drink and heated a can of soup. (Pea soup, in honor of the fog.) According to sea lore, pea soup should be avoided onboard a boat. The belief is that it brings up the wind. I am at a dock, I'm not at sea, and the wind is already blowing strong! I missed my walk, but I enjoyed seeing a beautiful rainbow as the sun gained power over the clouds at the end of the day. The pretty colors of the rainbow were such a treat to see after the last few days of gray rain and blustery winds. A mug of rum and a rainbow. Sweet. I am lucky.

A Great Big Adventure on a Good Little Boat

October 15
At Morrison's Marina

I woke up to gale-force winds and they didn't let up all day. Maybe the pea soup last night really was a bad idea. It is cold and horrible. The awful weather just won't let up. I get to travel for a day, and then I get weathered in for two to three days! I can't get out of this system of storms. The miserable weather and I are traveling at the same speed. Oh well, my little boat and I are safe here and I've meet some friendly people.

I took a walk into the peaceful town of Beach Haven on the barrier island called Long Island. The town must be a hopping summer resort town, but now the season is over and most of the specialty tourist shops are closed.

New Jersey to Maryland

The main road through town is quiet, with very little traffic. I like this. I walked less than a mile across the island to visit the beach on the Atlantic Ocean. The ocean was rough, with enormous and powerful waves crashing on the beach. There wasn't a soul to be seen. The wind was so strong that I had a hard time standing upright! I am glad not to be on the ocean today! I'm lucky that my *Summer Wind* is safely docked at a marina away from this unbelievably brutal day on the ocean. I walked for a couple of hours, enjoying the sights and stretching my legs.

October 16
Still at Morrison's Marina

I am captive here in New Jersey! The winds are still blowing gale force, and the temperature is bitter. There are whitecaps in the marina! I spent lots of time tending my lines and fenders and listening to the weather predictions. It looks like the storm will be with us for at least another day or two. For the rest of the day I read, walked, and shivered. I walked to the beach again and stood facing the impressive power and force of the wind and waves. The ocean was amazingly rough!

New Jersey to Maryland

I greatly respect the sea and am in deep awe of its powers.

~Thorleif Thorleifsson

I met Marlene and Jerry as they were walking down the dock to their boat. They recognized me as that lady who was sailing to Florida on *that little boat*. I didn't hesitate a moment when they invited me to dinner aboard their cruising powerboat. That night as I walked toward dinner with my new friends, I was guided by the warm glow of their comfortable and cozy home on the water. Marlene and Jerry were as warm as their boat. We had a hot and delicious dinner and interesting conversation. Marlene and Jerry cruise to Florida every year and they are here visiting friends while waiting for the weather to break. My new friends are waiting for the weather to break and I'm waiting for the weather to break, so we are in the same boat! A break in the weather—a long break—would be a good thing!

October 17
Another Day at Morrison's Marina

Lying in my snug cabin, listening to the horrible winds whipping through the rigging, made me remember the violent storm that tore through our property in Rye. It was about ten years ago that the tremendous winds from what was later called the "No-Name Storm" raced through the seacoast area of New Hampshire. We lost dozens of massive trees and portions of my extensive gardens were damaged. During the quick, tornado-like winds, I had been standing in our gazebo and I watched as the wind blew the rain horizontally and ripped trees out of the ground by their roots. The wind crashed through the woods and I thought it sounded like a freight train barreling toward me. I was in awe; it was such a powerful act of nature!

Here in Beach Haven, the winds are still blowing a gale. There is no letup yet. It is just too windy and rough to leave the safety of the marina.

I've met some more people here. I enjoy their company and relish the time that I spend aboard their warm and comfy yachts. A sport fisherman and I got to talking about the Little Egg Inlet, which is just south of this marina and one that I will have to navigate past. He said that there has been shoaling and the sands have shifted, making our charts inaccurate. He invited me aboard his boat to look over his charts and showed me the location of the new shoals so that I would be able to avoid these problem areas. There is nothing like local knowledge. Running aground wouldn't be pleasant, especially since the inlet will still be rough when I pass through, even after the winds calm down. He and I listened to the weather, and I decided that the wind should let up enough for me to leave tomorrow.

I thanked my new fisherman buddy and made the rounds to pay my dock bill and say goodbye to all my new friends who have opted to stay put for another day or so. I will miss them, but we promised to keep in touch.

A Great Big Adventure on a Good Little Boat

I need to keep traveling south. I want to be warm. This weather is getting tiring. I want the sun to shine and the water to be blue and sparkle. I remember how sunny and warm the Bahamas were. My parents and brothers and sisters sailed into the Exuma Islands on the *Sunbeam* in November and we reveled in the heat and bright sunshine. The clear, turquoise waters around the islands impressed us. We could see the coral heads in the white sand on the bottom through the sparkling waters. It was funny; the islanders were wearing wool caps and jackets. We thought they were crazy, as crazy as they thought we were wearing our T-shirts and shorts!

October 18
Beach Haven to Corson Inlet, New Jersey
ICW mile 90
39°13 '/ 74° 39.10'

After another fitful night, I slipped my dock lines at 0725. The wind had died quite a lot. I had no issue leaving the marina and I had no problems with the shoaling conditions at the Little Egg Inlet, thanks to my fisherman friend. As I had figured, the inlet was still quite rough and I got wet, but no big deal, I've been wet before. I didn't run aground and that is what counts.

Once past the choppy inlet, it was a pretty trip through the low and marshy lands of the New Jersey coast and her barrier islands. I passed Grassy Bay, which is land, not water.

A Great Big Adventure on a Good Little Boat

Goes to show how low and marshy the area is. This section of the ICW is narrow, with twists and turns that I found very enjoyable. I wasn't able to sail, but there was lots of nature to see and I wasn't getting salt water in my face. To me, it was like taking a leisurely hike through a pristine and quiet forest. I was moving on the water and enjoying the sights and sounds of the world around me. This is living. Quiet and easy passages like this one allow me time to think and realize how lucky I am. Today I am free; I have no regrets and I have no fears. I am living in the moment. There is no room in my head for anything but what is right here at this very moment. This is real freedom and happiness.

For quite a while in the distance, I could see the tall buildings of the city of Brigantine on Brigantine Island. The next city looming on the horizon was Atlantic City. If I remember correctly, we came into the Absecon Inlet at Atlantic City aboard the *Sunbeam* many years ago. I remember that it was terribly rough and many of us onboard were sick from being tossed around in the violent Atlantic. In spite of being sick, we were all topside to see the sights of the city as we entered the very turbulent inlet.

We finally got into calm water and I can't remember whether we anchored or docked, but I do remember going below, still with a sensitive stomach, and seeing that a huge container of chocolate syrup had broken open. The gooey and smelly mess covered everything. The smell was overwhelming. It was gross. Maybe that is why, to this day, I am not all that fond of chocolate.

The *Summer Wind* and I traveled past Atlantic City, continuing south in the waterway, bypassing the Absecon Inlet. Beyond the city I powered past the huge windmills that I assume help keep the wheels of Atlantic City turning. These windmills were gigantic and, actually, I found them pretty in a sculptural sort of way. At ICW mile 67, the Route 30 Bridge blocked my path. I radioed the bridge tender to request an opening and got no answer. I proceeded closer to the bridge so that I could read the posted operating times and found that I had just missed an opening. I circled in the waterway for half an hour and then again headed toward the bridge. As I got close to the bridge, I hailed the tender on the radio again. This time I got a response. He called back with an attitude and said that I should read the sign. I thought that I had, but there was another sign. The bridge was closed due to construction. He could have told me that a half-hour ago. He must have sat on a rabbit this morning! Oh well. I had to backtrack

A Great Big Adventure on a Good Little Boat

to Atlantic City and travel through the Absecon Inlet and out into the dreaded North Atlantic.

I motored through a calm inlet and surprise, surprise, into a calm and beautiful Atlantic! It was a great day to be on the outside in the ocean. I motored into the wind and raised my sails, happy to take advantage of the light winds and the open waters.

It was so nice to be able to sail on a friendly sea. I find such a great sense of freedom and peace when the sailing conditions are like this. There is no stress. The sails are full and the seas are quiet. I could fall asleep! I sailed close to shore to enjoy the shore-side views. I saw Trump's Taj Mahal Casino. It was very impressive to see the building from the water. I felt rich just sailing past that grand structure. Not everyone gets a chance to enjoy this view. The beach was gorgeous. It was so long and so white and it seemed to glow in the sunshine. There were no people on the beach today; the sun was shining, but it was still cold and breezy. I read in my guidebook that Atlantic City's famous boardwalk was the first of its kind and that the original boardwalk was built in 1870. It has been rebuilt several times over the years and runs southwest from the Absecon Inlet for four miles.

New Jersey to Maryland

It was a pleasant sail for the almost eight miles to the Great Egg Harbor Inlet. I started the outboard and lowered sail to enter the inlet. This inlet was scary! I saw only breaking waves and a bridge, with no apparent way to make the passage to the bridge. It looked impassible! I am so low on the water aboard my boat, which is a great disadvantage when the waves are high. The only way possible to make out the channel is to keep sailing toward it. Finally, as I continued farther into the channel, I was able to see the buoy and make my way through the inlet and back into the ICW. The chart showed a low bridge, but it has been replaced with a high one. Hooray! Bridges that have to open for me can prove difficult at times. Sometimes I have to wait and maneuver, trying to stay in the channel, possibly dealing with a current, a skinny waterway, or both. With my little outboard, this can be a challenge, especially when you add other boats to the mix. A high bridge is a good thing.

After passing Ocean City just south of the inlet, the ICW led me through Peck Bay, which is very shallow except in the narrow waterway of the ICW. The small Peck Bay led me into Crook Horn Creek, which is surrounded by low and marshy land. At this point, I was starting to look for a place to anchor for the night. My charts and the cruising guide showed no anchorages in this area. It was terribly windy and, because there was no high ground or trees to block the winds, finding a protected place to rest for the night was proving to be a problem. Finally, at about 1645, I anchored just off the waterway at about ICW mile 87 at marker 309, near the Corson Inlet. This was a relatively protected spot and I enjoyed an undisturbed evening.

I only use my phone at night to preserve battery power and, after the saltwater spray my phone received in New York, I don't like to keep my phone in the cockpit while under way. When I settled in for the night, I turned on my phone to receive a message from one of the friends I had met at the Beach Haven Marina. There is another storm coming up the coast! Just what I need!

October 19
Corson Inlet to Cape May Harbor, New Jersey
ICW mile 115
38° 57.'/ 74° 53.45'

Marshes filled with birds border this part of the ICW and I found it very peaceful to meander through these quiet waters. I saw cormorants and ibis. There were lots of ducks, including Brant and Wood ducks and other ducks that I couldn't identify. I saw one or two brown pelicans and the ever-present gulls.

Today was an enjoyable contrast to the rough and windy ocean and the open bays that I've traveled through. I know that there will be many more open and potentially nasty waters to traverse, so I appreciate the quiet areas. Here, there is time to pause and enjoy nature and the peace and solitude of a leisurely boat ride. There is no schedule here. There is no place to be except right here. I can let my boat drift and I can let my mind drift. I can think to the future. No wait, I have no future. I have no plans. Maybe I should become a vagabond and just wander about on the sea for the rest of my life.

I saw no other boats today until I entered the Cape May Harbor. Four sailing cruisers sailed in from the ocean and entered the harbor just ahead of me. They anchored off the Coast Guard Station as I continued on to Utsch's Marina for gas for the outboard and fuel for my cook stove. The marina was a busy place, and I had many eyes on me as I pulled up to the fuel dock. My outboard didn't die when I idled and I made a good landing. After restocking, I joined about six sailing vessels in the anchorage. I could hear the cadence of the cadets marching and "Taps" as I anchored. It is exciting to be here. My little boat and I have come a long way and I am satisfied with our abilities. The *Summer Wind* has successfully fulfilled her duty as a sea-worthy vessel, and I have been an able captain. We are a good team. There is hope for us yet!

New Jersey to Maryland

I love Cape May. I've visited by car a couple of times and love the character of the city; I especially love the Victorian architecture. Years ago, my daughter Ericka gave Don and me the gift of a long weekend at a beautiful Victorian bed-and-breakfast here. It was a fantastic and thoughtful gift and I had a marvelous time. In fact, I was so inspired by the Victorian "painted ladies," both here and in San Francisco, that I built my own painted lady. My tribute to this period is a gorgeous home in Rye, and it will stand for many years as my signature house. I am very proud of my painted lady.

I loved building houses. The first home I built was a post-and-beam Cape. I love the simplicity and the clean lines of a Cape. The last house I built was my "painted lady," with 27 outside walls and fancy trim work on every surface. I appreciate both the simple structures and the complexity and intricacy of the Victorian-era homes. I put my heart and soul into each one of my projects, and it showed.

I miss walking into lumberyards, hardware stores, and paint stores and being known by name. I liked being a "favored customer." I miss being a regular. It was fun to be recognized as the woman who built "that fancy house in Rye." After Don left, I built my own separate business and clientele. Many of my customers would have no one else work on their projects. That was a nice feeling.

My favorite project was the restoration of a 1908 cottage on tiny Monhegan Island, off the coast of Maine. The restoration of the "Four Winds" began with the yard sale at my home in Rye. The court had ordered me to vacate our marital home and I was selling most of the contents. My first step was to call an auctioneer. Then I held the mother of all yard sales. Tom came to check out the sale. Tom asked, "Who built this amazing house?" I told Tom that *I* had built it. He was impressed with both my design abilities and the quality of my workmanship. He mentioned that he owned a cottage on an island and how difficult it was to get anyone to work in such an isolated area. Tom asked if I could deal with the difficulties of working on an island. "Of course I can cope with working on an island; I spent years building houses on islands!" I exaggerated the truth a tad; hell, I exaggerated a ton! I was a kid when we built houses in the Bahama Islands. I needed the work, and I knew that I could somehow do the job and I could do it well.

After my initial visit to the cottage, I knew it was a project I could sink my teeth into. In fact, I was scared about getting in over my head with such a massive job. As it turned out, it was just what I needed.

Tom had told me that the cottage needed some "cosmetic" work! Ha! The "Four Winds" hadn't been worked on for over 30 years! The back porch was rotten, the front porch was too tender to even walk on, the steps off the front porch fell down when I walked up them to take a picture, and the east side of the cottage was sinking into the ground. This was a *major* restoration. What had I gotten myself into? I was scared to take the job. Tom's project was more than I had bargained for. This was a major job, but I had no choice. I was alone and I had a home to maintain and bills to pay, so when I returned to New Hampshire with my report to Tom, I told him that I couldn't wait to start his project. Meg and I had a job!

Tom trusted my every decision, from the design, materials, and construction methods down to choosing colors for the interior and exterior. He gave me free rein. I started his "little project" by jacking up the building and pouring new footings. I recruited two builder friends to help me with that part of the job.

With the help of a local woman—Zoe—I replaced all the siding and windows. I built new decks on three sides of the cottage and, to his delight, I built Tom a beautiful mahogany and cedar outside shower. Tom loved my work and I had lots of fun working for him. He even loved Meg!

Although I would enjoy visiting Cape May again, I don't plan to go ashore. It might prove too painful. Don and I had a wonderful visit here and I don't think I could handle those memories. They are too fresh. Besides, as an excuse, I spent too much money on dockage while I was weathered in at Morrison's Marina. Without a little skiff, I can't get ashore without paying dockage. The cold is biting my heels; I just want to keep traveling. I still have a long way to go, and I want to be on my way. Another storm is supposed to hit here soon. I'll listen to the weather tonight, and I hope to be lucky enough to get through the Cape May Canal and into a safe anchorage off the Delaware before the weather comes in again.

New Jersey to Maryland

October 20
Cape May Harbor

The heavy rain and high winds humming through the rigging woke me up at around 0300. I got up to a howling wind, whitecaps in the harbor, and spray in the cockpit. I let out more scope in my anchor rode (line) and checked to make sure that my little boat wasn't dragging. Another storm has caught me! I had been planning to leave today and travel through the Cape May Canal and get a few miles up the Delaware before the stormy weather attacked me again. This weather wasn't supposed to happen today!

The other boats in the harbor are also captive here. I am sure that they are all much more comfy than I am. They have cabins and heat. I can see the warm glow of their cabin lights, and one night I heard music and laughter. They were making the best of the situation. Anchored close to me is another solo sailor. His is a sturdy little sloop; he has a larger cabin than mine and he can cook below and out of the wind and the weather. He probably has a head!

At 0500 it was still rainy, windy, cold, and rough. My boat was jerking at her anchor with every wind gust. I am uncomfortable, wet, and so cold, but my anchor is holding, which is a very good thing! By 1245 the wind had died down a bit and the rain had been replaced with fog. A hint of sun started to filter through the fog and clouds. The harbor was still sporting a good chop, and as I sat in the cockpit the spray was moisturizing my face. During the day I spent my time trying to figure the tides and currents through the Cape May Canal and up the Delaware.

The Delaware is 56 miles of swift currents, with very few protected anchorages. Most cruisers can make the passage up the Delaware and into the Chesapeake & Delaware Canal in one day. There is no way that I can travel that many miles in single day. I don't mind leaving my anchorage before dawn, but I have no desire to be in unfamiliar water, trying to find a safe place to anchor in the dark. I need to find one or two anchorages off the Delaware so that I can be safe and secure as the sun sets. I checked my running rigging because I hope to be able to raise sail and take advantage of the open waters of the Delaware.

There will be lots of huge commercial ships on the bay, so I finally rigged my radar reflector. I have found the leaks in my cabin top—actually they found me—one drips into my ear and one into my eye. This is why my bunk and sleeping bag are always wet. Everything is too wet to fix, and I don't have the right caulking to do the repair. Next stop, it will be on my list.

Everything is damp! I am waterlogged! My fingers and toes are wrinkled and I am cold. I should have brought a pair of long pants to wear under my foul-weather gear; the shorts just aren't hacking it! Socks would be nice too!

A couple of sailors came by in a small inflatable boat. They are sailing aboard a pretty 32' sloop that is anchored downwind and beyond my boat. Lita and Kristopher were returning from a wet ride to shore. It had been so rough that they had almost swamped their small skiff. They came by to say hello and we complained to each other about the awful weather. We are all tired of waiting.

This next leg of the trip has me a little nervous. I want to figure the currents and the tides right. I want to find a safe place to anchor. I'm anxious to start on the next portion of my trip. The Delaware is a big and open body of water and can get very snotty. I don't know what I'm worried about; I've been in rough and miserable seas before and my boat and I have been fine. I just need to get sailing. A mug of rum will make things better.

October 21
Still waiting in Cape May Harbor

Everything is unbelievably damp. This waiting is getting very tedious. All of the cruisers and I are still here and just biding our time, waiting for the weather window to open so that we can continue our voyage to warmer climes. Without a skiff, I am captive on my little boat. I don't want to pay for dockage since I spent too much while I was stuck at the Beach Haven Marina in New Jersey, and I just can't bring myself to spend more money so soon. Plus, I don't want to be stuck at a marina where I have absolutely no privacy. Life at anchor in the bay is uncomfortable and boring, but at least I have

159

my privacy. I will have to wait out the storm here at anchor.

Thank goodness for my books. As you can imagine, with no other stimuli, I do read a lot. Every marina that I've docked at has a book trading library. I drop off the books that I've read and pick up new books. Unfortunately, most of the books at the marina libraries are fiction. I prefer biographies, and of course stories about traveling. I especially enjoy sea stories. I spend a lot of time reading my cruising guides. I like to read about the cities and towns along the ICW. I will miss visiting many of the noteworthy places listed in the guides, but it is still fun to read about them. I find myself writing interesting excerpts from my books on the inside of my cabin top, just above my bunk. The cabin top is littered with penciled writing. Many of the quotes and sayings listed in this book are from the writings above my bunk. The mold from the dampness makes it hard to read some of them. I just scribble around the condensation drips and spots of mold.

Lita and Kristopher stopped by tonight and invited me aboard their boat for dinner. I never refuse a dinner invitation. I dug up a bottle of wine from my stash in the bilge, jumped aboard their dingy and, after a wet and wild ride, I enjoyed a dry, warm, and friendly visit with my new friends. It was a wonderful evening. Lita and Kristopher have sold everything they own and they've moved on board their pretty boat named *Way Happy*. There is so much room in their boat! The main salon was finished with rich, varnished mahogany. There was a navigation table and a snug working galley where the couple produced a delicious meal. They even had a boat cat that lounged on their forward bunk. All the comforts of home! I hadn't thought about how much I've been roughing it! But, I love my little boat and my big adventure, and I wouldn't change too much!

Lita and Kristopher plan to sail to St. Petersburg, where they have jobs lined up. Dave, the solo sailor who is anchored close to me, joined us and we had a fun evening together. Much of our talk was about our experiences during our travels. Most of Lita and Kristopher's and Dave's voyage down the coast has been outside the ICW, and their stories were ones of rough and scary passages out on the stormy North Atlantic. My stories related cold, wet, and rough days in the open waterways of the ICW, but I also included tales of my escapades around the marinas and the interesting characters who I have met. I am pleased about my choice to travel down the ICW. It may be a slower voyage, with less sailing, but I've enjoyed seeing the countryside and meeting other cruisers.

During the visit, Lita showed me a copy of *Anchorages Along the Intracoastal Waterway*. This book is great and I must have a copy. It is a "Skipper Bob Publication," and it provides information on the best—and some of the more obscure—anchorages along the ICW. Many of these anchorages are not mentioned on the charts or in the coastal guidebooks. What a fantastic book! I want a copy. I need this book!

While I was aboard the *Way Happy* enjoying her owners' warmth and hospitality, I happened to look beyond the other anchored boats and saw my little *Summer Wind* in the distance. Oh-my-gosh, she is *so* small and she rides *so* very low in the water! It's no wonder that many people exclaim: "You are sailing to Florida in *that*?" My boat is so tiny. I actually found it amazing to see how truly small she looked.

After a home-cooked meal and an exciting and warm evening, Dave rowed me back to my home and back to my reality. That night, stretched out in my bunk, waiting out the weather, I thought about my friends in New Hampshire. I miss them. I miss my range of friends. I miss calling Vivian and Paul, inviting myself to dinner, offering to bring a butterfly leg of lamb for Paul to grill and maybe a bottle of wine. They always greeted me and I was able to satisfy my need for companionship. After a hard day of lawyer business or work, I could swing by Mary and Bob's home and know I'd be received with open arms and offered a drink and dinner. Karen and John were another fantastic couple of friends. I was always welcome to talk, drink, eat and sleep there. Sue and Leo had the knack of inviting me for dinner when I needed company. My Aunt Martha and Uncle Ansel were always there for a quiet meal and peaceful conversation. Marty and Steve, until they moved, always had an open door for me and for Meg. I knew I could pop into their home and be comforted, fed, and put to bed with a hot water bottle to warm my feet and my pathetic soul.

All of these friends are beyond what I can say. I couldn't have survived my trauma without each one of them. I am so fortunate. I miss their friendship and support. They haven't left me, I've left them. I'm not sure I've done the right thing. I guess only time will tell. I do know that I will never forget the special—and necessary— support of these friends.

My little boat rocked me to sleep and, in spite of the cold and wind, I slept well. It had

A Great Big Adventure on a Good Little Boat

been a memorable night with my new friends. I wish them safe travels.

October 22
Another day in Cape May Harbor

I woke to another morning of spray in the cockpit and the promise of another windy and cold day. I had been up several times during the night and was slightly encouraged by the sight of a few stars and a sliver of moon peeking through the clouds. This latest storm may break soon. The winds and cold this morning weren't promising though. The wind was still blowing with a vengeance and the anchorage was still quite choppy. All my clothes are wet, all my bedding is wet, the wind is howling, and my boat and I are shuddering. It will be better tomorrow. Tomorrow the sun will shine and the earth will be warm. My orders to the weather gods.

A Great Big Adventure on a Good Little Boat

Sometime during the day, I heard an outboard and poked my head from out of my damp cabin. The couple traveling aboard a green-hulled sloop, also at the anchorage, was heading inshore in their dingy. They swung by and asked if I needed anything. What luck! I asked for a Skipper Bob book. They knew of the book and offered to try to find a copy for me. I gave them $20. I want to get my hands on that book, so I crossed my fingers.

My phone has not worked since its saltwater bath off Liberty Island in New York. I wasn't paying attention and a fast boat's wake swamped my cockpit and my phone. I have found that salt water is almost instant death to a cell phone. I radioed to my new friend Dave via my VHF radio and asked him to call my brother Willy in Florida so that Willy could pass the word to everyone that I was OK.

While waiting out the weather, I read a bit of interesting information about Cape May. I had been familiar with the beautiful architecture of the buildings here, and I knew that this is an active fishing port. What I hadn't known was that this point of land was the end of an important Indian trail. The Indians used to take off from here to hunt whales in the bay. The area is also a natural barrier for birds migrating the

New Jersey to Maryland

East Coast flyway. During the fall, migrating land and sea birds funnel down the Cape to wait and rest. They wait for good weather. They wait just as we are waiting today. Birds of a feather.

My friends from the green-hulled boat returned from their trip ashore. They were soaked and looked cold and wretched. It had been a rough trip back for them, but they found my book! I invited them aboard and offered them rum, but my accommodations weren't very welcoming, so they continued on to their boat. I was very happy to get this informative book. I have a feeling it will prove to be very helpful in the future.

The wind is starting to diminish—not enough to leave yet, although I may try to leave tomorrow. The canal is not a problem with the wind and rough seas, since I will be protected there. The problem happens in the Delaware Bay. The bay is an open body of water: in these strong winds and rough seas, my boat and I might actually be in danger.

There is much you could do at sea with common sense...and very little you could do without it...

~Anonymous

A Great Big Adventure on a Good Little Boat

Hopefully, by tomorrow the wind will diminish enough so that I can continue heading south. My plan is to get through the canal, enter the Delaware, and sail to a calm place to anchor off the bay in the protected Cohansey River. This stop-over will bring me just over halfway up the bay. If I get an early start, I will be in good shape to get through the Chesapeake and Delaware Canal that next day. I found this potential anchorage with the help of my new best friend, Skipper Bob. Actually, I found three possible anchorages. This is my typical method. I like to plan a couple of anchorages along my day's voyage in case I encounter a storm, engine problems, or I just plain get tired.

I joined Lita and Kristopher for a few hours this afternoon. They plan to leave tomorrow also. With their friend Dave aboard the *Azure,* Lita and Kristopher plan to travel on the *Way Happy* in the ocean; I will miss them.

This evening, while warming my tummy with a rum and tonic, I heard "Taps" playing at the Coast Guard Station. Being here and listening to "Taps" makes me think of my parents. They both served in the Navy during the war. I've thought of them often, especially during this trip. I would love to be able to call them each night to tell them where I am and what the weather is like and what I'm doing. Dad would tell me how I should have sailed or how I could have avoided this or that. He would have done it this way and I should have also. I would still have enjoyed the chance to share my experiences with them. I might have even made Dad a little proud. Just maybe.

Mom and Dad's passion for sailing and adventure has been passed down to most of their kids.

My brother Greg is an avid sailboat racer and owns a few boats that he's restored. They are gorgeous. My sister Cindy and her husband Tim are busy remodeling their home and have kids with busy social schedules, so their boats are go-fast boats, enabling them to speed to a vacation spot and enjoy the destination. Sailors take pleasure in the voyage, while power boaters' desire is to reach their destination. To each their own. Obviously I am in the first group. What power boater would be happy to travel down the coast at walking speed?

I remember a boating trip with Cindy and Tim and their kids. We were just spending a day of enjoying the beach and water. Our return voyage is what stands out in my mind. We were aboard their twin-engine cruiser and made short time of the cruise to our destination. We were able to speed over the waters of the Gulf to our beach spot. As I remember, we left late in the day, expecting to make a quick return home. Of course, as things worked out, Tim lost power in one engine. No big deal, but we decided it would be safer to limp home in the ICW rather than return via the Gulf.

When we finally reached Cindy and Tim's dock, it was after 3 a.m. I loved that boat trip home! We had to work together to search for the ICW markers. We had a common goal and each of us became necessary; we worked as a team. To me, that's what boating is. We're literally in the same boat. We are in the same predicament and each must do his (or her) part for the whole to succeed. Mom and Dad taught us this, not with words, but with actions. We—my brothers and sisters and I—have been exposed to this kind of attitude our whole lives. It's part of being a large family; it's part of living and sailing on a boat; it's part of moving to remote areas where there is no one to rely on but one another.

I slept well tonight thinking about finally moving on. The waves in the harbor had calmed a bit and the rum warmed my tummy. The almost gentle rocking of my *Summer Wind* lulled me into a peaceful sleep.

October 23
Cape May Harbor to Cohansey River off the Delaware Bay,New Jersey
39° 20.62' / 75° 21.98'
(There are no ICW miles on the Delaware Bay)

As usual, I was up early and found that the wind had dropped and the harbor was calm. Finally, I can leave today. Hallelujah! My friends aboard the *Way Huppy* and the *Azure* arc getting an early start, but I have to wait until about 0900 for favorable currents in the canal and the bay. My outboard is just four horsepower and I need to rely on following tides to make headway in most of the canals and waterways. I hate to wait. The waiting was killing me, so I weighed

171

anchor at 0830. After all my worrying about dragging, I had a hard time pulling the anchor up out of the mud. It was so stuck that I couldn't haul it up by hand and I had to use my cockpit winch to pull it up. I spent so many sleepless nights worrying about my anchor dragging; what a waste of time that was.

My one-hour trip through the canal was uneventful. The current eased as I got near the end of the canal, and I had a following current in the Delaware for the rest of the day's travels. I had no traffic in the canal until I reached the Cape May Ferry terminal. Two of the massive ferries were docked there. Just as I was astern of them, I heard three horn blasts indicating that one of the ships was backing out of her dock and into the canal. The ferries are huge and use the entire width of the canal to back out of their docks. Of course, one of them had to back out just as I was passing. I don't think that the skipper even saw me! I cranked up my little outboard and hightailed it out of there as fast as my little engine could move me. Respect tonnage!

The chop and waves in the Delaware soaked me to the skin within minutes. Fun times! I was disappointed that there would be no sailing today because, again, the wind was on my nose. I had planned to be able to sail all the way to the Cohansey River, but now, in this cold, wet, and rough bay, the closer, alternate anchorage in the Maurice River was looking very appealing. I was so unbearably cold.

The frigid bay water assaulted me and dripped down my neck, soaking my clothes under my foul-weather gear. My GPS, my charts, and everything in the cockpit were doused with the constant deluge of the Delaware Bay waters. After a while, I kind of got so used to being so miserable that I decided to go a little farther on to Back Creek to anchor, though Back Creek was still shy of my goal destination of the Cohansey River. In spite of the fact that the wind was on my nose, the current was with me and I was making good time. I hated the thought of wasting a speedy travel day by stopping early.

The wind was supposed to be five to ten knots today. It was more like 15 to 20 and gusty. I am headed north. (Actually northwest.) Why am I going north? Why is the wind out of the northwest?

Since I was so cold and wet already, I decided to go all the way to the Cohansey. No sense stopping now. I want to keep going and travel away from this weather that keeps plaguing me. It wasn't until 1700 that I entered the Cohansey River and found a place to drop my anchor. I secured my boat, plotted tomorrow's course, and made myself a rum drink. I was exhausted and still shivering from the cold. I hadn't eaten all day. It was just too rough and too cold to do anything other than brace myself and stand at the tiller and steer. Today, the wind blew my gas cap away and I broke my funnel as I was trying to fill my gas tank while under way: it was one of my roughest days of travel since I left the North Atlantic.

The tide is flowing so strong in this river that my little boat, at anchor, is making a wake. My phone still doesn't work; I worry that family and friends are worried. I slept in the cockpit so that I could keep one eye on the stars to make sure that the boat wasn't dragging in the strong current. My cruising guidebook describes the Cohansey River as a river full of sharp bends and switchbacks: on the chart it looks like a bit of blue silly string as it squiggles into the New Jersey shore. The book didn't mention anything about the strong current! I'll have to be alert tonight.

When I woke at 2200, I was wet with dew. The boom had been dripping on me. We weren't dragging, so I went below to get some sleep. I didn't sleep well; I was too wet and too cold.

New Jersey to Maryland

Even though I don't have a job waiting for me in Sarasota, I may be warm there. I hope so. I don't know if I will be happy in sunny Florida. Yes, my sisters and brothers will be close and there will be no snow to shovel, but I loved living in Rye for 40 years. I have 40-year friendships there. I have connections there. I do love New England. I miss my old life, but I have to accept the fact that it is gone. I have been set free. Now I have to make sure that I make the best of my gift. Don't screw it up, Linda.

A Great Big Adventure on a Good Little Boat

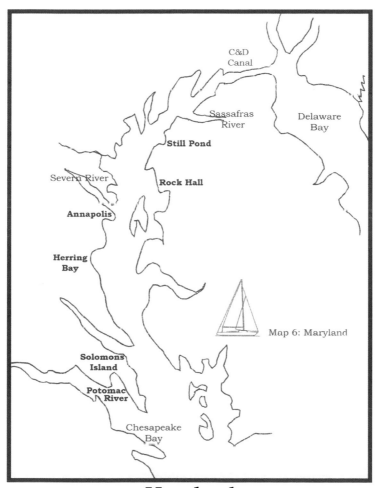

C&D
Canal

Sassafras
River

Delaware
Bay

Still Pond

Severn River

Rock Hall

Annapolis

**Herring
Bay**

Map 6: Maryland

**Solomons
Island**

**Potomac
River**

Chesapeake
Bay

Maryland

A Great Big Adventure on a Good Little Boat

October 24
Cohansey River, NJ to Still Pond Creek, Maryland
39° 20.' / 76° 07.92'

After an uncomfortable night of trying to warm my frozen body, I got up at 0500 and was underway by 0530. It was still cold and as dark as the devil's heart. There was a thick fog and the river was full of twists and turns with a strong current. This must be a test. I passed a small boat that was sitting against the shore. It was still dark so I was able to see only the silhouette of the boat and her occupants. They had rifles and I hoped that they were goose hunting, not sailor hunting.

Maryland

Once I got back into the Delaware Bay, navigating was easy, but I was not happy that I was still heading north. I was told that when I got into the Delaware Bay, I should just head for the big nuke plant plume; for two days now, that's what I've done. Today, I finally passed it. Another milestone! Next goal...the Chesapeake & Delaware Canal!

Today's trip was lovely. It was an easy ride up the Delaware Bay. This was a nice change from the weather these last two days. The wind is still out of the northwest, making sailing impossible, but it was an enjoyable day to be on the water. Only three huge ships passed me and we were far enough apart that their wakes were not an issue. I had figured the tides right and I enjoyed a favorable current all day. By gum, I might be getting the knack of this. Today I made seven knots most of the way up the bay and through the C&D Canal.

The canal was beautiful to travel through. I have motored through here at least once before, when I crewed aboard the *Lynx*, the beautiful 78-foot topsail schooner from Portsmouth, New Hampshire, to Baltimore. If I remember correctly, there are five high bridges and a railroad bridge with a closed height of 40 feet.

The canal is 14 miles long and connects the Chesapeake and the Delaware bays. In 1822, enough money was raised to get federal funding for the canal and the digging began. More than 2,600 men dug and hacked away with shovels and pickaxes for seven years. Amazing! The canal opened to ship traffic in 1829, and back then it was only ten feet deep and 66 feet wide. In 1919 the United States Government bought the canal and made it part of the ICW. The canal was deepened to 12 feet, widened to 90 feet, and the four locks were removed. Today the canal is 35 feet deep and 400 feet wide! It is remarkable to think that such a marvel was initially dug by hand. We are very lucky to have this shortcut. I am lucky to have this shortcut!

Wow, I am anchored in Still Pond Creek and it *is* still. I am in Maryland and finally out of New Jersey. Hooray! I hear the sound of geese and it makes me smile. My heart feels warm and I think I might sleep tonight. It was a comfortable traveling day; the wind was on the nose, but the water was calm and I didn't get wet. Staying dry makes all the difference in the world! It's still cold but the sun was shining all day.

I got to the Delaware end of the canal at 0900 and into Still Pond Creek at about 1530. I am sitting at anchor, in a beautiful creek, and not another soul is here. It's just the wild

Maryland

Canadian geese and me. Still Pond Creek is very small, with enough room for maybe two or three little boats. Trees grow down to the edges of the water, and their reflections on the smooth waters almost touch my boat. I can hear the wonderful sound of honking geese. The geese will probably land and rest on the still waters with me. I'm probably fortunate that it has been so cold because this might be a mosquito haven otherwise.

I'm glad to have Skipper Bob with me because I would have never noticed this creek on the chart. I followed the skipper's directions and entered a small cove off the Chesapeake, but I couldn't see any markers to indicate the entrance into the creek. I kept heading toward shore and to where the markers should be. Finally, I saw the first set of red-and-green day markers, and then I saw the second set. From where I was, the channel looked too narrow to be viable. I was thinking that this is a joke, a pirate trick maybe. Skipper Bob must be part of this hoax: lure a boat in and then rape and pillage and burn the evidence. Wow, maybe I should go to a dock where there are people. I must be losing it. I braved it out and entered the narrow passage into the possible trap. No trap— the markers are actually over 20 feet apart and they led me into a quiet and secluded piece of the world.

My clothes are dry and my bedding is drying in the sun. I've done my navigating for tomorrow, the sun is setting, and the rum is good. Life is wonderful! I may never leave. This is a definite "return to" place! I am happy to be in Maryland and in the Chesapeake. I am headed south—a good thing. I did a victory dance when I left the Delaware Bay and another upon entering the Chesapeake. I raised my arms, did a little jig, and walloped out a big victory yell!

This pond is so protected and quiet. The sun is setting and I am enjoying another rum and a meal. I actually cooked tonight. I sautéed an onion and added an Indian curry-with-mushroom thing. I added noodles and feasted. This is living. I can't believe how lucky I am to be enjoying such an exciting adventure.

Life is funny. The "ups" are so exciting. Don and I had so many ups. We did so many things as a family. Our home in Rye was special because it represented family togetherness. We hosted the best parties. For Don's parents' 50th anniversary, we rolled up the oriental rugs, moved back the furniture, hired a five-piece jazz band (his parents' favorite group), and we danced until we dropped! Our daughters Angela and Ericka worked hard to make sure to invite all of their grandparents' friends and keep the affair a total surprise. What a party! We had many unbelievable get-togethers. They were so much fun. They were so much work. We all worked together and made them happen. The good ole days. Good memories.

My days can be challenging. I usually leave before daybreak, after a restless sleep, hoping that I have figured my tides right—flooding in the Cape May Canal, ebbing in the C&D Canal. Big ships and huge wakes are always a threat. All but the smallest powerboats can be obnoxious, making wakes that break over my bow, soaking the whole cockpit and me. Even a one-foot chop can result in a wet and cold me. My charts get drenched, and my glasses get soaked and salty, which makes seeing difficult.

I protect my GPS with a baggie secured with a rubber band. The salt water coats the baggie, making it impossible to read the GPS screen through the film of salt.

It can be an issue finding a safe place to anchor at night. And the bridges can be a challenge. But I sit here now—full tummy, drink in hand—in a beautiful, secluded, and peaceful bay, on a happy little boat—and I wouldn't change a thing. The sun is setting and the geese are honking. Life doesn't get much better than this. It's like childbirth: you forget the bad parts. Or the bad parts are worth enduring because the good parts are so good.

Most of my day is spent standing at the tiller, with no food except for a couple of dried apricots, a few nuts, and a Corinita. I do have what I call my snack bar, which consists of a zip-lock baggie filled with nonperishable goodies like almonds, dried fruits, and my baby-sized Snickers bars. I usually stick to eating the nutritious foods in my snack bar, but on occasion a candy bar can be comforting. These snacks and my Corinita beer are often both my breakfast and lunch.

Of course a security is necessary, but security is only one aspect of life—man must also have things to fight and strive for, and so enhance the dignity of his life.

~David H. Lewis

Today was easy and dry, with no wet charts and no wet glasses. No water dripping down my back and into my eyes. No freezing cold. Life is great. I feel great. My good little boat and I have made it to Maryland! I think the worst is over. No more open ocean and I am headed south. I still hear the geese—I love geese. Last night I heard gunshots. Probably goose hunters. I felt bad—geese mate for life. It's sad to lose your mate.

I feel like I've lost too much these last few years. My life as I'd known it for 37 years is gone. My husband is gone. I no longer enjoy knowing that there is always someone to cover my back. I miss being there for him. I miss our work on the boat, setting moorings in the harbor. I miss all the building projects we accomplished together. We always said that between the two of us, we could do anything. And to think that he left 37 years of love, companionship, compassion, caring, and work, for a redhead. Amazing! Go figure.

My relationship with my daughters is gone. I miss my girls.

I miss the big, gorgeous Victorian home I built in Rye. I miss my extensive, award-winning gardens. I miss hosting weddings in my gardens. I miss my work as a wildlife rehabilitator. I miss my cut-your-own Christmas tree business. I miss working with my customers. I miss all of that life. My birds are gone and my dog is gone. I am 64 years old and every aspect of my life, except my relationship with my sisters and brothers, has ended.

So much is gone. But I still have the memories, and I try to focus on the happy ones.

A Great Big Adventure on a Good Little Boat

I am lucky to have these memories. Nothing is forever and everything has a time span. Everything ends.

> *What will see me through the next 20 years (and I am less sure of those 20 than I was of "forever") is my knowledge that even in the face of the sweeping away of all that I assumed to be permanent, even when the universe made it quite clear to me that I was mistaken in my certainties, in my definitions, I did not break. The shattering of my sureties did not shatter me. Stability comes from inside, not from the outside...*

~Lucille Clifton

Living in the past is not a place I want to be. I have to work at living in the present, living in the moment. Every experience is a building block of our character and every experience—good or bad—is important to the next steps of our lives. So I smile, enjoy, and continue my adventure on this earth, praising my lucky stars that I have the wherewithal to undertake this journey to free myself of the past and start a new life.

Maryland

October 25
Still Pond Creek to Rock Hall Harbor
ICW mile 21 to ICW mile 38.5
39° 08.'/ 76° 14.'
(The Chesapeake Bay starts at ICW mile
0 at the bridge at Chesapeake City in the
canal.)

I left lovely Still Pond at 0830 after a quiet
and restful night. I don't know why I left! It was
such a comfortable hideaway and one I'd like to
return to. There are many more miles to travel,
so I must weigh anchor and sail on. On my next
voyage, I want no destination, I just want to sail
and explore until I need to or want to stop. I
have discovered my next occupation! I could
become a vagabond. A hobo with a home. I'll just

keep traveling until I run out of places to visit! Back to reality, but I'll keep the vagabond idea in my head.

I motored the short distance into Worton Creek (on the eastern shore of the Chesapeake) with the intention of buying a phone. I was hoping that there would be a town close by so that I could replace my only means of communication. My waterlogged, nonworking phone is one of those "smart phones" and my only connection to the Internet, the National Weather Service, and e-mail. I miss it! I am still very concerned that my friends and family may be worried about me because I haven't been able to contact them.

I tied up to the fuel dock at Worton Creek and the place seemed deserted. There was no one in sight, no one had greeted me or helped me tie up. After walking around for a while I saw a man working on his boat and I asked him about getting a ride to town. He told me that the closest town wasn't close at all and the marina was pretty much shut down for the season. I found the marina's owner and bought a few gallons of unneeded gas so that I felt comfortable asking to use his phone. He invited me to call whomever I needed to, so that no one would be concerned about me. I hadn't planned to stay here; it was to be just a stop to buy a phone. After thanking the marina owner, I cast off my lines and traveled the short distance to my destination for today: Rock Hall Harbor, again on the Eastern Shore.

Both of my voyages today were short, but wet. The Chesapeake Bay was absolutely terrible! The water was dark, cold, and rough, and of course the wind was on my nose again. I was glad not to be motoring far today. It was hard to leave the quiet and relatively warm harbor of Worton Creek and motor back into the choppy waters of the bay. The creek was so welcoming and the bay was so nasty, but I wanted to travel closer to Annapolis today, so I headed back out into the challenging bay. It was another cold, wet, wind-and-spray-in-your-face day. Wow, I can't get south fast enough. I am getting the crap beaten out of me!

I reached Rock Hall cold and wet, but happy to be there. I tied up at the free town dock. No one else is here, although the docks to my stern are filled with boats, mainly work boats. Since this area is known for its oysters I assume that most of the boats are oystering boats. After talking to a couple of guys at the dock, I found out that there are quite a few crabbing boats here also. There are a number of yachts, but this appears to be a working town.

A Great Big Adventure on a Good Little Boat

I walked to town just to walk around and see the sights and get a bit of exercise. I found the town of Rock Hall to be a quiet town. There were the typical stores, like a grocery store, drug store, and a gas station. What was missing were the fancy, high-end specialty shops. This is a real, down-to-earth town. I could live here.

After working up an appetite, I enjoyed some oysters on the half shell at the restaurant near the dock. The oysters were local and delicious. While eating, I overheard a couple talking about the Great Circle Route. My ears perked up. The Great Circle Route is a trip I want to make someday. The route is a cruise up the East Coast of the United States, across the Erie Canal to the Great Lakes, the Trent-Severn, and the Georgian Bay, down the Mississippi and Tennessee rivers to the Gulf Coast of Florida, and back to the East Coast.

I wanted to hear more about the couple's plans, so I walked to their table and introduced myself and found out that they are in their late 60s, newly married, and waiting in Rock Hall for some repairs on their Island Packet cruiser. They plan to begin their Great Circle voyage next spring. I love to meet boating people. They always have a story to tell and an exciting adventure to share. This couple was fun to talk

Maryland

to. We had a great visit and I hope they have a fantastic adventure.

You are never too old to set another goal or to dream a new dream.

~C. S. Lewis

At the town dock there is a larger-than-life-size sculpture of an oyster fisherman. Obviously this is a town that is proud of its heritage. My cruising guide describes Rock Hall as a great stop for anyone traveling either north or south in the Eastern Shore of the Chesapeake. Years ago the Rock Hall Crossroads was an important way station for travelers. Both Jefferson and Washington passed through here en route to the Continental Congress in Philadelphia. I wonder if Washington slept here too. In the 19th and 20th centuries, Rock Hall was also a stopping-off place for the wealthy fleeing the city for the cooler, healthier air of the Atlantic Ocean.

Today Rock Hall is a waterman's working harbor, where the oystermen still putt out of the harbor at dawn and return to down a few beers in the late afternoon. I witnessed the return of these men and saw them unloading their catches while popping a beer or two, and basically enjoying what they were doing. They seem to be happy. I feel comfortable and like it here. This is a good place.

Maryland

October 26
Rock Hall to Annapolis
ICW mile 38.5 to ICW mile 53
30° 58' / 76° 29'

Whew! What a miserable, three-hour trip I had from Rock Hall to the Chesapeake Bridge! It felt like it was ten hours! As soon as I left the comfortable harbor of Rock Hall, I could see the bridge, but the wind was strong, on the nose, and there was a short, nasty chop. I thought that I would never get to the bridge. At full throttle, I was only making three knots. It was horrible and frustrating. I was soaked to the skin and shaking from the cold. The bay didn't look all that nasty from the quiet dock at Rock Hall.

A Great Big Adventure on a Good Little Boat

The salt water in my eyes prevented any thoughts of sightseeing. I was thankful to have the huge bridge to aim for. Visibility was too poor to make out any other navigation aids. Once I cleared under the bridge, my ride was less violent and the rest of my cruise into Annapolis was almost comfortable.

Actually, what I call the Chesapeake Bridge is two bridges. The proper name for them is the William P. Lane Jr. Memorial Bridges. I've never heard the bridges referred to by that name, but that's what the chart names the bridges, so it must be correct.

I had decided to tie up at the City Dock, the same place where my family had docked at when we lived aboard the *Sunbeam* 50 years ago! I tied up at exactly the same dock space we did back then. I don't know why, but it was important for me to be in this space. It was a connection.

Sailing into Annapolis was thrilling. I recognized a lot of the area, but at the same time everything was different. I remembered the outer harbor, which in the summer we were there was filled with yachts. Today, in October, it was quiet and empty. I recognized the Naval Academy on the shore ahead of me.

The Academy looked larger than I remembered and the buildings seemed to glow in the bright sunshine. The inner harbor wasn't as crowded as I recollect, but it *is* the end of October and many boats are probably on the hard for the winter.

I tied up at the same dock space the *Sunbeam* had occupied all those years ago. It was like I had been there yesterday. It was a special moment for me! I wanted to be here for my Mom and my Dad. Maybe they are pleased to see me here? Anyway, I'm here in Annapolis and I'm looking forward to visiting this wonderful city.

The City Dock certainly has changed! I remember the dock filled with working boats. The *Sunbeam* had been tied up between a research vessel and a commercial fishing boat. We were the only yacht there and we didn't look too "yacht-y"! The *Sunbeam* looked like an old fishing schooner. She was built as a racing schooner many years ago. The dock is on a narrow waterway that dead-ends, and back then a lot of nasty things collected there and floated back and forth with the tide.

Today this very same place is called Ego Alley. It is occupied with fancy and expensive yachts. (Until I tied up.) The park is still here, but the people walking and enjoying the vista are nicely dressed and they eat in fancy restaurants, not on park benches. The marine supply store that for years and years was the mainstay on the waterfront has been replaced by yet another fancy restaurant. As with many waterfront areas in the country, this one no longer relies on the working class to make it viable.

The pier at the City Dock is very high, and I was lucky that the only ladder on the pier happens to be at the *Sunbeam's* old dock space. I visited the dock master and he wanted to move my boat to a different spot. I told him why I wanted to stay there and he was nice enough to accommodate me. He was an agreeable guy and he understood. He was amazed that I have sailed from Maine in *that* boat, and solo for most of the way to boot.

The showers were my first stop after securing my dockage. I used lots of hot water and washed my body with my clothes on, to wash my clothes, and then I stripped down and washed myself really well. Both needed a good scrubbing and the heat of the water felt so good after being so cold for so long. I soaked up as much heat as I could! I had forgotten to bring a towel, so I had to use my dirty sweatshirt to dry myself. (Thank goodness that I hadn't washed it as well; it would never have dried in the cold and damp weather.)

Maryland

The very next stop was Buddies Restaurant for a huge plate of steamed blue claw crabs. Crabs and beer, life can't get much better. I stuffed myself! I felt so full that I may never eat again! The crabs were delicious and worth every bit of the voyage from Maine! I waddled back to my boat and spent the evening drying my charts and my clothes.

There were many people walking by, but because the pier is so high and my boat is so low, many people didn't even see me. The high dock afforded me my privacy.

It was in 1962 when my family sailed into Annapolis. My Mom and Dad had sailed their 65-foot schooner, the *Sunbeam*, down the East Coast, making this city the first place they stopped to complete the restorations of the boat and ready her for a long voyage. They left New York with seven kids and not much else except a lot of guts and a need for adventure. We kids were the crew! I am the oldest and I was about 15. The youngest, Joyce, was just out of diapers! Dad had the dream to sail to Australia, a place where he felt that "a man's success and satisfaction could be measured by his ability." Dad had ability!

The *Sunbeam* started her life in 1922 as a racing schooner and for many years she raced across the Atlantic. She was sleek and quite fast. During Word War II she was commandeered by the Coast Guard to sail up and down the East Coast watching for German U-boats. The Coast Guard painted her gray and attached "USCG 1923" on her hull.

During the first few years of the 1940s, Nazi U-boats prowled the shores off the United States, sinking ships at will. The unlikely defense the United States deployed was a ragtag group of seaman, officially called the Picket Patrol. Unofficially, this motley group was called the Hooligan Navy. All of the sailors were ranked 4F for one reason or another and couldn't serve in the traditional military. With donated sailboats from mostly well-to-do tycoons and WWI machine guns mounted to their decks, the "fleet" sailed off our shores to engage the enemy head on.

I don't know if they engaged any enemy, but they rescued many of our fighting men from the sea. One of the members of the Hooligan Navy reported that after 160 allied cargo ships were blown up off the Long Island coast, he joined the ragtag navy. The wooden sailboats were undetected by the U-boats and the sailboats sighted and reported many U-boat positions.

Maryland

It is a fact that a Hooligan Navy member met up with a U-boat commander after the war and the U-boat commander told him that he "hated you bastards"; he'd traveled 3,000 miles only to be detected by a *sailboat*!

Among the many civilians who joined the hunt for U-boats was Ernest Hemingway. He and his friends made many patrols aboard his fishing boat, *El Pilar*. With his crew of friends and plenty of alcohol, he stalked the waters near Cuba. His plan was to find a U-boat, power in close, throw hand grenades into the open hatch, then run like hell! Fortunately for lovers of literature, Hemingway never spotted a U-boat.

The *Sunbeam* was quite a beauty, even in her later years. Dad found her as a retired old lady on the hard at a marina in Marblehead, Massachusetts. His desire to travel and his love of sailing triggered his purchase of the old wooden schooner. My Mom agreed with and supported Dad's plan and was ready to leave the life she knew for one of adventure and challenge.

Our lives changed after that monumental day. As a family, we worked on the *Sunbeam* until she was ready to take seven kids and two adults on an extended voyage across the ocean. We were in the process of restoring her back to the beautiful and vibrant sailing vessel she had once been. Her restoration would be a

A Great Big Adventure on a Good Little Boat

continuing effort during our lives aboard the *Sunbeam*.

We lived aboard the schooner at the dock here in Annapolis for about a year. Mom was a registered nurse and got a job at the local hospital. Dad and we older kids worked onboard, preparing the boat for sea. The youngest kids were taken care of by all of us. My sisters and brothers and I learned how to sail in the Chesapeake. We would sail up the Severn River, dinghy ashore to pick up Mom after her work at the hospital, and then we would go sailing.

Dad had graduated from the Naval Academy and there was no way that he would let the Naval cadets out-sail and out-maneuver his boat and his crew on the water, regardless of the fact that his "crew" was young kids. So we learned to sail, and sail well.

I remember maneuvering through the crowded Annapolis harbor under full sail, and then sailing into the narrow waterway at the City Dock to parallel dock, under sail, with no engine. People on shore would applaud us! We kids loved the attention. While we were out sailing, if we saw a camera aimed at us (it happened quite often) we would fight for the prestigious position out on the bowsprit.

Maryland

While we lived in Annapolis, we chartered the *Sunbeam*. Our customer was Senator Jacob Javits of New York. He and his friends came onboard and we sailed around the Chesapeake showing them a good time. They were nice people, but I didn't like the charter. I didn't appreciate having to cater to our passengers' needs. We never chartered again, so maybe my parents felt the same way.

I remember an older couple who lived aboard their sailboat in the harbor at Annapolis. The man was an inventor of sorts and had designed a unique method to lower his boat's masts for easy passage under bridges. Mr. Inventor and his wife had a small terrier-type dog. The dog would jump overboard to relieve himself and then climb up the straight ladder back onto the deck!

On occasion Dad helped the older man. One day the inventor needed something done on the top of his mast, and Dad offered to be hauled in a bosun's chair. The old man started his electric winch and neglected to look up. Dad yelled and yelled to no avail. (The old guy was hard of hearing.) Dad's shoelace had caught in a part of the rigging and by the time Mr. Inventor realized that Dad was in trouble, Dad had been pulled out of the chair and was hanging on by his fingertips!

A Great Big Adventure on a Good Little Boat

Annapolis was a fun place for us kids and we enjoyed our time here. When we weren't working or sailing, we older kids spent our time tooling around the harbor making our own friends. Except for having to work on the boat, we had a lot of freedom that kids miss today. I have many fond memories of Annapolis and I love being here.

Maryland

October 27
Annapolis

My first full day in Annapolis has been very enjoyable. I woke early and sat in my cockpit, eating my leftover crab with my coffee. It's the middle of the week and there aren't too many people around, which affords me some privacy aboard my open boat.

Yesterday afternoon I had walked into a small mom-and-pop breakfast and luncheon place called Chick-n-Ruth's. I wanted to find out what time they opened for breakfast. The shop is very small, crowded and noisy, and I remembered the place from when we lived here aboard the *Sunbeam*. I asked a cook behind the counter what time they opened. (I found out later that he was the owner.) He asked me what time I wanted him to open. I played his game and asked him if I could get breakfast at seven. He said that I could get breakfast then, but I should wait until eight because all the cruisers met upstairs at eight o'clock and I could come in then and join them. How did he know that I was a cruiser? Do I have a tattoo on my forehead? Maybe I should buy a mirror to have onboard.

At eight this morning (Wednesday) I walked down the street to have breakfast with some sailors. I had no idea what to expect, but I had no better hot date. I entered the noisy place and walked upstairs. I was shocked. There were about 20 men and women seated at a long table and I introduced myself to the boisterous group. They welcomed me with open arms! These fascinating people are from everywhere and have cruised to everywhere. How fortunate I am to be here!

I sat next to Ursula, and as we ate and talked we became fast friends. She offered to take me to the Sprint store so that I could finally replace my phone. (Poor Ursula had to wait for over two hours while I purchased my new phone.) After the Sprint store she drove me to West Marine, where I purchased a Spot.

A Spot is a new electronic device that will allow me to notify a whole list of people, via e-mail, of my whereabouts and whether I am OK or if I need assistance. Ursula drove me to her condo and she set up my new Spot for me. We spent most of the day together and we had a great time. I am very thankful to her and will always remember her kindness.

Ursula is divorced; he got the house and she got the boat, and she was happy about that. Ursula sailed her boat from Guatemala and now lives in Annapolis; I asked her why she picked Annapolis. She said that Annapolis is the sailing capital of the world, so it is where she wants to be. Good choice, Ursula. How lucky I was to meet such a delightful and generous lady.

At that amazing breakfast I also met with Jeff and Elise. They invited me to dinner aboard their beautiful V40Sea Span sailing home. They were gracious and we had a wonderful evening. My friends Gerald and Marlene from Beach Haven called. They are in Annapolis and we will try to meet for dinner tomorrow. Who knew that my social calendar would be so full?

Last evening a sailboat arrived at the dock and tied up just ahead of my little boat. Aboard were five guys who sail together during this week every year. They are just a group of friends who enjoy sailing and getting away from everything for a week. I had gone over to help them tie up and we got to meet each other. They were impressed that I had sailed from Maine in *that boat.* They said that I was their hero and this morning one of them bought my breakfast! How cool was that! Thank you, guys. Have a great sail!

Annapolis is certainly the sailing capital of the world! There are sailors and sailboats everywhere, and the town caters to all of us. Sailors are welcomed. It is great to be here and to be a part of this sailor's haven.

I remember how awestruck I was 50 years ago at the sight of the capitol that is within walking distance of the dock. As kids, we made a field trip to the capitol and the other impressive buildings on the hill. I walked around the area today and enjoyed being here again.

I found out that Annapolis was a temporary capital of the United States. That was from 1783 through 1784. The beautiful city of Annapolis is situated on the Chesapeake, at the mouth of the Severn River, and is only 29 miles east of Washington, D.C. It was here that General George Washington resigned his commission as Commander-in-Chief of the Continental Army back in December of 1783.

I love the 18th-century homes and buildings on the tight, tree-lined streets of the city. Many of the street names date back to the colonial days. The small shops are filled with everything nautical. I particularly enjoyed browsing through one of the nautical bookstores.

The United States Naval Academy, established in 1845, has a huge influence on the city. I would have liked to visit the Academy again, but I just ran out of time. Everywhere I walked, there were Naval cadets jogging. These young men and women look so fit and clean cut. As they ran by, they made me feel old and out of shape, but I also felt very proud to be an American.

My visit here has been memorable and better than I expected. I am very happy to have had the opportunity to revisit Annapolis, a city that holds such an important place in my past.

October 28
Annapolis to Herring Bay, Maryland
ICW mile 67.6
34° 43.70' / 76° 32.60'

Wow, I didn't want to leave Annapolis and the great people I have met here, and I was sorry that I missed seeing my friends from New Jersey. They had to keep heading south and we just couldn't coordinate our schedules. My feet were getting itchy and another storm is coming. It's time to move on.

As I left the harbor, I sailed past the *Pride of Baltimore II.* The *Pride II* is a replica vessel launched in 1988. She replaced the *Pride of Baltimore,* which was an authentic reproduction of a 19th-century Baltimore Clipper topsail schooner. The citizens of Baltimore commissioned her on May 1, 1977. She and four of her 12 crew members were lost at sea on May 14, 1986. I remember that sad day.

The *Pride II* sails as a goodwill ambassador for Baltimore. I have been aboard her a few times when she was visiting in Portsmouth, and I knew her crew back then. I was a board member of the Piscataqua Maritime Commission in Portsmouth and we sponsored the tall ship visits. Over the years the PMC brought many beautiful tall ships into the harbor. The *Pride II* and the *Lynx* are my favorite topsail schooners. I do favor the smaller schooners, but as far as topsail schooners go, *Pride II* and the *Lynx* are fantastic vessels and I will never pass up an opportunity to visit them.

I was surprised to see that the *Pride II* looked somewhat shabby and not as pristine and sharp as I had remembered her. It is the end of the season and I guess that the monies to keep such grand ships in shipshape condition are hard to find these days. If I had tons of money, I would spend it renovating grand old homes and proud old boats. Maybe in my next life I can have that privilege.

It wasn't too rough in the Chesapeake until a rain squall hit me. With the squall came strong winds, and it rained so hard that it was painful to stand at the tiller and steer my little boat. It felt as horrible as the hail that would pelt down with a vengeance when I lived in New England. I decided to pull into Herring Bay on the western shore.

I didn't make a lot of miles under the keel today, only about 20. Maybe I can get an early start tomorrow to make up for lost time. It was still raining hard when I tied up at the Herring Bay South Marina. I docked at the first open dock that I came across. Not a soul was in sight. Who would be out in this miserable weather?

I secured my boat and hunkered down on my bunk until the rain let up in the evening. When the rain, no, sleet (yes, it was *sleet*) let up, I rolled out of my bunk and, while slip-sliding on the slick white docks, I braved the strong winds to explore my new temporary home.

I found that I've docked in a gorgeous place. In spite of the slippery docks I was taken aback with the beauty of my surroundings. The buildings, the pool, and the landscaping were professional and beautiful. It will probably cost me a small fortune to stay here! I sure know how to pick them! I still haven't seen anyone associated with the marina; actually, I haven't seen anyone since I tied up here.

Maryland

I walked past beautiful tropical gardens and huge palm trees. I am still in Maryland and I'm seeing palm trees? They are very large trees, not little potted trees. What's this all about? I took pictures on my new phone, and sent them to my northern friends. I bragged that I had made it to the South. Of course, I ignored the fact that just a short while ago sleet had made the docks white and scary to walk on.

What a fool I was! I jinxed myself! That night a full gale hit me in the marina. The sleet and wind that evening were horrible. The wind was battering my poor boat into the dock. The wind was blowing from the stern, making it very cold and uncomfortable to be onboard. I braved the cold and the wind and turned my little *Summer Wind* around so that she rode at the dock a little more comfortably and the wind and rainy sleet wasn't blasting into my cabin. With the wind on the bow my boat was much happier and so was I. While I was cold and wet and so wretched, I doubled up my lines and then crawled into my wet bunk, wearing my wet clothes, and tried to get warm on a blustery night! My fingers and toes were frozen. Needless to say, without gloves or socks or heat, it was a long and painful night. In spite of the cold and having to get up and adjust fenders all night, I did get a few hours of sleep.

A Great Big Adventure on a Good Little Boat

Anything that we consider to be an accomplishment takes effort to achieve. If it were easy, it would not be nearly as gratifying. What is hardship at the moment will add to our sense of achievement in the end.

~AWOL on the Appalachian Trail,
David Miller

Maryland

October 29
Still at Herring Bay Marina

It is so unbearably cold and windy. When I woke, there was frost on my deck and the docks were, again, slippery with frost. Wow, I might be south of Maine, but I am definitely not far enough south to be warm! This morning I slid along the dock to the marina's restroom and lingered there to soak up some heat. I was tempted to find a chair, bring a book, and spend the day sitting in front of the heater.

I found a restaurant across the street and I lingered there as I ate a hot breakfast. I sat next to the radiator. It is freezing and windy outside. The wind bites at my face as if I were back in New Hampshire. As I walked from the restaurant

A Great Big Adventure on a Good Little Boat

I could see the nasty, white-capped waves of the Chesapeake Bay. I couldn't believe how rough and horrible the bay was. The small-craft warnings are predicted to continue through Sunday, and today is only Friday. Looks like I'm stuck at yet another expensive marina! I *am* thankful to be at a marina, but I am pretty disappointed to be captive at yet another dock. I napped in my leaky cabin and then took a walk around the marina after today's rain and sleet had ended. I still haven't seen a dock master or any marina staff. Actually, I haven't seen anyone on the docks. Maybe I won't have to pay dockage here. Ha, fat chance of that.

Oh my gosh, I found a pair of socks on board and they are only damp! I put them on my painful feet and pretended that my feet were warm. My fingers are so cold and I know that I have no mittens or gloves onboard my little boat. Why would I need mittens? I was heading south! I had no idea that I would be so bitterly cold and subjected to so much miserable and stormy weather. Of course, I have warm clothes and foul-weather gear (everything is wet though), but I did not believe that I would encounter sleet and frost in Maryland. Just goes to show that on a boat, one must be prepared for every condition!

Maryland

It seems that I provisioned my boat pretty well, but not myself!

Lying in my bunk today, I got to thinking: I have made it about a third of my way to Florida. The hardest part of the voyage should be behind me. God, I hope so! My little boat is too small to be comfortable in these frosty conditions.

People are in awe that I have sailed this far in my little boat. I am in awe! I am uncomfortable, but I am happy. I love the challenges: every day I venture out of my comfort zone and the things that I know and understand. I relish every day's new obstacles; I am thriving on them. Every day I am scared, excited, and thrilled. Every day I am growing. I enjoy my time alone at a pretty anchorage and I enjoy staying at a busy dock, meeting other boaters, but moving on to another day of traveling alone and facing the new challenges is what I look forward to. What a rush! I want to make this voyage again; I am addicted. There's the Ulysses Factor again! The will-to-adventure.

My next trip down the coast will take place over the summer! No more freezing weather for me. I am done with the cold and the gale-force winds. My next adventure will be a longer one with no set destination.

I love my *Summer Wind*, but I think that I want to travel aboard a larger sailboat. I want a

215

head, a small galley, and an inboard engine. I want a small tender, so that I can row to shore and explore the sights there. My voyage has taught me a few lessons. Either that, or I am getting soft!

I spent the day listening to strong winds, and now, at 1700, there is not a whisper of a breeze. I should leave right now. It is so awfully cold and the rain is supposed to begin again. I am wearing every piece of clothing that I have onboard and I am still cold. I can't wait to get farther south into sunny skies and warm blue waters. Come on, King Neptune, help me out here.

Maryland

October 30
Herring Bay to Old House Cove off the
Patuxent River, Maryland
ICW mile 97.6
38° 19.20' / 76° 27.40'

It was a very uncomfortable night. It was so cold, and my sleeping bag and my clothes—my *everything*—are wet and wetter! Dripping wet. The boat banged against the dock all night. I spent the night adjusting the fenders and tending to my little boat. I'd get to bed and, after about 15 minutes, the wet sleeping bag would start to warm up, just about the time I'd have to go topside to adjust the fenders. After working outside in the drenching and freezing rain, I'd climb back into my wet sleeping bag and start the process all over again. This went on throughout the entire night. I was glad to see the sun rise. In the morning the docks and the *Summer Wind*'s deck were slick with white frost. Ugh. It was 38 degrees again! It could be worse; I heard that less than a hundred miles north of here over one foot of snow fell!

The seas were still gray and rough when I slipped my lines this morning, but the 15 or so knots of wind were on my stern for a change. Maybe I'm headed the wrong way! Oh, my gosh, I had a dry ride. I had not one splash of cold bay water in my cockpit. My charts stayed dry, my GPS stayed dry, and I stayed dry. What a joy. I sailed with my main and jib flying.

My friends Jeff and Elise left Annapolis today and we had planned to meet somewhere in the Solomons Island area. Solomons Island is on the western shore of the Chesapeake and up the Patuxent River. I like to anchor in still and secluded spots, so, after leaving the Chesapeake and heading into the Patuxent River, I avoided heading toward the crowded Back Creek. Instead, I motored up the less populated Mill Creek and finally found a perfect anchoring spot in Old House Cove. I radioed Jeff and Elise to tell them that I had found a quiet and safe place to anchor, and they agreed to meet me there.

Maryland

No other boats were here when I anchored. Oh, peace and solitude. Old House Cove is an extension of the Mill Creek near Solomons Island. This area was and still is a fishing village known for its famous Patuxent oysters.

I anchored at about 1400 hours. The sun was bright, so I pulled everything out of the cutty to dry, including my extra sails. Every inch of topsides was covered with wet clothes and bedding. I raised the spare sails on my halyards and they dried in the light breeze. The sun did its job, and I had just finished stowing all that dry gear below as Jeff and Elise pulled into the creek and dropped anchor near me. After they got settled, Jeff launched his rubber dingy, putted over to my boat, picked me up, and we ate dinner aboard their pretty yacht. I enjoyed an evening of yummy food, exciting conversation, and entertaining people. Life doesn't get much better than this.

Today is Dad's birthday. I miss him. He died in 2007. He would have loved to hear about my trip and be part of it. I know he always enjoyed the Chesapeake and he would have loved to tell me about the places I should visit along the way. He was a very special person to me. He had a lust for life and he was always able to bounce back from failures and obstacles.

A Great Big Adventure on a Good Little Boat

I remember his funeral service; there was standing room only. Many people spoke about Dad at the service and after they all had their say, I spoke. I told the crowd that my Dad was many things to many people. To me, Dad was strength and courage. It's because of his influence that I know that I will be able to weather any storm. I will not only survive, but I will prosper because his strength will always be with me. I can't fail, I will *not* fail. Thank you, Dad.

My Mom was a big reason that Dad was so resilient. She was strong, and she was always there for him. She supported his sometimes outrageous ideas. She was his biggest advocate. Dad was the dreamer; she was the strength and the support that he needed to succeed and fulfill his dreams. My parents taught me that it is important to have support and give support, and with someone at your side, nothing is impossible and no dream is too crazy. I miss both of my parents. I miss the support of a partner.

Don acted like an idiot! Don walked out of a partnership that is rare. We were a unique team. There was nothing we couldn't accomplish together. I supported him and he supported me. I didn't think he was crazy when he wanted to buy a big old dory that had been sitting and rotting for years. He wanted to restore it and go long-line fishing in the open boat, in the winter, in the North Atlantic. (Well, I thought that was a *little* crazy.) It was his dream, so I told him to buy the boat. We hooked the boat's trailer to the truck and halfway into the road, the wheels collapsed out from the trailer. Boat and trailer blocked a major road until the tow truck saved the day. It was funny. No one was hurt and there was no damage to Don's boat.

He did restore his dream boat, but he never fished from her. Sometimes Don's passions were a result of his huge ego. He needed to become the famous long-line fisherman of Rye Harbor. We were going to catch fish, and he would set me up with a building at the harbor so that I could make my seafood chowder and sell it to the tourists, while he sat around and bragged how he braved the mighty Atlantic to catch the fish for my chowder. Yet another project of Don's that created work for me! I didn't need more to do. He could go fishing, but my days were productive enough. I had no desire to spend my days cooking so that he could be the big man of the harbor. I did not want to cook chowder for the masses. I was enjoying building at the time and didn't want to change gears. He never did go fishing out of his dory.

A Great Big Adventure on a Good Little Boat

Don always supported my need to sail. He encouraged me to fly to Florida and race with my brother. He bought my *Summer Wind* for me and presented me with a new outboard for her. Whenever I sailed out of Rye Harbor, he'd drive along the coast, see my sail, and call on the cell phone to say, "Cap't Ahab, how does your sail go?" We worked, we played, and we loved. Who walks away from that kind of relationship? What happened?

As I lay in my cold little bunk, I thought about Dad and his power to overcome the obstacles in his life. He was lucky to have a strong partner. His soul mate supported him through everything. She didn't desert him. She stood with him and he succeeded. Don deserted our marriage, our family, and everything we had worked and lived for.

'Tis easier to suppress the first desire than to satisfy all that follow it.

~Anonymous

Maryland

October 31
Old House Cove to Old House Cove

I wanted to get an early start today, so I was up and heading out of the creek by 0500. It was well before daybreak. I tried to leave quietly and not to disturb the other four boats in our quiet anchorage. Over the evening hours my private creek got a bit crowded. I guess that the other cruisers had heard my conversation via the VHF radio when I told Jeff and Elise about my nice secluded anchorage and the other boats followed. Little did they know that they were following the blind! There was no wind to sail out of the creek, so I had to start up my outboard.

It is 1600. I am again anchored back at the Old House Cove, and I am enjoying my second

A Great Big Adventure on a Good Little Boat

rum drink. Let me explain. This morning I made coffee and reveled in the peace of my anchorage. The stars were beautiful. The wind was calm, with not a breath of air, and I sat in my cockpit soaking up the silence and the beauty of the pre-dawn. I thought that I would be able to make a lot of miles today. I motored out of the cove and through Mill Creek. When I reached the river I ran into a wall of fog. There was no visibility. None! This wasn't too big of an issue; I simply followed my GPS track, which was laid on my screen when I entered this area. (I had set my GPS to track my course. The screen shows a dotted line indicating my path in the water, and I simply followed that dotted line.) My only fear was being run over by larger and faster boats. I pulled out my foghorn, blew into it, and there was no horn noise! It didn't work. I had used it in the fog I encountered in the waters in New Jersey. Why wasn't it working now? In the dark, while under way, I couldn't figure out what the problem was. I needed to keep a lookout and steer. No time to deal with this problem now.

It was very early, so I hoped that no other boats would be on the water yet. I stayed close to the outer edge of the channel, just kissing the buoys, and running blind. I finally made it to the mouth of the river, out of the fog and back into the Chesapeake. I sighed a big sigh of relief and headed south. I was out of the blind fog. I poured myself another cup of coffee (too early for rum) and started to relax a bit. All of a sudden my boat jerked to a stop and my outboard choked and died. What now? I thought that maybe I had run aground. I was dead in the water. My GPS showed that there was plenty of water under my keel. What happened? It was still dark and I couldn't see anything.

I threw out my anchor to keep my position. It was calm, but I was in a strong current and I needed to secure my boat before I dealt with the engine. I lifted my outboard and found that the prop had been fouled with a crab pot warp. The area is filthy with crab traps. The crab traps are set on the bottom. Attached to each of these traps is a line with a buoy on the surface, allowing the fisherman to haul up his trap, which he hopes is filled with crabs. My outboard had caught the line from one of these traps. I could see the line wrapped tightly around my propeller.

My outboard sits on a bracket off the stern, putting the engine quite a distance from the boat. As a result, when I tilt the engine up and out of the water, I can't reach the prop. I couldn't reach that line wrapped around my engine's prop. I tied my knife to the boat hook trying to cut the mess out of prop. No luck. The strong pot warp was wrapped tight, with quite a lot of turns. I did a good job catching this crab trap! I tried to shimmy out on the outboard. At about halfway, I figured that with the current and the rock-and-roll movement of the boat, if I slipped off I would have a hard time climbing back onboard. I decided that this wasn't a smart idea. I wisely slithered back into the cockpit.

My only option was to bring the engine into the boat. This isn't easy at a dock, never mind at sea, but I had no choice. I took my mainsail halyard off my mainsail, and then attached it to the outboard to help lighten the load and to ensure that the engine didn't go overboard.

By this time the wind was starting to come up a bit and my boat started to really rock and roll. I decided to try the old knife-on-the-boathook trick one more time before detaching the motor and bringing it aboard. I did it! I was able to clear the line. I cut a bit at a time and finally got it all removed. Success! I'd be able to be on my way again.

Elated, I lowered the engine. I was so pleased with myself, until I found that the plastic gas line connector was broken and I had no spare. I had tried to get an extra connection before this voyage, but there wasn't one available at the time. Of course the Yamaha connectors are not common to any of the other outboards. I tried to repair my broken part with glue and a clamp. Nothing was gained, and I got glue on everything.

My outboard has an internal gas tank so it wasn't going to be a problem getting back into port under this slight wind situation. I was really disappointed though. I wanted to travel south, not back to port! So much for an early start. I had no choice but to head to a marina at Solomons Island where I might find a replacement part.

I resigned myself to the fact that I had to backtrack to port. I filled the engine's internal gas tank, started the engine, and headed back into the river and back into the thick fog! The fog was so dense that I had to pull off the channel and anchor. I could *hear* boats. I could hear their horns and feel their wakes. I never *saw* one of those boats. That was scary! I had no horn. I had only a winch handle and a cooking pan to make noise with. The thought of the sound they would make together made me laugh...I would sound like a demented cook! I was too embarrassed to use them. So there I was at anchor with no horn and no whistle. At least I was off the channel. Was I off the channel enough? Time would tell.

A Great Big Adventure on a Good Little Boat

It was a ghostly morning. Sounds are different in the fog. Everything sounds muffled, and it is impossible to tell what direction a sound is coming from. Hearing a boat's motor and not knowing where that boat is traveling is disconcerting. I knew where the channel was, and that's where the boats should be, but in the fog I couldn't be sure. I hoped that I was off the channel enough. I was very uncomfortable. I stayed put until the fog lifted enough so that I felt safe to travel again.

All of this had happened before daybreak. By 0700, the sun started to rise and break up the fog. I took a picture of a foggy and spooky sunrise. Today is Halloween and this morning's sunrise was so fitting. It was at daybreak that I heard, very clearly, the music of our national anthem. How cool and wonderful. Wow, what a morning! I found out later that there is a USAF base across the river, explaining the anthem. Eerie at the time though!

Finally, as the fog lifted, I raised anchor and motored to the marina dock with no more excitement. Lucky me, there is a West Marine within walking distance. I was able to get my gas connector, a new horn, and a whistle. I also bought some "life caulk" so that I could finally fix my cabin-top leaks.

Maryland

My gosh, there was a liquor store next door to the West Marine. What a great marketing plan: a marine store with a liquor store next door! I got myself a big bottle of rum.

That's my story. That's why I'm sitting here at last night's anchor spot. I am enjoying a rum drink and fixing the leaks in my cabin top. And it is barely 1600 hours! All in all, it wasn't too bad of a day. I made no progress, but I fixed a problem, I am at a safe place for the night, and this is a beautiful place to be. Life is good!

November 1
Waiting in Old House Cove

Wow, it is the first day of November and I'm still in the Chesapeake. Hell, I'm still in Old House Cove! The days are flying by and winter will be here soon. I have to keep moving; I feel like I'm in a race against the cold, and the cold is winning. At least it's not snowing. I had a great rest last night. It rained all night and I got up a few times, but I feel rested and *dry*! I have fixed the leaks. Rum and caulking seem to work well together.

I decided to stay put today since the weather is pretty rotten. I spent the morning reading and enjoying no drips in my cabin. Finally around noon the rain stopped, but it is still cold. I hope to leave tomorrow. If the weather were warmer and I had a little tender, I would be tempted to stay in my peaceful Old House Cove for a few days. I love to explore.

Many years ago, when my daughters Angela and Ericka were young, every once in a while I would take a field trip with them. Invariably, I got confused and we'd drive around for hours, hopelessly lost. There was no GPS then. I never minded being lost if I didn't have an appointment. What's the problem? There were roads and houses and people around. I looked at our detours as small adventures. We made driving in circles so fun that sometimes Angela and Ericka asked when we could get lost again.

On land, I do have a difficult time with direction. If my instinct tells me to turn right, I have learned to turn left because left is correct. Weird, because when I'm on the water or scuba diving I always know where I am and what my direction is. On the water, I can trust my instincts, thank God. I guess the water is where I'll travel from now on.

November 2
Old House Cove to Cockrell Creek off the Great Wicomico River, Maryland
ICW mile 136
37° 50.70' / 76° 16.90'

I feel so protected here that I rested well and had a good night's sleep. No dreams about failures, no dreams about what could have been, no dreams of what I could have or should have done. It was an excellent rest on my good little boat. I was up at 0300 and ready to get on my way. I enjoyed a leisurely morning, waiting for daybreak. I wasn't going to chance running into a crab pot line again—once is enough! This area is loaded with the traps and you need to see them to avoid them.

The morning was so quiet and comforting. I sat in my cockpit, sipping coffee and contemplating how wonderful my life of sailing is. I am relaxed, I am calm, and I have no problem dealing with whatever difficulty comes my way. (So far!) There is nothing that I can't handle. I am focused and I am free. For the first time in my life, I am free. It is an amazing feeling. I have never felt like this before, but sometimes it does confuse me. It is a wonderful feeling, but should I feel guilty? There are so many people who work hard just to feed their families. Here I am sailing around, enjoying myself. Why do *I* get to do this? On the other hand, damn it, I've worked hard all my life and why don't I deserve to be here, doing what I love to do? This is too deep for me. The coffee is good, the morning is beautiful, and I am ready to continue my voyage.

As soon as I entered the Patuxent River I was greeted with a thick shroud of fog again. Visibility was zero! What is it with this river? I powered past the tugboats tied up along the river. I knew that they were there, but I couldn't see them. Again, I anchored just off the channel to wait for the fog to lift. This river doesn't want me to leave.

A Great Big Adventure on a Good Little Boat

By 0900, I raised my anchor and started toward the mouth of the river and the Chesapeake Bay. The fog was still very thick, but I had my new horn and I had heard from a boat over the VHF that the fog cleared at the mouth of the river and that the bay was clear of fog. I finally made it out of the river and into the bay. I have finally escaped the foggy Patuxent River and returned into the Chesapeake!

I raised my jib and main in a light northerly wind. The wind was behind me. Maybe I was going the wrong way! After enjoying a short sail, the wind died, and there wasn't a breeze to be had. Down with the sails and on with the noisemaker.

I passed the Potomac River and continued my journey to the Great Wicomico River on the western shore of the Chesapeake. I had decided to anchor for the night at Cockrell Creek, just off the Wicomico. The creek looked to be small and protected, and I had read that there was a seafood store and deli there where I could dock and eat. My mouth watered all day anticipating the steamed crabs I planned to feast on that night.

As I traveled into the creek and headed toward the dock and the seafood store, my engine kept dying whenever I slowed down. I

Maryland

played the start-and-die game with my outboard until I got close to the dock and it just wouldn't start again. I pulled out my paddle and paddled my way to the dock. Another grand entrance. Oh well, at least here there seems to be no one around to criticize my poor docking abilities. I walked around the building and found that the store was closed for the season. I was not happy! All day I had been anticipating sitting in my cockpit tonight, at a safe anchorage, eating crabs and drinking rum. I wanted those crabs, and I was upset.

While I was tied up at the deserted dock, I checked the oil level in my outboard and it was fine. Maybe I got some bad gas and that's the reason for the outboard acting poorly. I hope that's all it is: bad gas.

After checking out my outboard and trying to decide on my next move, I realized that I couldn't stay at this dock. The flies were unbearable and the smell was overwhelming! It was so stinky! Engine or no engine, I wasn't staying here. I did get my outboard started and I headed away from the stench of that dock, and back out of Cockrell Creek. It wasn't until after dark that I finally found a place to anchor. I was desperate to end my day and of all places I could anchor, I chose an anchorage very near to the

A Great Big Adventure on a Good Little Boat

Menhaden Fish Factory, which ran at full steam all night.

The menhaden is a small, inedible fish, and the surrounding waters teem with them. In the 1900s, menhaden processing plants lined Cockrell Creek. These plants squeeze the oil from the fish, making meal and fertilizer. There is only one plant in operation now, and I am anchored in front of it. The menhaden fishing boats are huge; they remind me of the large shrimp boats in Key West.

I heated a can of broccoli-and-cheese soup for dinner. It tasted nothing like crabs; it didn't even taste good!

It was a noisy and smelly night.

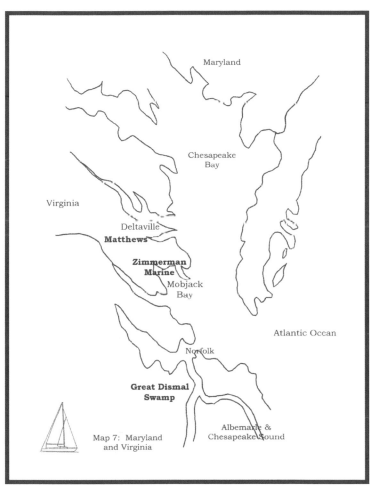

Map 7: Maryland
and Virginia

Maryland to Virginia

237

November 3
Cockrell Creek, Maryland to the East River, off Mobjack Bay, Virginia
ICW mile 172
37° 25' / 76° 21'

Today I killed my little outboard! It has been running rough and it wouldn't idle. As I entered Mobjack Bay just off the Chesapeake, it quit. It stopped dead. There was no sputter, no fading, and no warning. Just an ending. My boat coasted to a stop, and I dropped my anchor in the calm waters of the protected Mobjack Bay. Thank goodness I had powered off the choppy Chesapeake and into calmer waters before the demise of my outboard.

Maryland to Virginia

After anchoring, I tried to start the engine. It wouldn't start, and then the pull cord froze. It wouldn't move. The engine had seized up. I checked the engine's oil. There was none! How could that be? I had just checked the oil level last night at the stinky dock. There was oil then! How could that happen? I called my brother Willy and described what had happened. He told me that my engine was a goner, it was cooked, it was dead! I killed it! He was sort of kind, and told me that in each of our lifetimes, we cook an outboard. Once! He too has run an outboard out of oil. Comforting thought Willy, thanks. 'Twas just my time! Not very good timing on my part. Although, maybe it wasn't too horrible. I was in calm water and there were possible sailing destinations in almost any direction. I would just have to travel the way of the wind. After all, the *Summer Wind* is a *sail*boat!

While sitting safely at anchor, I looked over my charts and the cruising guide and found a full-service marina way up the East River, here off Mobjack Bay. The wind gods were with me, the marina was downwind. I raised my jib, weighed anchor, and sailed into the East River with the wind behind me. I sailed and sailed— where is this place? The river was getting narrower, with more twists, and the wind was diminishing with every turn of the river! With the wind behind me and no engine, I was sailing on a one-way voyage! Where the hell was I going?

Finally, I saw a tall mast off the river and I headed for the mast in the trees. There were no markers into the little hole-in-the-wall where I saw the tall mast, but I figured that if he could get in there, so could I. Besides, I had very few options at this point.

My silent sail into the dock shocked a man sitting on his sailboat when I called over to him and said hello. He jumped; he hadn't seen or heard me come into the dock. After he said hello, he told me that he was impressed that I had sailed into the narrow and tricky dockage. I told him that I didn't have a choice. He and I talked, and I found out that this is not a marina but a repair facility. He was here while his boat was being repaired. I am here without an engine. I'm going nowhere without power, so hopefully I can get some help.

This morning I had left my anchorage at 0500 and stayed in 30 feet of water to avoid fish and crab traps. The wind turned mean. I was so cold. The seas weren't bad, but they were on the nose and I was wet throughout the day. I was very uncomfortable. I don't know why, but I was extremely cold. The cold seemed to penetrate deep into my core, and I shivered all morning. I cheered as the sun finally rose on the horizon at about 0730, but it didn't do too much to warm me. I was still shaking with the cold. I encouraged the sun to keep rising and turn on the heat. I never felt it.

Mobjack Bay is protected from the wind. When I turned into it I enjoyed calm waters, I am thankful that my engine waited until I was out of the rough Chesapeake and into Mobjack Bay before it died.

I had read my guidebook incorrectly; I have sailed into Zimmerman Marine Inc., a marine facility where repairs and maintenance are done. My engine is beyond repair! This is a boat yard, not a marina. Well, I'm here, and they have welcomed me. The people are friendly and helpful. Unfortunately, they don't sell outboards, and the closest place I can probably get one is in Deltaville, about a 45-minute drive. Zimmerman has a courtesy truck that I can use as soon as they can find it.

I've sailed into a very laid-back place. After walking around though, I saw that these people are real professionals. Their work is of the highest quality. It was very extraordinary!

After much calling around, I found a West Marine in Deltaville that would order me a new outboard. I need a long shaft and nobody stocks them. It will have to come from the factory, so I have a four day wait. Sail and wait, sail and wait, sail and wait.

My friend Jeff keeps e-mailing me advertisements for "real" boats for sale on craigslist. He thinks my boat is too small for this trip! Imagine that! You know, he is right, but she's my boat and she and I have become a team. I have slogged through the hardest and the roughest part of this trip in my little *Summer Wind,* and I am not about to trade her in now. So, thank you, anyway, Jeff, but I will stick with the boat I have.

Thank goodness, there are showers here! I walked up to the shower room anticipating the hot water warming and cleaning my frozen and smelly body. Out of luck! There is only one ladies room and a sign asked that the boaters not use the shower during business hours. I was so disappointed! I will have to wait until tonight to take a much-needed shower. I haven't washed my only foul-weather pants since my shower in Annapolis. They can stand up by themselves and they may start to walk soon. I am surprised they haven't jumped ship yet!

I had done a good job fixing all the leaks in my cabin top while I was at anchor in Old House Cove. There have been no more puddles and wet bedding, up to now. Now it is so damp that the condensation is making drips in the cabin and again my bedding and I are getting wet! Go figure.

So I have found an engine, and now I just have to wait. I'll shower and clean the boat, take long walks, and read. I've met some great people here and I have enjoyed visiting with them. I even got invited to a musical jam session.

Another storm has attacked me. Oh well, I can't leave here yet anyway, and my *Summer Wind* is safe and I am comfortable. I hope to be able to pick up my engine on Tuesday, and I plan to do all my shopping that day. I'm low on many supplies, my food bin is bare, and I'm almost out of stove fuel. I want to fill all my gas cans too; the outboard used only about a gallon every three hours and less when I motor sail.

It is difficult to figure how far I can get in a day. Some days I get so tired of being wet and cold standing at the tiller. I like to leave early and quit early with enough daylight to be able to find a safe place to anchor and plenty of daylight to go over my charts and plan the next day's travels. I like to clean and re-organize the boat before dark, and of course there must be enough daylight to make a rum drink. About 1500 is a good time to be close to being able to anchor and stop traveling. This makes for a ten-hour day. I am tired by the time my day's voyage is done. By the afternoon, I am usually wet and wind- or sunburned. I have tried using sunblock, but the saltwater spray just washes the sunblock into my eyes so that my eyes burn and I can't see a thing.

As I've said, I wake up early, before daylight, and it's cold at that hour. I make coffee and enjoy a peaceful and quiet time before I weigh anchor and start another eight or ten or more hours of travel. Many times it is a spray-in-my-face day, and I am wet and cold throughout my day's voyage. In the afternoon I start to head into port. Late in the day the wind calms and the water is no longer spraying me, but my adrenalin is increased with concern about finding my way into another unfamiliar harbor or into a river or creek to find a safe place to rest.

When I find an anchorage, I drop and set my anchor, hoping that I am out of the channel enough and that my anchor will hold. Once I know that my boat is safe, I can look around at my new surroundings and admire the beauty of where I am. I sit back, warm my tummy with a little rum, and congratulate myself and thank my *Summer Wind* for another fine day. I am at peace. I work on my next day's voyage and plan that night's anchorage or port.

I usually plan on three possible stops for the day; I never know how beat up I might feel toward the evening. The *Summer Wind* is a small boat with no protection, and some days I can weather the storm and other days I just don't seem to have the stamina to travel for a few more hours. I like to have options and plans.

November 4
Still waiting at Zimmerman Marine, East River off Mobjack Bay, Virginia

Amazing, I'm in Virginia. My little boat and I have come *so* far! It has become an exciting event to cross the borders into another state.

The town of Mathews is a tiny place. There is not much here except the impressive boat yard, nice people, my little boat, and me. I like this place. The folks here are helpful and the river is pretty. I don't feel too bad about waiting for my new outboard today because the wind is blowing and the Chesapeake would be miserable.

246

Maryland to Virginia

I borrowed the yard's courtesy truck (they found it) and I drove to the town of Gloucester to buy thermal underwear and socks. I have been wearing shorts under my foul-weather pants and I had one pair of very stinky socks. Dumb, I know, but I was heading *south*. I was optimistic that I would be experiencing warm weather, and socks and long pants were unnecessary baggage.

I returned back into Mathews and found a small restaurant that had fried oysters on their "special" board. A beer and oysters—lunch can't get much better than that.

Back at the boat, I spent some time studying my charts and decided to travel through Virginia via the Dismal Swamp Canal rather than the more popular cruising boaters' route known as the Virginia Cut. Most power cruisers use the Virginia Cut. The Cut is heavily used by commercial traffic, and I have no desire to deal with all the nasty wakes of the huge commercial boats and fast cruisers. I'll opt for the slow and scenic route of the Dismal Swamp.

November 5 and 6
Still waiting

I read a page from *Packing for Mars* by Mary Roach. She was writing about how more and more people in our culture live via simulations. Simulation has become reality. But it's not the same. What *is* different is the lack of risk, the lack of sweat and uncertainty, and the lack of convenience that comes only with reality. There is no sense of accomplishment, no pride. My trip is definitely not simulation. This is the real deal! I feel a great sense of accomplishment at the end of each day. I feel the risk, the lack of comfort, and I feel the awe.

This would be a good day to leave: the wind is light and it is sunny, but the new engine hasn't arrived. Maybe tomorrow will be my lucky day. I spent the day drying clothes and sails, studying charts, eating, and reading. I may start drinking soon.

I did read some interesting information about the Virginia Cut and the Dismal Swamp Canal. The cut was completed in 1859 and is wider and deeper than the Dismal Swamp Canal. The cut is part of the ICW and follows the Albemarle and Chesapeake Canal for 50 miles—from Norfolk to Currituck Sound and Coinjock, North Carolina.

The Dismal Swamp Canal also joins the Norfolk area to the Pasquotank River and Elizabeth City, North Carolina. Besides all the traffic and wakes, there are several bridges and one lock to negotiate in the Virginia Cut. I don't like bridges! A lot of times it's necessary to wait for the bridge to open (many open on a set schedule—I always just miss the opening); it can be hard to maneuver while waiting because at times there may be a strong current in a narrow waterway. It makes cruising interesting. Although the Dismal Swamp has two locks and a couple of bridges, it is supposed to be—despite its name—the prettier of the two routes.

Slaves dug the Dismal Swamp Canal and I think that is why it is called dismal. I can't fathom how horrible it must have been digging the ditch with shovels. Imagine the mosquitoes. In the 1700s, George Washington and other entrepreneurs and politicians decided to build a canal to transport white cedar to be made into shingles out of the great swamp. Washington had hoped to drain the swamp and farm it. His scheme didn't succeed. Work began on the 22-mile canal in 1793 and pretty much finished up in 1805, providing a sheltered route between Norfolk and Elizabeth City.

Today the Dismal Swamp is a national landmark and is used mostly by recreational boaters. I found it to be very pretty and peaceful. The water is quiet and trees overhang the waterway from both sides, making it an intimate place. The Dismal Swamp was anything *but* dismal. When I finished my voyage and exited the canal, I wanted to turn around and travel it again! The Dismal Swamp is a magical length of waterway.

Maryland to Virginia

November 8
Still waiting in Virginia

At 1600 I received the call I'd been waiting for. My engine had finally come in and is waiting for me in Deltaville. I was tempted to wait until tomorrow morning to pick it up because I had planned to use the truck and make the rounds: get the outboard in Deltaville, go to the liquor store, then stop at the grocery store. I especially wanted to eat another oyster lunch in Mathews. I was looking forward to the oysters, but I was so tired of waiting that I decided to collect my new engine and do my entire running around tonight.

It was after 2030 by the time I returned to the boat yard. I was tired and hungry. Mike, one

A Great Big Adventure on a Good Little Boat

of the yard's employees, had made a big crock-pot of delicious soup; it was in the common room and he had told me that I was welcome to help myself. I did and it was fantastic and warm. Thank you, Mike.

Somehow I unclamped my old outboard and carried it up to the repair shop. I carried the new outboard from the back of the truck, down the dock, and onto the boat. I managed to mount the new and heavy engine on the bracket off the back of my boat. This bracket extends off the stern by about a foot, and the outboard weighs about 65 pounds; I weigh about 100 pounds. I was so afraid of dropping my new engine overboard. I could have waited until the morning when there would have been help available. I wanted to leave in the early morning. I wanted to leave when there was nobody around. I hate goodbyes.

After lugging and loading two five-gallon jugs of gas, I read the manual about the procedure of adding oil and starting my new engine. I followed all the directions and pulled the starter cord. She started and ran like a champ. Success! I can leave in the morning! Oh, it *is* morning! No shake-down cruise for my new outboard.

Maryland to Virginia

Earlier today I had talked to Alex, the yard manager about my dockage fee. He told me that there was no charge! He said that this is a repair yard, not a marina, and they don't charge dockage. What a unique place and what good people. I did leave him my old outboard. He said he could use it for parts. Thanks to Zimmerman Marine!

November 9
East River to Deep Creek Lock on the
Dismal Swamp
36° 43.50' / 76° 15'

After a couple of hours of fitful sleep, I left the dock in the dark and fog. I was so excited to continue my journey! I motored out of the twisting and turning East River, back into Mobjack Bay, and onto a calm Chesapeake Bay. I enjoyed a following sea, so I raised my sails and experienced a lovely sail into and through Norfolk. I had planned to visit Norfolk and play the tourist, but after spending all those lost days at the Zimmerman boat yard, I just wanted to keep moving.

Maryland to Virginia

Norfolk was incredible—an overload of tugs, cargo ships, barges, Navy ships, planes, jets, helicopters, lots of sailboats, and big fast powerboats with huge wakes. Wakes from all directions bombarded me and I rock-and-rolled through Norfolk. One passing tug did slow down for me. I gave him a big smile and a wave. He reciprocated.

The number of Navy ships at the docks was staggering. The docks were huge! The ships were huge! What an impressive area. I was surprised at the number of pleasure boats out and about. There was a big tug with a barge behind me and he was gaining on me. He made me nervous and I will blame him for my wrong turn, or lack of turn. I traveled the eastern route of the Elizabeth River instead of the southern branch, as I should have. It was about an hour before I realized my mistake. It was odd, though, the bridges matched the bridges on my chart. My GPS said that I was wrong, but I didn't believe that I could have missed my turn! Golly gee, the GPS was right.

I wanted to catch the Gilmerton Bridge before it closed between 1530 and 1830 and I missed it because of my wrong turn and long detour. I called the bridge tender hoping that just maybe she would open for me. She said that she would open at the scheduled 1830, almost two hours away. I turned about and was ready to anchor to wait when I heard a tug call the bridge tender. He had an appointment for an opening. Wow, I didn't know you could do that. Maybe it is just a commercial thing. I don't know. The tender radioed me and invited me to pass under her open bridge after the tug if I could get there quickly. I raced to the bridge and thanked her.

Hooray, I was on the road again. By 1730 I reached the Great Bridge Lock at the north end of the Dismal Swamp. The sun had been in my eyes all day, and I was weary when I anchored just to the north of the lock. The lock wouldn't open till morning. I was in sight of the lock; actually, I was anchored about 300 yards from it.

It was a spectacular night. The moon was nearly full and reflected on the smooth water. The trees on the close banks hung over me and I felt as though I was wrapped in a safe cocoon. I am lucky to be here.

Yesterday was my youngest brother's birthday. I called Willy to wish him a happy birthday. He is planning a birthday boating outing with family and friends aboard his 85-foot cargo barge. Willy built this impressive boat himself. He launched the *Exuma Trader* two years ago. I suspect all the family will join him out on the water and there will be fishing, kayaking, and swimming, with lots of good food and some drinking! The *Exuma Trader* has been my home since I moved to Florida. I've been helping him finish the boat by completing much of the woodworking projects onboard. That's my rent. Willy and I have a great relationship, and I hate to miss his birthday. I hate to miss any family get-together, especially a boating one, but there will be other barge outings. I am happy to be where I am.

A Great Big Adventure on a Good Little Boat

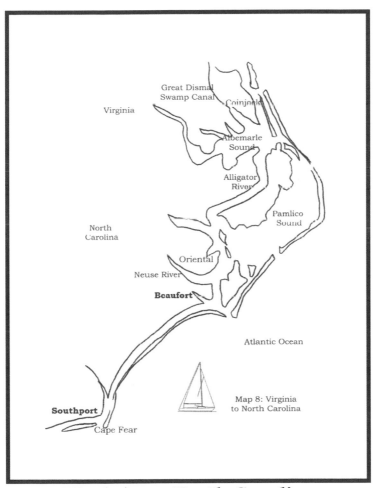

Map 8: Virginia to North Carolina

Virginia to North Carolina

November 10
The Dismal Swamp to Goat Island in the Pasquotank River, North Carolina
ICW mile 43
36° 20.59' / 76° 13.19'

I woke up early to a blanket of unbelievably thick fog. I was very close to the bright red lights of the lock, and they were all but invisible. It was so quiet and peaceful. I was sitting in the cockpit making a pot of coffee when I heard voices on my VHF. A woman was asking the lockmaster when he would open. He asked how close her yacht was to the lock. She replied that was hard to know because they couldn't see a thing. I knew where they were; they were just a few feet off my stern! I was pouring my first cup of coffee when I saw the three sailboats. All of us did a double-take; not one of us expected to see another boat so close.

The lockmaster said that he would wait for the fog to lift somewhat before letting us into the lock. I could hear their anchor chains releasing, and I chatted with the invisible sailors while we waited. Finally the fog lifted a bit and the lockmaster turned on the green lights, opened the gates, and invited us into his lock. I entered the lock last because I had trouble getting my outboard started. One of the other sailors stopped, re-anchored, and came onboard and helped me! That's boaters for you! Being last was a good thing, since the turbulence was less in the back of the lock because we were going into higher water.

While waiting for the waters to rise, I got to see and meet the other boaters. Two sailboats were traveling together and the two couples were from Canada. They were in their 30s, very nice, and I enjoyed our little visit. A younger couple taking a year off from work and life ashore to sail and travel owned the other boat. They were sweet. I wish them luck! The lockmaster was a happy guy. You could tell that he loved his job and enjoyed people. He had at least a hundred conch shells around his pretty gardens and he used them as horns. He tooted his horns for us. What fun.

After operating the lock, the lockmaster jumped into his pickup truck and raced to the drawbridge ahead of us. He reached the bridge and had it open and ready for our passage. We all thanked him and he wished us happy travels.

I had another lock to pass and another couple of bridges to raise for me today. In spite of the locks and bridges, I enjoyed this part of the voyage.

The other boats stopped at the Dismal Swamp Canal Welcoming Center, but I continued on. We met up and traveled together through the canal for a while until they left me in their wakes. I took a picture of the sterns of the sailboats as they sailed away from me. A common sight for my slow little boat.

I did find out more information about this canal. I assumed that the canal was named "dismal" because of the horrible conditions the slaves who were digging it were exposed to. My idea was wrong. In 1728, Colonel William Byrd II of Virginia had just returned from making a survey of the Virginia-North Carolina border for the English Crown. He and his party had to cut their way through dense undergrowth and thick forests of this swampy area. Byrd found the place repulsive and is said to be the one responsible for adding "dismal" to its name.

The digging of the canal wasn't started until after the Revolutionary War. The new nation was desperate for good roads; if the country was to prosper it needed an effective means of transportation. Both George Washington and Patrick Henry felt that canals were the best answer and favored a route through the Dismal Swamp. In 1793, construction began at each end of the canal, with most of the labor provided by slaves. By 1796, the canal construction was way over budget. The canal work stopped and construction of a road began, connecting both canal ends. Today the Dismal Swamp Canal is the oldest operating artificial waterway in the United States and is on the National Register of Historic Places.

Our country has so much history, and traveling brings it to life. Being here and seeing it creates a connection one can't gain through books. I don't remember history being this interesting in school!

As I traveled through the Dismal Swamp I felt that I was drifting down the Amazon with Hepburn and Bogart on the *African Queen*. This straight and narrow passage struck me hard. I was captivated and in awe. There is one other time that I have been so bewitched: in Mexico at the Mayan ruins of Chichen Itza. The overhanging trees in the canal and the closeness of the passage enveloped me like an old friend. I was comfortable here. I took a picture of a hand-operated barge that a farmer still uses to transport his cattle from one side of the canal to the other. I wish that I had seen him use it. I could almost hear the cows mooing. I must belong to a time in the past. That is where I seem to belong. I passed a huge sign welcoming me into North Carolina. How neat was that? I wish that I had taken a picture.

The Dismal Swamp was so beautiful and so relaxing. I could have fallen asleep and yet it kept me captivated. I didn't want to miss a thing. Throughout the canal I saw few signs that humanity existed. I was here and I was the only person that mattered. There are very few markers, so I just traveled through the middle of the waterway. I did meet up with a nasty-ass water snake and had he been bigger, he would have bitten my head off.

The cruising guide mentioned a place along the canal that advertised grilled breakfast and lunch food. My mouth started watering as I read. I was so looking forward to stopping there. I never found it and I was very disappointed. I didn't eat anything all day until after I anchored because I never lost hope that I would find that greasy spoon which would quench my need for some good, old-fashioned, bad-for-you grease. Oh well, canned chicken noodle soup is almost the same as a nice greasy grilled chicken. *Not.*

I reluctantly left the enchanting Dismal Swamp and headed my bow into the Pasquotank River. After the straight and thin waters of the canal, the meandering ribbon of the Pasquotank was stimulating. I wanted to find anchorage somewhere along this skinny, winding river before I reached Elizabeth City because beyond the city the river widens and a ferocious chop will likely greet me.

I found a sheltered place to drop anchor behind Goat Island, which sits in the river and creates a bend in the channel. Since I arrived here before dark I used the daylight time to adjust my engine mount. I thought that my outboard was too low in the water and I wanted to raise it up a little so that the engine would be higher and create less drag while sailing. I rigged the main halyard to the engine to get the weight off the mount. After removing the bolts and lowering the engine, I had to repeat the process because I felt that now the mount was too high. Finally I was satisfied with my work and rewarded myself with a comforting rum drink. The sunset was worth a picture and the moon was full and beautiful. There were geese honking and the rum was flowing. It was another great day and night to be who I am and where I am. I will enjoy tonight because tomorrow brings another large and open body of water and probably a chop and...a wet me.

Thinking about bodies of open water brought to mind one pleasant summer day in New England. A few years ago, I was sailing off the coast of New Hampshire with a couple who I'd recently met. We had a lovely sail until the wind died. The ocean was as flat as a pond—a very rare occurrence. We drifted for a while until I remembered that I was hosting an important dinner at our home that evening. I needed to get home and start cooking! We lowered our luffing sails, intending to start the outboard and tolerate a noisy trip back to Rye Harbor. My damn engine wouldn't start. Each of us tried, I checked the fuel, I pulled the spark plug, and I even cursed at it. Nothing worked. Finally, in desperation, I called Don on my cell phone. He did come out to tow us in but, for some reason he was extremely grumpy and I was embarrassed in front of my new friends.

The pressure of being late for my party was taking its toll also. To this day, I refuse to sail unless my day, and my companion's day, is free of commitments. When you are sailing, there can be nothing except sailing on the schedule for the day, and maybe the next! You never know what may happen when you are on the water. After all, look what happened to Gilligan!

November 11
Goat Island to the Alligator River, North Carolina
ICW mile 83
36° 20.70' / 76° 13.49'

There was going to be a long day ahead of me, so I was up and had raised anchor at 0530. I raced to make the scheduled bridge opening at Elizabeth City and made it with three minutes to spare. I continued down the Pasquotank River and it got wider and wider and finally opened up into Albemarle Sound. In spite of all the horror stories that people told me about the Albemarle Sound, I found it calm with friendly winds. I raised both my mainsail and my large jib and enjoyed real sailing for a few hours.

Virginia to North Carolina

Around 1300, the bay waters started to get choppy and nasty, so I reluctantly started my engine and lowered the sails. I began to feel the all-too-familiar attack of salty spray. Water soaked everything in the cockpit—including me —as I motored into the Alligator River. The sun was finally shining, and my face and ears were sunburned or wind burned, I don't know which. After another long but fine day, I turned off the open and choppy Alligator River and entered the narrower and more protected Little Alligator River.

It took a long time to find a safe place to anchor and finally, after setting and raising the anchor a few times, I settled on a semi-protected spot at the entrance of a creek off the river. I was too tired to eat or drink, so I just went to bed. Thank goodness that I had a mosquito net to drape over my open cabin doors because this place was a mosquito haven.

North Carolina juts out into the Atlantic and has three capes: Cape Hatteras, Cape Lookout, and Cape Fear. *Hmm,* I wonder why it's called that. Actually, I do know why it's called Cape Fear, and I can't wait to get past that inlet. There are no major ports and no natural harbors and, according to my coastal guidebook, there aren't many anchorages to be found along the ICW here. The Albemarle Sound and the Pamlico

A Great Big Adventure on a Good Little Boat

Sound are the two largest landlocked sounds in the United States.

Looking at the Pamlico Sound on the chart makes me cringe. This sound is large and exposed. If the past storms are any indication, it will not be an easy crossing. Well, I'll have to worry about that when it happens. There is nothing I can do about it now.

Do not dwell in the past, do not dream of the future, concentrate the mind on the present moment.

~Buddha

My adventure aboard my little boat is teaching me to concentrate on the moment. Some nights I find myself fearful for my future. Some nights I lie awake thinking of how I could have made different choices in New Hampshire. I wonder why my daughters and I are estranged. My heart aches for our lost relationship. Should I come clean and tell them that no matter what their father professes, he had a lady friend in the shadows for six months before he told me he was leaving me. Do they even know that *he* left me, *I* didn't leave him? Should I tell them how sudden it was for me? How devastating it was for me? How I had no one to turn to because I was *so* ashamed?

My brother and sister-in-law were the first to know. I was too embarrassed to open up to anyone else. I believed in my vows, and for better or worse, Don and I would be married until our dying days. Once he made his decision to leave, he was so cold. I told him that we couldn't walk away from 37 years. "Let's get help"; I was willing to do anything to make our relationship work. He looked at me with ice cubes for eyes, shook his head, turned, and said, "Too late." He walked away. That's when I knew he was right. I had no chance in hell to change anything. He had everything planned. He was in control, as usual. That is, until *I* filed for divorce! For perhaps the first time in his life, he was speechless. For a very few moments, he wasn't in control.

Our divorce was so painful, and it devastated the entire family. And the hurt is still with us. It's taken me six years of battle, legal fees, and court appearances to force him to pay me what *he agreed to* in court on the day of our divorce. I guess he didn't realize that he married someone who hangs on like a bulldog! I have finally received full payment, but I am devastated by his method of securing the funds.

A Great Big Adventure on a Good Little Boat

It isn't even a bittersweet victory. It's just bitter. It's done. I feel sick.

Do not destroy tomorrow by turning back to yesterday's sorrow.

~Anonymous

November 12
Alligator River to the Dowry Creek
Marina, Pungo River, North Carolina
ICW mile 135
35° 40.56' / 76° 03'

As usual, I was off anchor early and I entered the Alligator River-Pungo River Canal. The wind had started to build during the night, and my poor little boat shuddered with the gusts. After a restless and miserable night, I was glad to get an early start. The Alligator-Pungo River Canal is very pretty, straight and narrow, with low marshlands on either side. The low lands provide no shelter from the wind, and I was bucking strong headwinds that were building all day. The canal will bring me into the wide and exposed Pungo River, and I knew that since I was experiencing a soaking chop in this skinny canal it will be a lot worse in the open river. All I could do was take a deep breath, hold on, and thank my little boat for enduring everything I plan to put her through.

By gum, it was worse. It was horrible! I had water breaking over my bow and water pouring into my cockpit. I couldn't read the GPS, I couldn't read the charts, and I couldn't see any buoys or markers! In the canal I had been making five-and-a-half knots. In these violent waves and vicious winds, I was making only two knots and at times less. I was afraid that soon I would be making no headway at all!

I saw a larger sailboat ahead of me lose the dingy that she had been towing. The crew was having a rough time retrieving it, so I called via my VHF radio to offer assistance. I was relieved to have my offer turned down. I wouldn't have been much help, but I had to offer. I saw the boat circle for the third time. They were finally able to retrieve their dingy. The poor yacht had lines dragging and she looked ragged. Her crew must have been exhausted.

As I continued up the river, I encountered the worst, most treacherous waters that have assaulted my boat since the beginning of our trip. We were in danger of foundering. Water was coming into the cockpit from all directions and my tiny bilge pump was working nonstop and barely keeping up with the deluge of the Pungo River waters. This was the first time I was afraid during my voyage. I needed to make quick decisions, and they had to be the right decisions. I had to get out of this situation—and fast.

My first possible port of refuge was Dowry Creek. I only knew this because I had been studying the charts. My charts and GPS were useless to me in these rough waters. At this point, it was all I could do to hold on and keep myself from losing my footing. We were in real danger now.

I didn't hesitate to point my bow toward where I thought the protected creek was. As I approached the channel, the first markers finally appeared and I was able to make my entrance into the creek relatively easily. The chop calmed and the wind reduced as I motored through the channel toward the harbor. I was so relieved to be out of danger! I did find it a bit disconcerting to see a sailboat high and dry on the bank at the harbor entrance. I stayed in the marked channel, and I headed toward the dock, where I saw two dock hands ready and waiting to handle my lines. They were a welcome sight.

A Great Big Adventure on a Good Little Boat

I was soaked to the skin, exhausted, and felt as though I'd been through hell. I was so relieved to be out of the rough and horrible seas. It felt comforting to be secure at a friendly dock in a protected harbor. It is funny, though; you get into port looking and feeling like a drenched rat: wet, cold, and miserable; the harbor is calm and quiet and warm and all the people are dry. Such a contrast! It is amazing, but you know that every one of those people has experienced the same conditions. Maybe that's why the boating community is so tight knit.

Cruising has two pleasures. One is to go out into wider waters from a sheltered place. The other is to go into a sheltered place from wide waters.

~Howard Bloomfield

I had planned to just get fuel and then anchor beyond the dock, but when the fuel guy mentioned that tonight was Pot Luck Dinner Night for boats at the dock I decided to stay. Wow, how lucky can I get: a safe harbor, friendly people, and hot food.

The dinner was held in the warm and cozy common room at the marina, and the food was delicious. What a joy to be in a comfortable and dry building, enjoying tasty food, and meeting exciting people. I didn't have to brace myself against the rocking and rolling of rough waters, and I ate tons of food. It felt so good. I was a little embarrassed because I had nothing to contribute, but that didn't stop me from stuffing my face.

Another solo sailor who I'd met in Annapolis is here, and we traded experiences of our travels. She sails a larger boat and she has a companion now. It is a small world, and I met some great people at this little marina. One of the couples has invited me aboard for hot coffee and fresh cookies. She insisted on making me a bag of goodies for my snack bar. Another sailing couple generously gave me one of their ICW books. After such a tortuous passage, and getting into this friendly marina, it was so fantastic to visit with these cruising people. Cruisers are a special breed; they are friendly, helpful, and willing to share what they have. Dowry Creek Marina is one of the stops that I will remember and plan to return to.

November 13
Dowry Creek to Broad Creek off the Neuse River, North Carolina
ICW mile 175
35° 05' / 76° 36'

There was frost on the deck this morning! I can't reach the warm weather fast enough! I was sad to leave all my new friends at the marina, but they will be leaving soon too.

The Pungo River was a lot calmer today than it was a few days ago. My sails propelled my *Summer Wind* down the river, and I had a pleasurable but short sail across the Pamlico River. I had to lower sail and motor when I entered the narrow Goose Creek. The powerboat cruisers were thick as flies there, and they all powered past me, leaving memorable wakes. I was able to raise sail again when I proceeded into the Bay River and the open Neuse River. I found a protected location to set my anchor in Broad Creek, just off the Neuse River. It was a very enjoyable day to travel. I sailed most of the day; the sun was shining and I was a little warmer than I'd been in the last few days. Every day that I can raise my sails and head my bow south is a good day.

I often sit in my cockpit and watch the sunset; I enjoy hearing the geese calling, and revel in the solitude and peace of being right here, right now! I am so comfortable at these times. I was built for this. I am in my element. I am challenged every day, but I am in charge of my destiny. After 64 years, I am doing exactly what I should be doing! I found out what I want to be when I grow up. This is it! What a thrill!

Perhaps I need to be alone because I don't have the strength to pursue my own happiness when I am with others. I let others influence me too much; I want to please others at my own expense. I avoid confrontation whenever possible.

On this trip I am truly myself and I am living, I am who I want to be and I am doing what I want to do. Maybe I am just being selfish, but I don't think so. I've paid my dues. I've worked, married, worked, raised a family, and worked some more, and I believe that I have earned my independence. If this is selfishness, it is a good thing, and I'm all for it. It is time for me.

> *Everyone needs to find time for him- or herself.*
>
> ~Me

November 14
Broad Creek to just north of Bogue Inlet,
North Carolina
ICW mile 226
34° 40' / 77° 04'

This morning the Neuse River was kind to me, and I enjoyed sailing until I entered the skinny Adams Creek across from the town of Oriental. Everyone had told me to sail into Oriental, a friendly and popular cruisers' port. I had been headed there, but the winds and seas held me up and I had to take refuge in other places. At least 20 boats came out of Oriental as I passed this well-visited port. I guess it is popular, a bit too crowded for me. I don't like the trailer park-style of anchoring. I do appreciate my privacy.

All of us were headed into the constricted entrance of Adams Creek. These larger and faster cruisers passed me. I am always the smallest and slowest cruiser. Once the confusion and wakes of the cruisers passed, it was a tranquil and enjoyable cruise to Beaufort, North Carolina. I continued on past Morehead City, where I was tempted to stop to eat some real food, but it was such a favorable travel day that I didn't want to waste one minute of it. Today the wind was light and the seas were calm. The comfortable sailing days have been few and far between, and I have to take advantage of the decent weather and travel as far as I can during a good day like today.

I've been having issues with my new engine. It uses oil. It is brand new and I don't think it should be using so much oil. I was very careful with the break-in procedure, and I check the oil every morning. After cruising, by midday the oil light will sometimes blink on. This scares me. I don't want to cook another outboard; it was a very expensive mistake. When the oil light flickers, I have to pull off the ICW, anchor, and add oil.

Virginia to North Carolina

I called the factory and described my use of the outboard. They told me that, with the way I was working the new engine, it should use oil. They told me to keep adding oil until the seals seated and that there was no problem with my engine. So that's what I do: I keep adding oil. I have run aground and dropped my VHF radio overboard while tending to my little engine. Lots of fun!

I powered past the Beaufort Inlet. I wanted to stop here because my Dad and brother and I spent the night at a marina here many years ago. We were transporting a powerboat from Annapolis to Florida when we made a stop at this port for fuel and food. There was a big buffet dinner that night and we enjoyed a fantastic smorgasbord. The memory of the food brought back fond recollections of that voyage so many years ago.

I always enjoyed being with my Dad. A long time ago, when Dad had found the *Sunbeam* up in Marblehead, he and Uncle Ernie traveled by car for many hours to Massachusetts from Long Island on weekends so that they could ready the *Sunbeam* for launching. I always tried to get Dad to take me with them. It was a very long trip for a little girl. Dad did not make any potty stops, and I never asked.

A Great Big Adventure on a Good Little Boat

The *Sunbeam* was on dry dock, and I loved the adventure of climbing what seemed like 100 feet to the deck of our future home. I remember the cold, the lack of comfort, and the thrill of being with my Dad. Another joy that I recall was the lobster dinner that Dad treated me to on the last work night at Marblehead before heading home. Lobster was what Dad called "adult food," which had to be earned. I felt deserving. I loved my adventures with Dad. They could be painful, but they were always exciting.

I continued on. It killed me, but I powered onward and past Morehead City and food. This section of the ICW is close to the North Atlantic and a barrier island protects the coast, the ICW, and me. Because the inlets are close together and the Waterway is close to the ocean, the water has become a beautiful blue. I saw lots and lots of dolphins, and it was fun to watch them feeding and playing. I could watch these fascinating creatures forever.

I remember reading about a famous seventeenth-century sailor and one of his experiences with dolphins. He was sailing off a coast, at night, and he was not sure of his position. Sometime during the dark evening he was accompanied by a pod of dolphins. He felt that the mammals were herding him toward a direction away from his current course. Ultimately, the dolphins saved him and his boat from disaster. They led him away from a rocky shore. He was convinced that the intelligent sea mammals saved him from death.

I think that the dolphins I was seeing today would be capable of such an amazing feat. My companions today enjoyed swimming across my bow and diving under my boat. As they left the surface I called to them "dive, dive, dive." They even nudged me a few times. What fun!

All sailors know that dolphins swimming with a boat will bless her with good luck. Fishermen and sailors believe dolphins have the best interest of men at heart, and when the dolphins are around, the boat is under their protection. I always talked to my dolphin friends and thanked them. It was a gorgeous day. The sun was shining and the wind was calm, and I felt almost warm again.

Finding a place to anchor proved to be a problem. All along the North Carolina coast it is difficult to find good anchorages. This part of the ICW consists of a narrow channel in the shallow waters of Bogue Sound. It is difficult to find a spot to anchor and be off the channel. I finally anchored just off the waterway. There isn't much protection here, but if the wind doesn't

A Great Big Adventure on a Good Little Boat

build over the night, my *Summer Wind* should be safe. I will have to be alert.

November 15
Just north of Bogue Inlet to Sloop Point
in Topsail Sound, North Carolina
ICW mile 264
34° 23' / 77° 36'

It was another nice day to be on the water. I could get used to this. The dolphins were my companions again. I never tire of watching their sleek bodies as they effortlessly sail through the water. I felt protected and blessed. Some days are so peaceful and serene that at times it feels like I am the only person on earth. I could go on like this forever. I feel that I am in touch with the earth, just another piece of it like the birds and the dolphins. I want to stay in this place and be connected with the natural world.

A Great Big Adventure on a Good Little Boat

...for to be on the water is a comfort to the
soul...

~Carlton Michel

I could make this my new occupation! I could become a professional vagabond. Oh well, back to the real world.

As I was cruising along, enjoying the peace and quiet and the marshes and the many birds, I came across a large and impressive sign with an unlit amber light on each corner. It read: DO NOT PROCEED—LIVE FIRING IN PROGRESS WHEN FLASHING. Wow, I was glad not to see the amber lights flashing. What would I do? I guess I would have to anchor and just wait. I wonder how long the firing would last? How loud would it be? It might be cool to see things being blown up.

I was entering Camp Lejeune and its firing range. I passed old tanks and other military equipment that were the targets of the live firing that I was happy to be missing. The camp sits along the banks of the ICW, and as I sailed past the barracks I saw men walking around. I waved, but no one waved back.

Late in the morning, I had noticed that I had been alone all day yesterday and this morning; there were no other cruisers. Where did they all go? One beautiful antique cruiser did pass me. It looked like an old Elco. The Electric Launch Company ("Elco") started building electric luxury yachts in 1893, debuting their classic electric launch at the opening of the 1893 Columbian Exposition in Chicago. The company wanted to appeal to a larger market and built gasoline-powered yachts also. All of the Elco yachts are crafted using the finest materials, and they are outfitted with details that set these luxury yachts apart. The Elco Company is still in business.

The fine ship I saw today was all varnished wood and very sleek and elegant. What a lady! It was a thrill to see one of these marvelous yachts. She is the boat you would expect to see in an old classic black-and-white movie. She had passed me yesterday and I passed her while she was at dock this morning. Then four big and fast cruisers passed me. The cruisers and I have been playing the passing game for days. It is fun to recognize and wave to each other.

I made it to the next bridge right at its scheduled opening time. That's a first! When the sun shines and the day is warm, everything seems to go right. I anchored in a channel close to the barrier island and a nice-looking community of homes and docks and boats. All

A Great Big Adventure on a Good Little Boat

the boats in this area are powerboats. The water is too shallow here for much sailing possibilities. It was a protected and quiet location to drop anchor and spend the night. It was another wonderful day to be me. I am blessed!

November 16
Sloop Point to just south of Carolina Beach Inlet, North Carolina
ICW mile 295
34° 04' / 77° 53'

It was another marvelous day to be cruising. What an enjoyable way to travel! I could sail on forever if the temperature was warm and the seas were calm! The ICW here is a skinny channel through the marshlands of North Carolina. I love the solitude and peace of this remote area. The marshes are alive with birds, and the dolphins are still playing tag with me. These happy sea mammals keep a smile on my face, and I love talking to them. I find myself talking to all the wildlife during my travels in the quiet and peaceful areas of the ICW. When I hear them responding, I will start to worry.

I anchored off the ICW early and changed the oil in my outboard. This job was hairy because the drain plug sits over the water and I have no spare plug if my one-and-only one was to drop into the drink. I tried to buy a replacement plug when I bought the outboard. Can you believe that the dealer doesn't stock such a critical part? That marine store didn't even carry an extra fuel filter! Unbelievable. Besides having no desire to lose my oil plug, I also didn't want to dump oil into the water, so I rigged a plastic garbage bag around the outboard to catch the oil and the one and only plug if I dropped it. I carefully unscrewed the plug, trying to keep hold of it as it became slippery with the engine's oil. My plan worked well. I didn't lose the plug and no oil escaped into the sea. After replacing my one and only plug, I removed the oil-filled garbage bag and poured the spent oil into an empty oil container. I filled the engine with the recommended amount of fresh oil and cleaned up my mess. I was happy to get that job out of the way. I had been so nervous about losing that damn plug.

It was still early, so I made a rum drink and a nice dinner to celebrate my success. During the night a noise wakened me. I couldn't place the sound. Finally I realized that my keel was tapping the bottom ever so slightly. My GPS indicated plenty of water here, but my boat told me otherwise. Oh, well. I made a 3 a.m. move to deeper water and went back to bed. Sleep is never without incident at anchor and the rest of the night was uneventful.

This morning, just after daybreak, as I reentered the ICW, I heard another sound that I couldn't quite place. I looked around and, on a long pier that ran parallel with the waterway, I spotted the source of the mystery sound. Walking on the long dock was a man playing the bagpipes! He walked and played as he kept up with my boat. I was delighted. He serenaded the beginning of my day's journey. It was so lovely that it gave me goosebumps. What a special treat. As he reached the end of the dock, I blew him big kisses. He bowed and I sailed on. Now, that's the way to begin a perfect day!

I realized that the water is a pretty blue here and not the brown I saw in the rivers and areas away from the ocean. The low and narrow barrier islands are the only things separating the *Summer Wind* and me from the rough Atlantic. The inlets are close together in this area, and to the north of an inlet I may have a following current and pretty much fly past the opening to the ocean; once past the same inlet I can be bucking a strong current and be barely making any kind of headway. The many inlets are the cause of the blue waters and the many dolphins in the water.

My speed, or lack of speed, doesn't hold these sleek mammals' interest for long, but they seem to enjoy diving under my boat.

As I pass each inlet, I notice how rough the ocean is and I am very thankful to be in protected waters.

I find this area beautiful but exhausting. It is so hard to find a place to anchor or dock. I start looking for my home for the night at around 1400 because by then the sun is starting to get low and it is difficult to see. Heading south and west, the sun is right in my eyes all afternoon and I get weary. It is exhausting to stand at the tiller for 8 to 12 hours each day. The spray makes it difficult to see the charts and my GPS. I do get tired. I must be getting old.

Yesterday, I had spray in my face for only a couple of hours, just enough to wet my charts and salt up my glasses and make me cold. My radio isn't charging well, and I can't check the weather as much as I would like. I have a passage tomorrow that may be nasty if the wind is out of the south, making a weather report imperative. Damn, do I sound like a whiner?

I plan to stop at Southport tomorrow. My sister-in-law has a friend there who offered her hospitality, and I intend to take her up on it. It will be nice to wash clothes and have a long, hot shower and a home-cooked meal! I've never met Elizabeth, but I expect that I will enjoy my visit. How nice of her to offer her hospitality to a stranger.

November 17
Near Carolina Beach Inlet to Southport,
North Carolina
ICW mile 307
33° 54.86' / 78° 00.85'

I heard a weather report this morning and high, gusty winds were predicted. It will be a nasty day to travel, but I didn't want to stay at anchor another minute. All night the lightning and thunder and wind kept me awake. My little boat swung on her anchor like a crazy carnival ride. I knew it would be a miserable day traveling in the Cape Fear River, but I just had to continue. I traveled in the relatively protected waterway of Myrtle Grove Sound and passed through the restricted but tranquil Snows Cut, into the Cape Fear River.

Sure enough, as I entered the river, it was rough and I was blasted with spray and wintry water. I was uncomfortable, drenched, and not looking forward to dealing with being miserable for the next 10 or 12 miles down the river to Southport. I looked behind me and saw a huge cargo ship bearing down on me. God, she was so big! Does she see me? Is the *Summer Wind* even a speck on her radar? There was enough water outside of the channel and that's where I headed and that's where I stayed. Another ship was entering the river from the ocean with her bow pointed my way. Well outside of the ship-way I was safe from being run over, but her wake still gave me quite a hold-on-for-dear-life ride.

There was another gigantic ship coming toward me, so I continued to travel outside the channel. Three more massive cargo ships left me in their wakes. Really, I rocked and rolled until long after they passed me. As if that wasn't enough of a challenge, as I went by a big ferry terminal a large ferry was headed out. I wasn't sure of her course until I realized that I was very obviously in her path, and she seemed to have no intention of deviating from her route.

With plenty of water outside the ship channel, I was able to steer clear of my oncoming nemesis. Respect tonnage! After avoiding the huge and fast ships cruising through the river, I began my turn toward Southport. I thought that I was out of danger, and it would be easy sailing, but I was wrong. I had just cleared the ferry terminal when thick fog settled in and blanketed the area. I couldn't see a thing! I stayed off the channel as best as I could. I was nervous about being run over since the waterway narrowed as I powered closer to Southport, and I was forced to reenter the busy channel. I heard three cruisers pass me; I saw only one of them. This was scary. I used my GPS chart plotter to help me find the Southport Marina. The strong winds and current made my docking less than graceful, but I was so happy to be at the dock and safely out of the foggy ICW.

I called my hostess from the dock, and Elizabeth couldn't believe that I had found my way through such a horrible and foggy day. I didn't tell her how difficult my day had been.

What a wonderful lady. Elizabeth picked me up and brought me, along with my smelly laundry, to her lovely home, which overlooks the ICW just south of where I had docked my little boat. Elizabeth and her husband Robert enjoy watching the ever-changing marshes and the meandering river of the waterway. The sunsets are a spectacular sight from their home. All of the houses along the ICW in this area are far from the actual water. There are expansive marshy lowlands that make up the waterway borders and many of the homes have long docks connecting the homes to the water.

Elizabeth and Robert have been living here for a while and, like most people I know, they are always making improvements. Elizabeth's taste in decorating and colors was impressive; their house was beautiful and stylish.

I showered, and as I stuffed my stiff and stinky clothes into the washer, I was assaulted with the strong odors of grime, salt water, and many days and nights of wear. After I felt human again, with a clean body and clean clothes, Elizabeth and I drove into town to do some sightseeing. Of course a visit to a restaurant was included in our outing.

We also made a trip to Wrightsville to replace my VHF. The radio wouldn't keep a charge and I needed it replaced. Elizabeth and I returned to her home, finished my laundry, and talked and relaxed until Robert joined us after work. We enjoyed cocktails as he cooked thick, juicy steaks on the grill. This was the first red meat that I've eaten since my departure. The steaks were delicious. It was a lovely evening. I stayed overnight and slept in a real bed for the first time since I left Kittery in the beginning of October. The bed was warm and dry and fluffy soft. The bedroom window afforded me a peaceful evening view of the ICW. Thank you, Elizabeth and Robert, for a delightful dinner, a warm bed, clean clothes, and best of all, your friendly hospitality.

When you are good to others, you are best to yourself.

~Anonymous

November 19
Southport to Calabash Creek on the
North Carolina/ South Carolina border
ICW mile 343
33° 52.41' / 78° 34.20'

Elizabeth drove me back to my boat at about 0700. I slipped and slid down the dock ramp. A layer of ice coated the docks and my deck. What the heck was this? This is North Carolina; there shouldn't be *ice* here! This is the South, isn't it? I guess not south enough! I thanked my new friend Elizabeth for her kindness, released my dock lines, and pointed my bow in the direction of the south and—hopefully—warmth. As I traveled down the ICW, I blew my horn and waved as I sailed past

A Great Big Adventure on a Good Little Boat

Elizabeth and Robert's home. (I hope it was their home, since I made a spectacle of myself.)

It was chilly, but because of a pleasant breeze behind me, I flew my jib all day. I was motor-sailing and grateful for the calm and comfortable voyage through a meandering section of the waterway. Two cruisers were about to pass me, so I turned my VHF radio on. (To save power, I don't keep my radio on all the time that I'm cruising.) I heard someone calling over the radio: "Little blue sloop, look to your starboard, I'm waving at you." I looked, and sure enough, there was a guy aboard a 24-foot sloop waving at me! He was anchored in a small cove off the waterway. Weird, I guess, but I answered his call and he invited me to raft up to him and offered to make me dinner. It was early in the day, but how could I resist an offer like that?

I lowered my jib, turned around, and rafted to his sailboat. His name was Steve, and he had heard about me from other cruisers. Well, he did make me dinner and we enjoyed talking for most of the night. Steve was a nice guy, but I had no desire to cruise with someone. I enjoy being alone. He was lonely, and looking for someone to sail with, but I am not lonely. I enjoy sailing alone. We parted ways in the morning.

Virginia to North Carolina

After studying my charts, I realized that Steve and I were anchored in Calabash Creek and we were floating on the North and South Carolina border. I've traveled into another state! I have just sailed through ten states and I am entering the waters of the eleventh state on my voyage. I think it might start getting warm now. God, I hope so!

A Great Big Adventure on a Good Little Boat

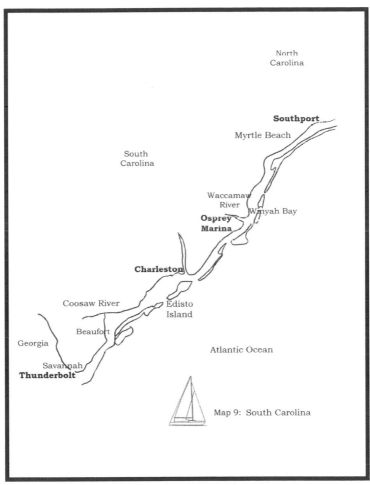

North
Carolina

Southport

Myrtle Beach

South
Carolina

Waccamaw
River

Winyah Bay

**Osprey
Marina**

Charleston

Coosaw River

Edisto
Island

Beaufort

Georgia

Atlantic Ocean

Savannah

Thunderbolt

Map 9: South Carolina

South Carolina

November 20
Calabash Creek to the Osprey Marina,
South Carolina
ICW mile 373
33° 40.85' / 79° 02.48'

Today's run was through a pretty area of South Carolina. I traveled under five fixed bridges. When traveling under these high bridges there is *no* stopping, *no* radioing, *no* waiting, and *no* maneuvering. My progress was slowed because I had to call and wait for the opening of two low bridges today and, as I was biding my time, trying to keep my position at the third low bridge, I lost my VHF radio—yes, *again*! I had radioed the bridge tender and he told me that he would open in a few minutes. As

South Carolina

I sat on the *Summer Wind*'s transom, a cruiser called and asked the tender to wait the opening for him. Then yet another two boats called. I ended up waiting for over 20 minutes! What's that about? The bridges never wait for me! By the time the bridge opened, there was a flotilla of one powerboat and three sailboats, including the *Summer Wind*.

While waiting, I had to work at keeping myself in place against a strong current. There wasn't a lot of room to come about and I was playing at backing up with my engine. Well, anyway, I unhooked my VHF so that I could have it with me on the transom and it went overboard. My new, "floating" radio sank like a rock! I just bought this one in Southport while I was visiting Elizabeth. I was more than upset to lose another radio. I still have lots of bridges to call and I need a radio. I decided that I would try to cruise with the other two sailboats, letting them call the next few bridges, until I could find someplace to stop to get another VHF. Eventually, one of the sailboats turned into the tiny Osprey Marina, just off the ICW, so I followed. Why not?

The entrance was very tight and the larger boat had a difficult time maneuvering and tying up to the fuel dock. Again, I had to practice backing up while I was waiting for him. At least I had no radio to drop into the drink while I was backing and waiting! Finally, I got to the fuel dock and rafted to the larger boat (the fuel dock was that small).

I asked if there was anyone who could take me to a marine store to get a VHF radio. The boat next to me offered me their spare VHF; it had battery issues, but I could have it. I thanked them, but I had a long way to go and didn't want problems with my radio. The dock master offered to drive me to replace my VHF as soon as he could get us off the fuel dock. I decided to stay for the night and powered to my new dock location. The dock master finished his work of situating all the boats for the evening, and then he drove me to buy another radio. I hope this is the last radio I need to buy, not just for this trip but for the rest of my life!

After returning to the marina, I showered and cleaned up my boat and settled in. Deb and Walt, my new neighbors on the dock next to mine, invited me aboard their boat for cocktails, and I had the opportunity to meet some of the cruisers that had been playing tag with me for the last week or so.

It worked like this: they would pass me in their much faster powerboats, reach a marina, and dock overnight or longer. My days were longer and started earlier, but I was much slower. These fast-cruising boaters would have a nice breakfast and a leisurely morning at the dock, and then pass me during the next day. I was the tortoise and they were the hare. I had been seeing their boats for days now, and now I got to meet the people aboard them.

Most of the cruisers have made this voyage many times. It was fun to be around happy and adventurous people. It was a stimulating and entertaining night.

A Great Big Adventure on a Good Little Boat

November 21
Docked at the Osprey Marina in
South Carolina

My Florida relatives want me to join them for a rambunctious family Thanksgiving dinner. Thanksgiving has always been a very important holiday for me, a total family gathering with lots of people, too much delicious food, and plenty of good wine. My New Hampshire family and I have broken up, so it made sense to fly to Florida.

I considered the Thanksgiving visit, but I hated to leave my little boat and break up my voyage. Once I committed myself to the Florida visit though, I couldn't wait to see all my brothers and sisters and their families. I made arrangements to fly out of Myrtle Beach on

South Carolina

Tuesday morning. After meeting with the dock master and paying the bill to cover my time away from the *Summer Wind*, I spent the rest of the day walking around the marina, critiquing the boats there, and meeting all the boat people.

I met a couple with four young kids. The family was traveling aboard a large fancy powerboat. I realized that this was the same boat that powered into the South Mills Lock in the Dismal Swamp. As I remember, her name is *Our Home*, and she powered very close to my boat, towering over my low stern like a skyscraper. Other than the fact that the kids were running wild and the family obviously had lots of money, they reminded me of my family's adventure so many years ago. Those kids were very lucky, as were we.

November 22 through November 28
Thanksgiving in Florida, then back to the
Osprey Marina, South Carolina

What a wonderful Thanksgiving! I am so glad that I made the effort to fly to Florida for the celebration. Family and friends gathered at Willy and Leona's home for an afternoon of eating and drinking and laughter. Earlier we had converted his pool table into a beautiful and grand dining table, complete with a pretty and unique centerpiece. Willy made an oblong box with holes in the top. Leona placed pots of 'Dusty Miller' in the holes and arranged dried fall leaves around the base, camouflaging the pots and the wooden box. Three small poinsettia plants topped off the arrangement. Willy discreetly added a string of tiny lights and the result was lovely.

We all pitched in with food contributions to create an outstanding feast. There must have been 25 of us sitting at Willy and Leona's table, happily stuffing our faces. It was so much fun to have everyone together and see all my family and fantastic friends happy and healthy. I'm so glad I flew here to share the holiday with them. It was such a fun visit, with lots of good laughs, delicious food, and great people. Thanks to all of you for making this a memorable holiday.

My Florida Thanksgiving helped me more than my sisters and brothers will know. Since Don left, I have dreaded all holidays. Holidays are torture for me. My grown daughters involved their father and took care of him during the holidays; I was on my own. Yes, I had many friends in New Hampshire, and I was never without an invitation to join their families for a home-cooked meal and a welcoming family get-together. I was always so grateful to my gracious friends, but I always felt out of place. I felt like the odd man out. This was due to me, not because of my kind friends and their families. My Florida Thanksgiving was the first one with my family in six years. It was very special.

I remember the first Thanksgiving that Don, the girls, and I had after Don's mother died. We

A Great Big Adventure on a Good Little Boat

always celebrated Thanksgiving at Don's mother and father's home, and she cooked the conventional turkey with all the fixings. Thanksgiving was always at her home and Christmas was always at mine. We were all uncomfortable facing our first holiday without her. It was going to be a difficult time. I realized we needed to jump out of our traditional gathering, so, instead of our Thanksgiving foods and our normal Thanksgiving setting, I decided to change everything and make a new and fresh beginning for all of us. We met at our home, and I served steamed clams and lobsters. Basically, I served a New England Clam Bake. Everyone had a good day. We hadn't forgotten Don's mother on that day, but we were able to enjoy a family get-together and toast her. Yet her special holiday wasn't thrown in our faces. We were happy and we honored her by not trying to replicate her special meal.

After a rough return flight from Sarasota, I didn't get back to the marina until very late. The marina was closed, the docks were dark, and there wasn't a soul to be seen. It was quiet and a bit eerie. The rain was coming down in buckets and the cold was penetrating. Welcome home, Linda! As cold and hard and cramped as it was, I was happy to be back in my damp bunk. I realized that I missed my boat and my voyage and that I love this vagabond lifestyle. I guess that I'm not a vagabond because I have a destination and a home, sort of....I think I would be happy without a specific end to my journey. Maybe Florida will be just a resting place until I get those itchy feet again.

It was tremendous fun to be with family. They are very supportive and I'm looking forward to spending more time with them. Cindy and I had fun together, as usual, and I was able to get to know Leona better. My stay was a short one; I wanted to return to my *Summer Wind* and my adventure. I enjoyed my visit, but now I am anxious to get moving. I had paid my dockage fees through today, so I plan to continue traveling on my little boat in the morning.

November 29
Osprey Marina to the Little Minim Creek,
South Carolina
ICW mile 417
33° 11.25' / 79° 16.25'

I left the dock at about 0830. The dock office wasn't open, but I was hoping that I could say goodbye to the friendly staff at the Osprey Marina and get some of the coffee from the pot they started in the morning. I enjoyed and appreciated the crew here. They always wore smiles and went out of their way to be helpful. I felt very comfortable about leaving the *Summer Wind* in their capable hands. Though the marina is small, it provides many of the amenities of a larger marina. I enjoyed my visit and hope to come back on my future travels.

I left the marina and reentered the quiet and skinny section of the ICW, but I could feel the southwest wind building. There won't be any sailing today with this southerly wind. The ICW continued to widen as I proceeded into the Waccaman River, which was still relatively calm and pleasant. The Waccaman and the Great Pee Dee Rivers joined and widened into the wider and choppy Winyah Bay, where I got hammered with strong winds and rough water. This bay is another section of open water and it was rough, cold, and wet. The wind was blowing at about 20 knots, gusting to 25, on the nose again. It was like someone had turned on a wind and wave machine! I wanted to pull into Georgetown, but it was too rough and wet to read the charts. I couldn't see the chart with the salt water running down my eyes and glasses. I decided to continue on into more protected waters.

Finding a comfortable anchorage tonight might become a problem. There are many little creeks off this area of the waterway, but there is nothing but marshes along this section of South Carolina. The lack of high ground and no trees will provide little to no wind protection.

After consulting my best buddy "Skipper Bob," I decided to try to anchor in Minim Creek, which is just a tiny creek off the ICW. I anchored in about eight feet of water where the creek widens a bit, and I hoped I wouldn't hinder other boats from passing. It had been a long, wet day, and I was happy to pull into the tiny creek. My friend "Skipper Bob" said that trees protected this area. Well, they weren't trees, they were low shrubs, but my anchor held, so I stayed. I was cold and uncomfortable and the wind buffeted my little boat, but I was too tired to even think of finding another place to anchor. I went to bed wearing every bit of clothing I could find onboard. As the night wore on, the wind did diminish and my sleep wasn't interrupted too often.

As I tried to keep warm, I thought of my comfy bunk aboard Willie's *Exuma Trader*. As warm and dry as it was, and as comfortable as I felt visiting with my Florida family, my little cold and wind-blown boat is where I am and where I am happy to be. I need to be here now. So thank you family, for affording me a welcome respite from my adventure. And thank you, *Summer Wind*, for the welcome rescue from being enveloped by caring people before I've had a chance to be totally comfortable in my new skin. I need more *me* time. I need time to work on who I want to be. I need time to figure out what I want to do and where I want to go. I need my little *Summer Wind* voyage with all its challenges and eye-opening experiences.

November 30
Little Minim Creek to Dewees Creek, South Carolina
ICW mile 454
32° 50.39' / 79° 45.25'

It was another frosty day of motoring. My butt cheeks hurt from shivering all morning. My hands and feet were stiff and in pain. The wind is still out of the southwest. How can a south wind be so cold? At least it's not raining or, worse yet, at least it's not snowing!

All day I had been cruising through the narrow waterway. On either side of my tiny world were lowlands and marshes. The grassy marshlands are extensive here and there is little sign of higher ground. I saw no trees today. I found the area unspoiled, and it was relaxing just being here. The waterway crossed several rivers and I traveled through the Santee Swamp. At times I traveled through straight, connecting waterways, and in other sections of my watery road my passage took me through wider, meandering rivers. This day would have been enjoyable if I hadn't been so blasted cold. I decided to anchor early, since I knew I couldn't make Charleston before dark.

At the crossing of Dewees Creek I headed northwest into the creek, where I saw what looked like a sand bar with hundreds of birds standing on it. These birds appeared to block the entrance to the creek. What the heck is this about? I motored closer and the birds flew off. They weren't standing, they were floating on the water's surface and it wasn't a sand bar—it was water! That was a bizarre image. It made me question my ability to see what was real. Am I going a tad loony? I'm usually a sensible person and I don't like questioning myself. Maybe I just need to rest and regroup. It has been a long and cold day. I shivered all day.

I reached a relatively good spot and set the anchor. The current was swift and the wind protection was minimal, so I let out all of the anchor rode available. I hope it's enough. Thank goodness the weather had warmed up and I stopped shivering. A rum drink will help even more.

I settled into my new locale and realized that the marshes were alive with birds. The flock of birds was feeding and then vying for a roosting branch for the evening, and they became louder as the sun started to settle low on the marshes. They provided me with tonight's entertainment.

I heated a can of vegetable noodle soup and crashed into my bunk. The soup warmed my tummy, but did nothing for my hunger and need to eat "real food." I like to chew my food; soups just don't hack it. I have no refrigeration onboard, so mushy canned foods have to suffice. Sleep came quickly, and although I woke up several times during the night to check my position, I woke up rested. I plan to dock in Charleston tomorrow and stay for a day or so to enjoy one of my favorite cities.

South Carolina

November 31
Dewees Creek to Charleston, South
Carolina
ICW mile 469
32° 46.50' / 79° 56.50'

My secluded anchorage in Dewees Creek became crowded as the sun went down. Five sailboats joined me during the twilight hours. They anchored downstream of the *Summer Wind,* so my privacy stayed intact. You just never know about these hidden anchor spots. Maybe Skipper Bob is their best friend too!

As the sun rose, so did we sailors. We woke to a pleasantly favorable but very light wind. It seemed like there must have been an anchor call because the fleet of sailboats and I entered the

A Great Big Adventure on a Good Little Boat

ICW in unison. All of us were sailing toward the next bridge—the Ben Sawyer Memorial Bridge—which is closed between 0700 and 0900. Quite a few bridges are not open to boat traffic during rush hour, allowing cars and drivers to get to and from work; the Ben Sawyer Memorial Bridge was one of them. This bridge has a closed vertical height of 31 feet. If I motor-sailed, I could clear my 32-foot mast under the bridge at low tide without waiting for an opening.

The taller boats meandered slowly down this lovely section of the ICW, killing time until the scheduled bridge opening. I made it to the bridge in plenty of time to take advantage of the tide and I still had time to enjoy the scenery. I found the area very pretty, with marshes and birds and quaint waterfront communities with quirky homes and lots of docks and small powerboats. The marinas looked friendly and inviting.

At each bridge there is a sign marking the height of the bridge above the water level. Since I was traveling under a 31-foot bridge at low tide, the height gauge showed that the clearance was 34 feet. These height markers are a great aid to boaters, but I have a complaint about them: as an older single-hander, I find it hard to steer and read the numbers, even with binoculars; the result is that I have to power in very close to the bridge before I can read what the closed height is. The charts also record each bridge's width and height. I do rely on my charts, but I wasn't sure about the tide drop in this area and I wanted to guarantee the clearance of the bridge by reading the numbers posted at the bridge.

I enjoyed cruising through the area. I applauded myself for clearing the bridge with a foot or two to spare. I have to admit though, my masthead clearance looked scary.

I did find that until I got into the Deep South, the charts name the bridges. Not the case as I traveled further south. This isn't a big deal except for the fact that the bridge tenders get somewhat indignant if you don't call them by their bridge's name. This is where the *Cruising Guide* is worth its weight. The guide includes an ICW bridge list, listing not only the name of the bridge but also where it is via the ICW mile and its latitude and longitude. Very helpful! Also included is the type of bridge—fixed, bascule, or swing—and the closed vertical clearance of each bridge. Another helpful bit of advice is the VHF channels that the tender monitors, as well as the opening schedule and restrictions of each particular bridge. I wouldn't leave home without these guides.

A Great Big Adventure on a Good Little Boat

I loved this quiet passage until my GPS quit at the entrance of Charleston's active harbor. I had just passed under the Ben Sawyer Memorial Bridge and I was enjoying the calm waters in the remaining quiet area of the ICW before entering the hubbub of the busy Charleston Harbor. The screen just went blank! I was depending on it to get me through Charleston Harbor. Obviously, I was too dependent.

Last night I had plotted my waypoints so that I could easily follow the channel and not get sidetracked by all the big boat traffic, the merging rivers, and the ocean inlet of this crowded port. With a blank GPS screen, all my planning was gone. I was not a happy camper.

While cruising in the waters of Charleston, trying to avoid the ship traffic, steering, and working to reactivate the GPS, I got turned around. I wasn't sure where my next buoy was. I was stressed! It brought to mind something I had read: when he was asked if he had ever gotten lost in the woods, Daniel Boone once said, "I've never been lost, but I was bewildered for a few days." I was *bewildered*!

As I had anticipated, there were huge ships entering the harbor from sea, and they made huge, nasty wakes—making navigation even more difficult. Damn, it made *standing* difficult!

South Carolina

Finally, the sailboats that had been behind me entered the harbor and as they headed toward the marina, I shamelessly followed.

I docked at the same marina where my parents and siblings and I had docked so many years ago. We had stayed in Charleston for a couple of months way back then. This is a copy of an article written in a Charleston newspaper. I will quote it in its entirety, errors, inaccuracies, and all. It is titled "Nine is a crowd on Yacht *Sunbeam*—New York family heads 14,000 miles down under to get away from it all. A young married couple with seven children and a hankering for adventure have arrived in Charleston on the first leg of a 14,000-mile voyage to Australia aboard a small schooner.

"We just wanted to get away from it all," explained Willard F. Petrat, 40-year-old former naval officer and New York building contractor who skippers the schooner *Sunbeam*.

He has as crew his wife Jessie and seven children aged from 16 to 3.

Mr. Petrat bought the *Sunbeam*, a 60 foot veteran of ocean races, after she was laid up at New York and virtually retired. He spent six years of his spare time rebuilding her.

Last Spring he gave up his construction business, uprooted the family from their home, upped anchor and set out on a voyage that will take them more than halfway around the world.

327

A Great Big Adventure on a Good Little Boat

"We were fed up with the city life, and I thought Australia would be a good country for a new beginning," Mr. Petrat said yesterday.

As he sat repairing sail aboard the *Sunbeam* at Charleston's Municipal Marina, his three boys, four-girl and one-wife crew arrived on deck. "I thought about taking on an experienced crew, but I couldn't have a better one than the one I've got," he said with a smile.

Mrs. Petrat is his 'first mate' and she helped in the rebuilding of the schooner. She and the older children can take a turn at the helm, and most of the young sailors can lend a hand in the galley and the chores of swabbing down.

Sailing across the Pacific does not mean a holiday from school. "All have correspondence courses up to high school level which Jessie and I supervise," Mr. Petrat explained.

After their first taste of stormy weather on the trip from Annapolis to Charleston, the family did not suffer seasickness, according to their skipper.

From Charleston the Petrats will sail for the Caribbean, and make the Pacific crossing from the west coast sometime next year.

Mr. Petrat is an old hand at navigating Pacific waters. He did it as a lieutenant commander in World War II— aboard a submarine.

As a graduate of the Naval Academy, he joined the U.S. Navy in 1937, and made three war patrols with his ship across the Pacific to the Gulf of Siam and the Java

Straits. "I think I'll enjoy it more sailing on the surface," he said.

That's the end of that newspaper article. It portrays Dad as an idealist. He wasn't. He wanted to travel and he had seven children. To set the record straight, the article also makes it sound as though Dad worked single-handedly for six solid years refurbishing the *Sunbeam*, when the fact of the matter was that my mother, siblings, and I spent long hours working as well. And, contrary to Dad's comment, most of us *did* get seasick. We were young and a novice crew. He couldn't afford better. We were for the most part willing, we were young and moldable, and we had no choice. We were a captive audience. For me, it was a great experience. My time aboard the *Sunbeam* will always be with me. I am a strong and capable person because of my experiences traveling on that great yacht with my family.

We never did sail to Australia. When we finally sailed to Florida and crossed the Gulf Stream, we cruised to the Bahamas. Nassau was exciting for us kids, but it was too expensive to stay long, so we set off for the out-islands of the Exumas, a chain of islands south of Nassau which, at that time, were very isolated.

We worked our way down the beautiful chain of islands. I remember being amazed at the clarity of the water. It seemed shocking to be able to see through the clear waters. We could see huge coral formations, sandy areas, and fish. Lots of fish!

We arrived at Staniel Cay just before Thanksgiving. I remember that we were anchored off the Staniel Cay Yacht Club and the weather turned nasty. We had to stand 24-hour anchor watch for a few days. Two of us were always on duty to make sure the *Sunbeam* didn't drag her anchor.

Although the waters teemed with fish, we had no snorkeling gear or slings to be able to catch the fish. We had no fishing gear, and no money to buy gear. That Thanksgiving dinner was a couple of cans of Spam!

Dad talked his way into a paying job for us. He designed a home for a wealthy Frenchman on an island close to Staniel. We moved our floating home, anchored off Foul Cay, and we all began work on a beautiful island vacation home for a rich French couple.

Over the years, we built quite a few homes and an airstrip on different islands in the Exumas. We earned money and bought snorkeling equipment and Hawaiian slings. (Spear guns were outlawed for fishing in the islands.) We used the readily available Hawaiian sling, which consisted of a stainless steel shaft and a screw-on spear point. The shaft was powered by rubber tubing attached to a block of wood with a hole in the center, placed in the hole, and powered by pulling back on the tubing. The shaft was not attached to the line. We learned very quickly that to lose a shaft meant going hungry. Even if we could afford to buy a new spear shaft, it would be weeks before we could receive it on the island.

We became efficient fishermen and never went hungry again.

The *Sunbeam* eventually was sold and we built ourselves a large and elaborate two-story houseboat. With labor, we purchased an island on the ocean side of Staniel Cay and created a magical, permanent home for the houseboat. We called it Hoi Ti Cay. We built a moat around the houseboat island and connected the island and the houseboat with arched bridges, stone shark pens, turtle pens, and steps into the water where we could sit and feed a plethora of small tropical fishes. The tiny fish would come up to your toes and nibble at them. A free pedicure!

The houseboat is long gone, but much of the stone walls are still standing. The first Monday in August is "Jessie and Bill Petrat Day" on Staniel Cay. The islanders walk to the ruins and enjoy a picnic and a day of fun and frolic in

A Great Big Adventure on a Good Little Boat

honor of my Mom and Dad. A big thanks to Mom and Dad. There were good times and there were bad times, but they are times I will always remember. I am a better person for them.

I've always enjoyed my visits to Charleston. Founded in 1670, Charleston is the oldest city in South Carolina and was originally called Charles Town. Situated on the west bank of the Ashley River, Charleston was planned to be a great port town. It did become that. Charles II of England, as a gift for their loyalty, granted the town to eight Lords Proprietors. Because Charleston was the capital of the Carolina Colony and a stepping off point for English expansion in the late 1600s, the colonists erected fortifications around the settlement to protect it from Spanish and French assaults. The fortifications also were protection against Indian attacks and pirate raiding parties.

Two of the original buildings that once protected this walled city still stand. In the mid-1700s, Charleston grew to become the wealthiest city in the South. In 1773, Charleston protested the Tea Act by confiscating local tea; Boston wasn't the only town to make tea protests. The city resisted British attack in the Revolutionary War and even painted the church steeples black so that they would blend in with the night sky.

During the Civil War, Charleston sided with the South. On April 12, 1861, a shore battery shelled Union-held Fort Sumter into submission; the Confederacy held the fort and the city for the next four years. After the Civil War, the lucrative rice and cotton plantations faltered as the commodity-based economy declined. A gradual growth began again in the 20th century, and with it came tourism.

Charleston began protecting her historic buildings, which created new tourist attractions. Hurricane Hugo struck in 1989 and damaged over half of the homes in the city's historic district. I have visited this beautiful city several times, and I was looking forward to doing the tourist thing: sightseeing and eating local foods. On my previous visits I enjoyed visiting the old homes and seeing the southern gardens and architecture.

First things first, though—I need to find out what is wrong with my GPS. I called my knowledgeable friend Paul, the friend who did a lot of the wiring on my boat. After our phone consultation and some testing, I found a corroded internal fuse connection. I cleaned the fuse connections and tightened loose battery terminals. That is the extent of my electrical expertise! It worked; I had power to my GPS and a live screen. Thank you, Paul.

I enjoyed strolling around the city. I didn't get to the historic district because it was quite a distance from the marina and I just had too little initiative to get myself there. As a kid, I remember our visit here and I recollect that we had a good time, but kids always have a good time.

I recall having Dad, or maybe it was my brother Carl, hoist me to the top of the *Sunbeam*'s mast in a bosun's chair so that I could scrub it. A cameraman from a local paper happened by and shot a picture. To this day my sisters and brothers complain that I will do anything to get my picture in the paper! They were just jealous!

My brother Carl remembers that we kids often went crabbing in the dingy. We found a perfect place where the crabs were plentiful and huge. We caught crab after crab after crab, and we filled the bottom of the boat with so many angry, snapping blue-claw crabs that we had to stand on the seats to paddle home. We found out later that we had caught these crabs near a sewer outlet, which accounted for their large size. We ate them anyway. I don't think that was the last time we caught crabs at that spot.

South Carolina

I'd also visited Charleston a couple of times with my then-husband. We had fun exploring the historic homes. I particularly enjoyed touring a house that had not been restored and which the Historic Society had no plans to restore. We were able to see how the inhabitants lived and understand the progress of their lives as they aged, closing off one room after another as they were no longer able to maintain the large house. Two elderly ladies were the last people to occupy this particular house and, by the time of their deaths, they were living in just one room. This unrestored home allowed us to see the original furniture, wallpaper, and everything that the inhabitants lived with in the 1800s. I appreciated the Society's attempt to preserve that amazing home.

On another visit Don and I bought a huge plaster gargoyle. It was so large and heavy that the store owner offered it to us at a bargain price. I think he wanted to enjoy watching us struggle to fit it into the small car that we were driving! It *was* a struggle, but we succeeded. Don and I always had fun together.

Maybe those memories are too recent for me to make the effort to tour the city. It is too soon since Don left. After so many years of togetherness, all the firsts that I experience by myself can be very difficult and emotional.

A Great Big Adventure on a Good Little Boat

I remember the first time I went to a restaurant for dinner alone. (Traveling doesn't count.) I'm talking about deciding to drive to a local place to sit by yourself and eat a nice dinner. I've seen single people eating out many times. Most bring a book to read. I decided that I would not do that. At first I found that it was awkward and hard not to feel sorry for myself or feel like a loser; there is no one who wants to join you for dinner. Finally, I realized that I enjoy eating alone on occasion, and it is OK to be solo and there is no stigma attached to being by yourself.

I will have to plan a visit to Charleston on my next voyage down the coast after a little more time has passed. Besides, I need to keep moving. I want to be sailing. While I am sailing I am able to keep my feelings at bay. I worked on my GPS, walked around on the dock, and visited with other boaters.

Later in the day I met George and his friend. These guys are traveling aboard a boat and visiting Charleston. He had a rental car and that night we drove to a good Taiwanese restaurant where I let them order for me. It was a pleasure to eat a delicious meal with two interesting men. I enjoy Taiwanese food—I enjoy *all* food!—but I'm not familiar enough with it to order for myself. We ate and drank and it was a fun way to spend the evening. I do love Charleston, but I think I'll be on my way in the morning.

December 2
Charleston to the Edisto River, South Carolina
ICW mile 506
32° 37.14' / 80° 23.74'

At 0700 I left Charleston and enjoyed a few easy miles until my GPS went blank again. There still are many miles left on my trip, and I have become dependent on this tool. I want it to work. Besides that, I paid a lot of money for this GPS Chart Plotter and it *should* work. At about mile 476 in the Stono River I saw what looked like a marine repair dock. I tied up and asked to use their power to charge my GPS's internal battery. I sat there and charged the battery for an hour and a half. Damn it, I hate waiting.

South Carolina

I called the factory while waiting for the charge to complete, but the technician wasn't helpful at all. He wanted me to hardwire the unit directly to my twelve-volt battery. How the heck was I supposed to do that? There was no possible way for me to accomplish what he wanted me to do. These techs are in a nice, warm, and comfy lab, and I am in the field on a boat. I called my friend Paul, and he agreed with me that there was no way that I could hardwire the GPS to the batteries with the materials at hand.

I did the only things that I knew how to do. I started at the source of power—my twelve-volt batteries—and checked them with my voltmeter. The batteries were fully charged. My solar panel is doing its job well. I checked my fuse bus bar and found power there. The next possible problem in the power line was that inline fuse connection. This is the connection that I had cleaned in Charleston. The little copper connectors looked OK, but I used a piece of fine sandpaper to clean them again. Those darn tiny fuse connectors were the culprits. The GPS screen lit up and the power icon at the top of the screen indicated that my navigation wonder was back in action! Problem solved, for the moment anyway. Now I know where to find the potential problem with this unit. The real problem is one of salt and moisture. There is not one place onboard the *Summer Wind* to escape this condition! Thank goodness I didn't opt to use a laptop for my electronic charts.

During the time that I was docked and playing with the GPS the current had increased. The current was powerful. My *Summer Wind* was broadside to the current and she was jammed against the dock. I had to use lines to pull her free. It was all I could do to free my *Summer Wind* from the strong pull of the tide.

Once I got going again, it was a lovely day. The sun was bright and I was warm. I actually took off my heavy foul-weather jacket for the first time since the beginning of this voyage. A red-letter day!

I enjoyed this quiet section of South Carolina. The straight canals and winding rivers were calming to my soul. It is very remote and my only company all day was the birds, the water, and the marshes. I was at peace with my place in nature and with the solitude in this part of the world. I felt as though I was the only human on the earth. I was alone and my only company was my little boat and the wonders of the natural world.

Peace may be creeping into my soul. Maybe I can be happy again. I anchored off the ICW in

South Carolina

the South Edisto River in a lot of current, but my anchor held well all night, and I slept well.

December 3
South Edisto River to Beaufort, South Carolina
ICW mile 536
32° 25.55' / 80° 41.22'

I was up and off the anchor by 0700. A beautiful sailboat cruiser passed me. I recognized her as a Herreshoff. No wonder she turned my head. The Herreshoff yachts are sleek and distinctive. Nathaniel Herreshoff was a famous naval architect. He revolutionized yacht design and produced a succession of undefeated America's Cup defenders between 1893 and 1920. There is a Herreshoff museum in Bristol, Rhode Island, and it's on my list of places I have to visit. Herreshoff's boats are gorgeous, and it was a real treat to see this beauty. We played tag for part of the day. I tried to raise her by radio without success. It would have been nice to talk to the skipper about his boat.

This has been an interesting journey through South Carolina. I traveled out of the South Edisto River into the Ashepoo River via a little cut, which is a waterway connecting two rivers. These cuts are straight and close, making me assume that they are man-made. Another cut delivered me into the bigger and wider Coosaw River. The seas were following and I enjoyed power sailing all day. I had to double-check my direction because the wind and the tide were with me. I must be going the wrong way! I have been so used to tide and wind in my face.

I was racing to make the Lady's Island Bridge opening on the hour. The bridge opened early and my little engine got a real workout trying to get to the bridge before it closed. The tender did wait a bit for me. A big thank you, Mr. Bridge Tender.

I pulled into the fuel dock at Beaufort. My fuel consumption has been minimal. The last time I got gas was at mile 373 and this is mile 536. I used seven gallons. That's 163 miles on seven gallons. Fantastic; that's just over 23 miles per gallon. This is an economic and satisfying way to travel.

I realize that my days have been filled with horribly cold temperatures, strong unfriendly winds, and sometimes very heavy seas, but I am thriving on every moment. I believe that with each obstacle my little boat and I overcome, we grow stronger. I will survive and prosper. What other option is there? I may just have to not stop!

There was a Christmas boat parade tonight and it passed right off my dock. How wonderful is that? I met a couple who is cruising on a big powerboat. We enjoyed cocktails and a perfect view of the parade on their upper deck. From this perch, each boat passed before us. We saw every one of the millions of lights and we heard every bit of the seasonal music many of the boats blasted through their speakers.

I think we saw more of the parade than the judges did. It was a great parade, with about 30 boats decorated every way you could imagine. There were lights, moving reindeer, Santas that Ho-Hoed, and lights that spelled out Happy Holidays. It was a fantastic display. The boaters put a lot of effort into this parade, and they had a ton of fun. What amazing imaginations they had. The Christmas spirit caught us all, even the Bah Humbug people like me.

As I lay in my cozy bunk that night, I realized that today's parade made me think of Clarence. Clarence was my 1950 Chevy pick-up truck. He was painted black and wore a shiny chrome front grill. He had a list to the left, so he had a crooked grin. Other than his beautiful new paint job, a new shiny grill and back bumper, Clarence was original. He still had his horsehair floor matting and leather seat, with "three on the column" and a starter on the floor.

I was the third owner of Clarence and I *loved* driving him. He only poked his nose out of the garage during the no-snow months in New England, but we made an exception when Clarence, Meg, and I participated in the Rye Christmas Parade. I lost Clarence in the divorce.

It's not that I don't like the holiday. I would just like to hide on that day. In the past, I could not get enough of the Christmas season. I loved the music, I loved the decorations, and I loved the special family day of Christmas.

I loved our Day of Making Cookies, when Don and Ericka and her boyfriend Derick and I would spend a whole Tuesday (our business was closed on Tuesdays) and bake cookies. We baked hundreds of cookies to give as gifts.

A Great Big Adventure on a Good Little Boat

I loved tending my Cut-Your-Own Christmas Tree Farm. I got a big thrill seeing the parents and the kids who came to cut their trees. I treasured watching the kids racing around and playing with our dogs, as their parents tried to find the perfect tree. My customers' kids were young when I began selling trees; over the years I watched them mature into adults. I cherished that. I loved walking out into our field with Don and Ericka (Angela was living on her own, but always joined us for Christmas), hunting for and finding the best and biggest tree for our home. Our ceiling in the great room was 27 feet high and our trees were close to meeting that height. I miss the struggle of pulling such a heavy and fat tree through our double-door entry, and raising and securing each massive tree. In fact, the very reason for the construction of a pair of two opening doors was the anticipation of our humongous Christmas trees.

I miss our untraditional Day of Christmas. My daughters and their cousins would write a play and assign each of us a part. We all participated in a skit, and we laughed at each other and had a blast.

We made up ideas for a "Yankee swap." There are many variations of the "Yankee Swap," but we played it like this: we had categories, like a gift that no one could identify, a gift that you didn't pay for, and other bizarre ideas. Each person brought one gift per category and it was labeled for each group. Then we'd choose numbers and the person with the lowest number chose his or her gift. The second person could choose a wrapped gift or take the first person's gift. We never just sat around and opened gifts.

I miss the cinnamon buns that Erika and I baked for our traditional Christmas-morning breakfast. I miss the fire in the fireplace. I miss waking early to put the giant turkey that I had raised into the oven. I miss the smells, and I miss sharing our special day with our pets. I had my military macaw, Bart. My Meg and our other dogs Jake and Ben were joined by Ericka's corgi Tommie, and Angela's pugs.

The first Christmas Day I spent after Don broke up our family was beyond upsetting. My daughters made an effort and invited me for Christmas Brunch, and I appreciated it and I resented it. The big gathering was that evening with everyone except me. I was so sad and upset to have no family on the day that had always been so special. It was devastating. I had a hard time breathing. I drove to the beach and watched the waves crash against the shore. I envisioned me in those waves. It felt impossible to go on with life. I didn't want my daughters to see me so weak. I just wanted to fade into nothingness.

I miss my family—the ones who I love with all my heart. There is too much that I miss. That's why I want to be alone for Christmas. I no longer have a Christmas. I don't want to be a part of someone else's holiday; I want my old Christmas or no Christmas. Maybe someday, but not yet.

Earlier, when I had gone off to find food, I spied an older woman and man sitting on the back deck of a worn houseboat. The couple looked like locals, so I stopped to ask for the name of a good restaurant nearby. We ended up talking for over an hour. Helen is 91 and newly married—two years now. She was sitting with a friend and she made it clear that he was not her husband. She has lived on her houseboat for over 30 years and has no plans to leave. Helen told me about the big town Christmas parade tomorrow and gave me the name of a local restaurant. She told me that she has an extra bunk if I get tired of traveling. I think she was serious. I enjoyed a great meal of fried oysters at the restaurant that she had recommended. What a cool lady she is.

South Carolina

When you're traveling, you are what you are right there and then.
People don't have your past to hold against you. There are no yesterdays on the road.

~William Least Heat Moon

December 4
Docked at the Downtown Dock in Beaufort, South Carolina

After an early and hearty breakfast downtown, I walked around the dock to check out the boats. I zeroed in on a small sloop. The *Muskrat* was a real beauty. She is a 23-foot sloop, with a very traditional look and a wooden mast. Her freeboard was no greater than mine, and she drew my attention. Her owner Dave told me that she is a "Stone Horse," built in Massachusetts. He is only traveling 100 miles to his winter port and he couldn't believe that I was traveling all the way to Florida in my small boat.

South Carolina

The "Stone Horse" was originally built in 1931 and is a Sam Crocker (a well-known boat designer) design. She was built in the tradition of small, working vessels that evolved up and down the New England coast during the days of sail. She *was* a beauty! There is something so special to me about gorgeous, traditional sailing boats. I am drawn to them; I love to look at them and admire them. They give me goosebumps and —sometimes—bring tears to my eyes. My little *Summer Wind* makes me feel this way. She is very special to me.

There was also one of those solo, around-the-world sailboats at the dock. She was a boat that look likes a space pod. Her owner is French and he said that it was a great cruising boat. I thought it was impressive looking—but ugly. As my brother says, "Life is too short to own an ugly boat!"

I joined my new friend Helen and her husband and, after watching the longest Christmas parade I'd ever seen, I took a tour of the town.

Beaufort is this state's second oldest city and the entire downtown district is listed on the National Register of Historic Places. Period mansions line the streets, and palmettos—the state symbol—grow everywhere.

A Great Big Adventure on a Good Little Boat

Shipbuilding, rice, and cotton kept Beaufort prosperous until the Civil War. Beaufort led the Southern efforts to break off from the Union. I walked past the Secession House, where the Ordinance for Secession was drawn up so long ago. A Union armada invaded the town in 1861, and Beaufort remained in northern hands during the war. The Union's occupation probably saved the town from destruction. I walked past many beautiful and preserved homes that were used as Union headquarters, and most were occupied as hospitals for the wounded Union solders.

The majority of the grand mansions that are preserved are in the Federal style and are well maintained, with pretty gardens and grounds. I enjoyed my stroll around this quiet and very Southern town. I felt a real sense of history here.

The Federal period was between 1780 and 1820, and these lovely buildings can be found on the eastern seaboard, from Boston to Savannah. The style features a simple box shape with a symmetrical façade. Many of the northern buildings feature clapboard siding, often painted white, with symmetrical details like black-painted doors and shutters; brick siding prevails in the South.

South Carolina

I called three marine stores before I could find fuel filters and an oil plug for my little engine. In the morning I will borrow the marina's car to get groceries and the engine parts, and then I will be off to another day of sailing.

I enjoyed Beaufort. It would be nice to return to the serene elegance of this antebellum town. I'd like to return in April to visit Helen and eat crabs at the soft-shell crab festival. I do love those softies!

December 5
Beaufort to Cooper River
ICW mile 567
32° 08.25' / 80° 53'

I left the dock around 1030 after a tummy-filling breakfast in town and a ride to purchase supplies. The Beaufort River took me into Port Royal Sound. The current and the wind were favorable again. I could get used to this! My jib and engine propelled my little boat and me into the Skull Creek. Thankfully, I saw no skulls today and none popped up out of the water.

The Calibogue Sound had a bit of an ocean swell, but I can't complain after the horrible conditions most of the sounds have handed me. It was another fine day with pleasing scenery in spite of the fact that it was overcast and rainy throughout my stint at the tiller. The dolphins were my companions for much of the day, and I enjoyed their occasional nudges. I wonder what they are trying to tell me. Maybe they were telling me to smile, to enjoy the simple act of living and being alive. So I smiled and thanked them, and appreciated the world around me.

I found a pretty and protected area to anchor in the Cooper River off the ICW. There were quiet marshes on one shore and trees on the other. There was no sound except that of birds squawking and dolphins blowing. The dolphins seemed to be feeding along the shore only 100 feet from me. They swam back and forth along the shore, leaping out of the water, making a loud ruckus, and then they'd quietly glide under water and surface at my boat. They swam around and under my boat, and then back toward shore to resume their loud feeding frenzy. The dolphins and birds provided all of the entertainment I needed for the night.

As parents, this should be the preferred pastime for our children. Children should be exposed to nature and encouraged to sit outside, to look and listen to the natural world. Even a small backyard is alive with bugs, birds, and growing things. "Big Bird" or any television show ever produced is no comparison to the wonder of nature.

There were no other cruisers today. The day had been mine alone. There were only tall fixed bridges to pass under, and it was a calm and easy day to travel.

South Carolina

December 6
Cooper River to Thunderbolt, Georgia
ICW mile 580
32° 02' / 81° 02'

Last night I had decided to go into Savannah, which is eight miles up the Savannah River. I reached the Savannah River and found the wind and the current running against me. The wind and current and the big boat traffic on the river made me rethink my plans. In the cruising guide, I read that I could continue down the ICW to the town of Thunderbolt, and from there it would be a quick bus ride into Savannah. This seemed like a much better idea than bucking the current for well over an hour. Dodging the wakes of the huge ships didn't appeal to me, either. Continuing on to Thunderbolt seemed like a good idea.

The Savannah River divides South Carolina and Georgia, so I have entered another state. It's always cool to think what I have accomplished, traveling so far down the coast of the United States.

I followed the Wilmington River and, on the way to Thunderbolt, I passed the famous Bonaventure Cemetery, which was featured in the best-selling book and later in the movie *Midnight in the Garden of Good and Evil.* My guidebook writes that it is one of the most picturesque sights on the coast. I don't know about that, but I saw that the cemetery sits up on a bluff and I could see an immense cross towering over the cemetery stones that stood shoulder to shoulder in rows almost down to the water. All of those dead people had a commanding view of the river. It was a very inspiring sight and the cross was huge.

Thunderbolt is a part of the Savannah metropolis. According to Native American lore, the town was named after a huge lightning bolt that struck during a storm and split a large boulder, revealing a fresh water spring that continued to flow into the 20th century. The small town thrived as a supply port for

South Carolina

Savannah, and the city's residents built summer homes here in the years leading up to the Civil War.

I motored along the ICW to the town of Thunderbolt and docked at a marina, only to find it closed for the day. I docked, and walked around until I met up with Petra. We got into a conversation and I asked her if she knew where I could catch the bus to Savannah. Petra said that she didn't know, but she had a friend who would know. Petra introduced me to Lucy, who lives aboard a 40-foot sailboat at the marina. Lucy took one look at my little boat and couldn't believe that I sailed from Maine, alone, in that little boat. She offered to drive me into the city and pick me up when I was ready to return to the marina. You meet the nicest people at marinas.

Savannah was just a ten-minute car ride, and Lucy dropped me at the riverfront. I had a fun time meandering along the waterfront.

My first stop was a restaurant. I devoured a delicious soft-shelled crab and drank a beer. After walking along part of the riverfront, I was sorry that I hadn't sailed down the river. There was a lot to see. River Street is paved with centuries-old cobblestones that were once ballast in the ships that sailed into port. I took a picture of the statue of the Waving Girl,

A Great Big Adventure on a Good Little Boat

honoring Florence Martus. Florence lived with her brother in the Cockspur Lighthouse. She fell in love with a sailor who asked her to marry him when he returned from his next trip. When he set sail, she waved goodbye with her handkerchief. He never returned, and for 45 years she waved her handkerchief to every ship that passed the lighthouse.

Savannah was first settled by a group of Englishmen led by General James Oglethorpe, who was given a land grant by King George II. Oglethorpe named the large landmass Georgia, in honor of the king, and Savannah as its capital. The city is laid out in grids, with homes and shops and churches built around squares. Each square is decorated with a park, featuring lovely fountains and benches shaded by oak trees draped with moss.

This is a very historic city. In 1864, Major Sherman presented the newly captured city to President Abraham Lincoln as a Christmas gift. The city may have been spared because the residents were so gracious to Sherman and his troops, and because of the fact that the Confederate forces had already withdrawn from the city before Sherman's arrival.

I walked through the squares, enjoying the lovely parks. I saw many beautifully restored homes decked out for Christmas. It was a warm and lovely day to be a tourist in a pretty southern city.

I intended to catch a bus back to the marina. There was a problem: I couldn't remember the name of the marina or the name of the town that the marina was in! I just drew a blank! I asked the bus driver if this bus went to The Marina. She looked at me and asked, "What marina, honey?" I meekly said that it was a marina by a big bridge. She was very kind and told me to climb aboard and we would find the marina, honey. I'm sure that she thought that I had a few screws loose, but she was a considerate soul. Thank goodness for southern hospitality!

After quite a ride, we found the marina. I was the only one on the bus at this point. I think it's pretty funny that I can navigate my little boat from Maine to Georgia and then I have trouble finding my way out of the city of Savannah!

I visited with Lucy to thank her for the ride into the city. I didn't tell her about my embarrassing return trip. Petra invited me aboard for cocktails, and I had an interesting evening with Petra and her husband. They are here for a respite from traveling and to make repairs to their sailboat.

A Great Big Adventure on a Good Little Boat

I love Savannah. Savannah was another first on my long lists of firsts since the death of my marriage, and it was almost painful to revisit this lovely city. Don and I drove to Savannah quite a few years ago to attend his brother Bob's wedding. Don and Bob's parents and our grown daughters were there with their boyfriends. Bob's grown daughters joined us, as did the children of Bob's wife-to-be. We were a large and happy group. We toured the city in horse-drawn carriages, toured the historic homes, and had a tremendous time in Savannah.

Visiting here alone is bittersweet. I love the city, but touring here as a single person is painful. Being by yourself is great when that's what you should be doing, but it's not too much fun when someone should be by your side in a city where there are lots of people walking together. There were couples and groups of people everywhere in Savannah. They made me feel lonely.

I admire the elegant beauty of Savannah, but I am ready to find a quiet place to anchor and enjoy the birds and the dolphins and being alone.

Docking at marinas and meeting fascinating people is stimulating, and I enjoy the break from traveling alone. I always miss the solitude of the isolated anchorages when I'm at a marina, and I never miss the marina when I am sitting at a quiet and isolated anchorage. When I get to a beautiful anchorage and I am secure after a day of travel, I am very happy to be alone. I am happy to be alone to enjoy a beautiful sunset or see the moon rise. My secluded world and I become one and I don't want to share it with anyone, well, maybe my dog. When I am at anchor it is just my little boat and me, here at this moment, and I am happy.

I will leave Savannah in the morning to find that little anchorage.

Live the moment, because life is filled with the unexpected.

~Anonymous

That night, lying in my comfy cabin, I thought of one of my best companions: Meg. My Meg was special. Ever since I was a kid, I've wanted a Blue Merle Australian Shepard. Her name would be Meg. In 2000, my thoughtful daughter Ericka located a breeder and we drove to meet the long-awaited dog of my dreams. She was there! I had finally found my Meg.

From that day on, Meg became my constant companion, and we were very seldom apart. Meg needed me and became depressed the few times I did leave her. She would actually become sick!

Meg was not the easiest dog to live with, either. Angela and I used to go to yard sales every Saturday. Of course, we'd have to take Meg. The second we left the car with Meg inside, Meg would bark. Angela and I pretended that Meg wasn't ours. "Who would bring a dog and let her bark like that?"

One Saturday I placed an anti-barking collar on Meg. We left her in the car as usual and headed to hunt out the day's bargains. As we got to the outside tables laden with treasures, we heard Meg barking. I thought, so much for an anti-barking collar! I must have left the window down more than usual because before I knew what was happening, Meg ran into me and I fell onto a display table. I knocked over the table and everything on it. Meg continued racing around, barking, and running into everyone and everything in sight. She was crazy! People were yelling and stuff was flying. I finally caught her. She kept barking and her anti-barking collar shot off a spray of citronella with every bark. The collar was making Meg bark! She was panicked. I threw off the collar and Meg was instantly fine and happy to be saved.

South Carolina

Angela and I tried to make amends to everyone before we sheepishly left the premises. We never returned to a yard sale in *that* neighborhood again.

My Meg died on Monhegan Island in 2009. She loved the island and on her last day we made our traditional evening walk to Lobster Cove, where she had always made the ducks fly. Not tonight. She slowly lumbered back to the cottage and together we sat on the front deck to watch the sun set.

That evening I sat with Meg on the floor and we enjoyed the quiet of the island. Meg's breathing became labored during the night. I hugged her and told her that it was OK. She could go. Her work here was done. I would be OK. I didn't mean it. I still needed her. I loved her. I didn't want to be without her. She was in pain. I hated that. I wanted her pain to end. I had to let her go. I had to let her go. Please let her go. She was so special. I need her. No, let her go.

She died with my love surrounding her. I cried until there was nothing left. To this day I miss my Meg and thank her for being my best friend.

A Great Big Adventure on a Good Little Boat

It's not what you take away from life that will ultimately define your existence, it's what you have brought to the party of life that makes you special to yourself and others.

~Anonymous

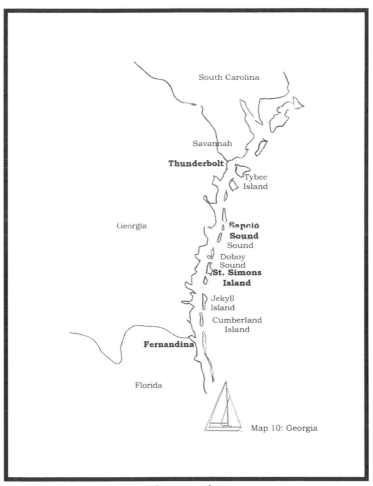

South Carolina

Savannah

Thunderbolt

Tybee
Island

Georgia

**Sapelo
Sound**
Sound

Doboy
Sound
**St. Simons
Island**

Jekyll
Island

Cumberland
Island

Fernandina

Florida

Map 10: Georgia

Georgia

December 7
Thunderbolt to an anchorage off the Isle of Hope Marina, Georgia
ICW mile 590
31° 58.80' / 81° 03.20'

I spent another day of dealing with the cold. The wind, the waves, and the current in my face made today's trip miserable. I only traveled ten miles. This was my shortest travel day yet. The wind was predicted to increase, so I decided to stop at the anchorage off the Isle of Hope Marina. I just couldn't bring myself to face the wide and windy area of the merging Vernon and the Little Ogeechee rivers. I must be getting soft!

I came across a fairly protected anchorage and the boats there looked snug and happy, so I stopped. I anchored upwind of a small sailboat, sans mast. In place of her mast was a stout flagpole and from this pole flew a huge Confederate flag. I know that I have arrived in the South!

There was another sailboat that caught my eye. She was dragging her anchor dead smack in the middle of the channel. One of the sailors at the anchorage said that he had reported her to the marina and he was told that the poor boat drifts back and forth with the current and they have no idea who owns her. I watched her drifting dance all day. It's a wonder that she hasn't caused a collision.

Sure enough, as predicted, the wind increased and I spent another sleepless night of listening to the wind and the rain and the shuddering of my little boat. It had started to rain early and it was just too wet to heat anything for dinner. I went to bed and tried to be warm and ignore the wind.

You know, many nights during this trip I've been too cold and the wind has been too gusty to be able to light my stove, and I haven't been able to make myself food. Yet, I never felt hungry at bedtime. I *do* like to eat. During my great adventure, I never felt hungry. I have lost weight, but I never feel the lack of energy or feel fatigued. In fact, I've never felt healthier or more fit. Amazing, considering that I've been eating canned and packaged food and very few fresh and natural foods. Maybe attitude, contentment, and peace of mind can outweigh the quality of the food we eat, for a while anyway.

Georgia

December 8
Isle of Hope to the Wahoo River, Georgia
ICW mile 628
31° 36.06' / 81° 13.06'

Look at my coordinates: I am heading south and west. I *will* get to Florida and it *will* be warm! Today was a nice day, with no more rain, and the wind had quieted a bit. I got a late start so that I could catch the opening of the bridge just a half an hour away. I made it on time for its scheduled opening. I radioed the tender and his opening was in perfect time with my speed. I didn't even have to slow down. How nice. Some of these tenders are very skilled at their trade.

This bridge could have been difficult to wait for, since the current and the wind were behind me and it was in a restricted area. I hate that scenario. The thought of running into a bridge is not an amusing one. This is the last bridge that has to raise for me in the state of Georgia. Hooray! There will be plenty of bridges that have to open for me in Florida, but this is the last one in Georgia and I'm thankful—for the moment. I'll worry about the bridges in Florida when I get there.

It was an enjoyable day of jib sailing through the pretty and calm marshes. A large sailboat passed me and I thought how nice would it be to just follow her and not have to navigate for a short while. I'm glad that it was just a thought because I saw her head on the wrong side of a day marker. I looked on the chart; she was lucky not to have run aground. I'll forget the idea of letting someone else do my navigating.

At one point, there were lots of helicopters flying overhead. I counted, and there were 15 of them. It seemed as though they were watching me! Yesterday there was a police boat that followed me for about five or six miles. Maybe I look suspicious. Do they think that I am running drugs on a slow boat to Florida?

Today was a good day. The winds were out of the northeast, a bit strong, and I was glad not

Georgia

to be bucking them. It is still cold—in the 40s. My hands were cold and my ears were painful all day. At least it's not raining! I anchored in the Wahoo River, just north of Sapelo Sound.

December 9
Wahoo River to Wally's Leg, Georgia
ICW mile 667
31° 15.54' / 81° 24.25'

I think that I am not very happy to be close to Florida and the end of my trip. I still have a long way ahead of me, but I feel my destination getting too close. I feel almost threatened by the ending of my voyage. I am afraid to be caught up in the ties of responsibility and the reality of earning a living. I am so happy traveling that I don't want my trip to end, and I'm starting to drag my feet. I used to raise my anchor and be on my way by 0530 or so; today, I didn't leave until 0800.

Georgia

I crossed three large and open sounds today: the Sapelo, the Doboy, and the Altamaha. These would have beat me up if the wind had been on my nose, but the wind was out of the northeast and not too strong. I enjoyed using my turbo jib to increase the speed of my little engine. I like flying my jib. It helps fill my need to sail and it just feels good to see that pretty white sail propelling me toward the Sunshine State.

Seven cruisers passed me today. Most of them were sailboats and I am always amazed that very seldom do I see a sail on these boats. They have a crew, and it would be easy for them to raise a sail. My mainsail is a pain to raise alone, so I use my jib and I use it at every opportunity. Oh, well. I guess cruising *does* make some people lazy. Maybe my boat is too small for me to get lazy.

There was a local fishing boat working in the waterway and I hailed to him, hoping to buy some crabs. I had a hankering to eat some crabs. He said that he was clamming, not crabbing. Too bad! We both slowed and cruised side-by-side for quite a while, talking. He was very impressed with my adventurous voyage and told me that if I needed anything in this area, all I had to do was to ask anyone to find him and he would be at my service. The name of his boat was *The Provider*. He was sincere and we had a nice chat. What a fun way to meet fascinating people!

All in all, it wasn't a bad traveling day. It was cold, but navigating was easy. There were several ranges and it was good to practice my navigation skills on them.

While at anchor, I was joined by two other cruisers. We had found a quiet and protected place to spend the night off the ICW and west of St. Simons Island. Most of the time, at anchor, we cruising boats respect each other's privacy and don't go visiting. We wave as we pass and try not to anchor too close.

After a hot mug of soup and a warm mug of rum, I realized that both my chart book and my cruising guide ended at the Florida border. I'll have to find a marina and some charts and a Florida cruising guidebook. These guidebooks make cruising so much easier, and I have come to depend upon them.

Georgia

December 10
Wally's Leg to the Morning Star Marina, Georgia
ICW mile 685
31° 10' / 81° 25'

All through the night there was a light drizzle and the morning was overcast. It rained intermittently all day, and with no cover I was wet and cold the entire time I was underway.

After leaving my anchorage, I motored down the meandering Mackay River into the open St. Simons Sound. The ICW exposed me to the winds and waves of the ocean, and the *Summer Wind* and I began our rock-and-roll dance.

I had planned to continue into the Jekyll Creek and dock at Jekyll Island but, according to my trusty guidebook, the marina on St.

A Great Big Adventure on a Good Little Boat

Simons Island has a courtesy car and a marine store close by. Although going into this marina meant backtracking, it would be worth it so that I could get the Florida cruising guidebook and some Florida charts. Besides describing the marinas and their services, the book lists all the bridges, their restrictions, and times of openings. There is also a lot of navigation information about many of the cities and towns a cruiser may want to visit, including a listing of restaurants and other services. It is an invaluable tool. I wouldn't leave home without it!

I traveled into port and picked up my charts; tomorrow I plan to go on to the Jekyll Harbor Marina and enjoy a tour of the island. It is only a one-hour sail, and it will feel decadent to be able to make a late start and have a leisurely sail.

I can't control the wind, but I can adjust the sail.

~Ricky Skaggs

Georgia

December 11
Docked at the Morning Star Marina, Georgia

All night the wind howled and my boat shook. Thank goodness I am at a dock. This terrible weather continued all day, with the wind gusting to 45 miles per hour and a wind chill of 42°. Another fun day in paradise. I was miserable and there was no way I was going to travel through the open and exposed St. Simons Sound to the Jekyll Harbor marina in this weather.

With no traveling to do, I hitched a ride to St. Simons Island and, in spite of the cold (I was wearing shorts), I enjoyed walking through the village. I ate a delicious crabcake breakfast and bought a pair of long pants because I was freezing. Even though it was so very cold, there were lots of people out and there was a small street fair going on with tent-covered booths. The wind kept the poor exhibitors busy just trying to keep their tents and umbrellas from blowing away. I think today is Sunday.

I enjoyed wandering around, touring the lighthouse, and walking along the waterfront until I worked up enough of an appetite to eat the best fried shrimp that I ever remember tasting. I walked the five miles back to the marina and almost got blown off the bridge. It's a good thing that I ate all those shrimp!

Georgia

December 12
Still at the Morning Star Marina

Late yesterday afternoon a cruiser came into the marina. He said it was dangerous in the sound. He and his boat had been beaten up. He was exhausted and glad to be tied up to a dock. We decided that a good meal would make the day better, so we made our way to the restaurant and sat down to a tasty dinner together, with rum drinks aboard his sailboat afterward. Eating with someone is a welcome change to my usual solo dining. I don't mind sitting alone, but a lively conversation with a human can be a good thing.

Today the temperature with the wind chill was 39°. The wind howled all night and all day.

A Great Big Adventure on a Good Little Boat

How long can this continue? I am so soggy and cold and bored silly. I borrowed the marina's courtesy car and drove to the grocery store just for something to do. I bought a whole roasted chicken and a bottle of wine and by mid-afternoon I was halfway through both. Reading, eating, and drinking is what I do when I can't sail! I have read one book and have almost through another.

While inspecting the boats along the docks, I met Gary and he invited me aboard his powerboat. He, his wife, and I sipped hot coffee and had a friendly and warm visit. Their boat was dry and toasty. What a luxury.

The wind is diminishing and the rain has finally stopped. It's time to get out of here and continue my journey. I had planned to visit Jekyll Island, but since I lost so much time to this latest bad weather, I'll forgo my visit and get further down the coast. I've just got to get out of this cold and threatening weather.

Georgia

December 13
Morning Star Marina to the Brickhill River, Georgia
ICW mile 697
30° 54' / 81° 27'

I left the frosty dock at 0730. I shut down my outboard, raised my main and jib, and sailed through the St. Simons Sound into the Jekyll Creek. Then I continued south into the large and open St. Andrew Sound. Oh, how wonderful! The outboard was silent and it was a gorgeous and calm day. Any winds less than gale force are such a joy! It felt so good to sail and be in such a beautiful area.

St. Simons Sound wasn't too choppy, but the St. Andrew Sound made me work; it was a real rock-and-roll time! There were ten-foot swells coming in from the ocean—some of them breaking. I didn't get wet because of the wind direction and that made all the difference in the world. It was cold with no sun, but the wind was behind me, and since I wasn't getting soaked it was not too uncomfortable.

I left the ICW to amble through the scenic and twisty Brickhill River. I wanted to see the wild horses of Cumberland Island, so I anchored early. I did see the horses! There were about six of them grazing on the marsh grass not far from me. They were bigger than I had expected. It was a real treat for me to see these beautiful creatures. As a kid, I always loved horses.

My first horse was an island pony. I named him Cody and I bought him with my own, hard-earned money. (My sister Debbie and I baked donuts and key lime pies and peddled our goods to yachtsmen arriving on the island.) My family was living on an island in the Bahamas at the time. We transported my blue-eyed albino pony to the island aboard our LCM-6, a World War II acronym for "Landing Craft Mechanized," also known as a "Mike Boat," which was designed for landing troops and tanks during Allied amphibious assaults. We used our LCM-6 to transport building materials for the houses Dad and the family built in the islands.

Georgia

Cody turned out to be an unbroken wild animal! He and I learned a lot during our time together. I rode Cody without a bridle and saddle. His bony back made it nearly impossible to keep my seat. I rode him at full speed up and down the beautiful one-mile long crescent beach until he was tired, then he'd make a sudden 90° turn and leave me spitting sand. Ours was definitely a love-hate relationship! In spite of that, I missed him when we had to travel on. I can't remember what happened to Cody, but I don't think we found him a retirement home for wayward horses in Nassau.

Cumberland Island is seventeen-and-a-half miles long and one of Georgia's barrier islands. Over half of the island is marshland, mud flats, and tidal creeks. Besides the island's band of feral horses, it is known for sea turtles, wild turkeys, armadillos, and a multitude of shore birds, salt marshes, and historic structures. The wild horses are believed to be descendants of horses brought to the island by early English settlers. I prefer the popular myth that the horses arrived in the 1500s with the Spanish conquistadors. Either way, I want to visit the island on my next voyage through here!

I was able to dry out most of my gear before nightfall. I have an oil drain plug being delivered to the marina at Fernandina, Florida, and I called to see if it had arrived yet. It still isn't there. They should have received it today.

Now, because my part hasn't been delivered yet, I'm in no particular hurry to continue on to Fernandina. I hate having to remove the oil plug over the water. I was successful at changing the oil once, but it still worries me not to have a spare plug. Without the plug, my engine is inoperable, and if the wind was unfavorable, I would be stuck until I could sail into a port. Maybe that would be a good thing. I hope that during my next adventure I don't have the compulsion to make progress every day! I mean, so I might have to wait for favorable winds if I couldn't use my engine. It happened before and I simply sailed into port.

I changed my oil tonight even though I did not have a replacement plug. I felt lucky. There was no way that I was going to run another outboard out of oil. I change my new engine's oil every 60 hours instead of the recommended 100 hours. I figure that I am running this little engine hard, sometimes for 10 or 12 hours each day. Hard work for a new engine. I baby it because I need it and it cost me a bundle!

My days' runs seem to be getting shorter and shorter. I do believe that I am dragging my feet! I realize now that I actually have many options awaiting me in Florida. I think I might buy a fixer-up house, live in it, work on it, and then sell it. Then maybe buy another or buy a larger boat and continue to sail. I could work on boats. I am a fantastic varnisher and an excellent woodworker. We'll see. I have options! I won't go hungry!

Tomorrow I will be in Florida and I have mixed feelings about approaching the end of my voyage. My brothers and sisters and their families pull me to Florida and I would love to be there, but I am getting so much satisfaction out of this trip in spite of the hardships my little boat and I have endured that I am dreading to have it end. Maybe my stop in Florida should be just an extended visit.

I wish I could be content to hole up here for a while. Maybe a week or so, just to relax, watch the birds, and reflect. My head isn't there yet. I am still too driven and I'm starting to get tired of it. In the past I've felt a bit crazy with my need to produce till I drop. This adventure is teaching me to slow down and appreciate the sedate pleasure of sitting and listening in a quiet place.

There is no schedule here. There is no place to be except right here. I can let my boat drift and I can let my mind drift. I can enjoy where I am and who I am for the first time in my life. I realize that I am happy. I am OK with my body. I am OK with my brain. I am OK with who I am. I need to be OK here and now. And I am. What a pleasure after so many years of raising a family, working, and being a vibrant part of society.

Those were very special times for me and they were necessary. Back in those busy days, there was never time to drift. For many years I felt that my life was spent reacting and not acting. There always seemed to be too much to do. Looking back, I know that most of those pressures were self-induced because I was so driven. I needed to do everything and I needed to do everything perfectly.

Priorities change with age and loss. That was then and this is now. I'm standing at the tiller and I am the captain of my boat. I have no need to be more than this. I'm afraid to lose this newfound contentment at the end of the voyage. I'll see.

The sea drives truth into a man like salt.

~David H. Lewis

Georgia

December 14
The Brickhill River to Fernandina Harbor Marina, Florida
ICW mile 717
30° 40' / 81° 28'

I left my calm anchoring spot and appreciated a slow trip through the Brickhill River with my jib up and no engine and rejoined the ICW. I decided to travel on this side trip off the ICW hoping to spot a few more horses and take advantage of the less-traveled route. I didn't see any horses but I saw birds—lots of birds. This area is so untouched and isolated. I loved the solitude of my detour. This is what life should be: quiet, real, with nature all around, and being satisfied with where you are and who you are.

A Great Big Adventure on a Good Little Boat

I reentered the ICW at mile 705 and that's when navigating became difficult. I found the buoys confusing to read, with two rivers merging into the Cumberland Sound, and there was a Safety Security Zone at the Navy Station. There were ranges, security boats, and warning signs: Do Not Enter Here, Restricted Area, Keep Out. I found it very complicated and intimidating. I had to pay attention and was thankful to have my chart plotter available to help me decipher my course through the maze of buoys, signs, and security boats.

Once past the challenging security area, I sailed into the St. Mary's Entrance, another inlet out to the sea and the open section of the Cumberland Sound. Even though it wasn't too rough, it was rocky and rolly because of a big ocean swell, but I didn't get wet so I had no complaints.

I lowered my sail in the Cumberland Sound just off Fort Clinch on the northern-most tip of Amelia Island. Yes, I have made it to Florida! Quite an accomplishment for a little boat and an old lady! Horrible weather has plagued me, but my little boat and I have worked and traveled well together. I am proud of the *Summer Wind* and I am proud of me!

Georgia

Fort Clinch is a nineteenth-century brick fort, built between 1847 and 1869 in a pentagonal shape. It was named for General Duncan Clinch, who was an important figure in the Seminole Wars. At the beginning of the Civil War, the fort was seized by Confederate blockade runners, then captured by Federal troops in 1862. This gave the Union control of the Georgia and Florida coasts and served as a base of Union operations.

Restoration of the fort began in the 1930s. In 1935, the state of Florida bought the fort and surrounding land. Today it is on the National Register of Historic Places. I thought the fort was unique and I circled, trying to get a picture of it, but I couldn't get close enough to take a good picture with my unsophisticated camera.

As soon as I entered the Amelia River I started to smell the petroleum. It was so stinky that I figured I would pick up my engine part at the marina and continue down the river and away from the unpleasant odor. I tied up at the fuel dock and found out that my part still hadn't arrived.

It was too early for the day's delivery, so I asked if I could just hang out at the fuel dock for an hour or so until the UPS truck arrived. Oh yes, I could stay, but the dockage per hour was exorbitant! I needed the engine part, so I decided

A Great Big Adventure on a Good Little Boat

to just pay for a night's dockage and take in the nearby sights while waiting for the delivery. Hopefully, my engine part will arrive later today or tomorrow.

Fernandina is an easy town to walk around, and I enjoyed stretching my legs and seeing the sights. Fernandina sits on the Amelia River and is the first Florida town south of Georgia. Years ago, the area served as a convenient port for slave ships, whose cargo then was transported overland a few miles north to Georgia. I bought some postcards to send as Christmas cards (I do not send cards at Christmas, but this is different) and I bought a book written by a local author. Of course, I found a restaurant close to the water and ate a delicious seafood dinner. After all, one has to keep up one's energy!

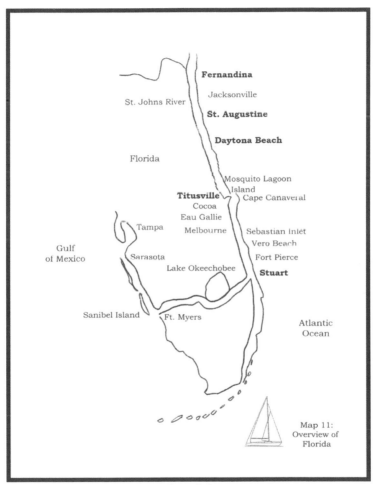

Fernandina
Jacksonville
St. Johns River
St. Augustine

Daytona Beach

Florida

Mosquito Lagoon
Island
Titusville
Cape Canaveral
Cocoa
Eau Gallie
Tampa
Melbourne
Sebastian Inlet
Gulf
Vero Beach
of Mexico
Sarasota
Fort Pierce
Lake Okeechobee
Stuart

Sanibel Island
Ft. Myers

Atlantic
Ocean

Map 11:
Overview of
Florida

Florida

A Great Big Adventure on a Good Little Boat

December 15
Fernandina to Sisters Bridge, Florida
ICW mile 739
30° 23.64' / 81° 27.59'

Wow, my engine part still hasn't arrived. I called UPS twice and finally talked to a woman who cared. She located my package and said that it would be delivered by noon. My dock space offered virtually no privacy, so I sailed out of that place minutes after picking up the part.

I had a nice visit in Fernandina, the people were friendly and helpful, but the place did smell and it was very noisy. All night a nearby plant—I think it was a cement plant—made loud noises and trains rumbled by. Did they have to blow their whistles every time they passed by my dock slip? I miss my quiet little anchorages.

I traveled south on the marsh-surrounded, twisty Amelia River into Nassau Sound. I was pleased to find calm waters where the Nassau and the Amelia rivers meet. Actually, I wrote on my chart "Like a Lake." I left the sound and entered the skinny Sawpit Creek, where I saw two fishermen in a small boat. They had their big outboard tilted up and they were using a tiny trawling motor. They waved me down and asked if I could tow them to a boat ramp just 300 yards upstream. I started towing them and continued further and further. That ramp was more like a mile upstream and my little outboard had to work hard to make headway. It was funny: these guys had nothing except two fishing poles. They were just two old farts fishing and having fun. I hope they never venture far from home.

It was beautiful, warm, and sunny, and I was able to take off my heavy foul-weather jacket early. This is the very first day I haven't had to wear it since the beginning of October. I love the sun!

There were huge flocks of white pelicans in several areas along the Sister Creek. They were so big and so white and there were so many of them flocked on some of the islands that it looked like the land was covered with snow.

Only two cruisers passed me today and my day was peaceful and easy. I anchored for the night just north of the Sisters Creek Bridge and three sailboats joined me to wait until the first bridge opening in the morning. We will pass under the bridge together. I hope to make St. Augustine tomorrow.

Florida

December 16
Sisters Bridge to St. Augustine, Florida
ICW mile 777
29° 53' / 81° 18'

The three sailboats and I passed under the Sisters Creek Bridge at 0700. They soon left me in their wakes, and I was alone again. My sail to St. Augustine was nice and uneventful. It was a lazy and comfortable day.

This part of the ICW runs through marshes and swamps, and I enjoyed a day of nothing but high bridges between the Sisters Bridge and the Bridge of Lions at St. Augustine.

I joined six or seven other boats waiting for the Bridge of Lions' scheduled opening. I remember this beautiful bridge from our visit aboard the *Sunbeam* so many years ago. The

A Great Big Adventure on a Good Little Boat

bridge is guarded by large marble lions and was completed in 1927. I tied up at the Municipal Marina and met Dick, Janet, and Richard, who were sailing on Richard's 39-foot sailboat all the way from Texas to Annapolis. Now, that's a long trip!

I was excited to find out that my friends aboard the *Way Happy* are here. They are the couple that I had met while waiting for the weather to break in Cape May Harbor. Steve, my solo sailor and dinner-making buddy along the ICW, is here also. It seemed like old home week. We had a great time catching up and telling tales of the adventures we've each had en route to this remarkable city.

After cleaning my little boat and myself, and rejecting an offer to shower with a male sailor, I walked into town.

I had been looking forward to visiting the oldest city in Florida. I remembered the lions and the fort and the wax museum from my visit aboard the *Sunbeam*. Funny what kids remember! I don't recall staying in St. Augustine for a long period of time, but I do remember the special charm of the area. The bridge holds unique memories for me also. As we approached the bridge sailing aboard the *Sunbeam*, the bridge stopped working. The *Sunbeam* was forced to come about in the confining approach to the bridge. We ran aground and had a difficult time getting ourselves free. Dad was more than upset about having his boat caught on the bottom. The bridge worked sporadically during our entire visit.

I found a great tapas restaurant on the second floor of a building and filled my tummy with fantastic ceviche and a beer at a table on the balcony. After this delicious snack, I went off to tour the city.

This city's history began in 1565, when Pedro Menendez and 700 soldiers and colonists landed here. St. Augustine is the oldest continually occupied European settlement in North America. The Englishman Sir Francis Drake burned the village and the wooden fort to the ground in 1586. John Davis, a pirate, burned St. Augustine again in 1668. In 1672, the Spanish Queen Maria Theresa ordered the construction of a stone fort. I guess the Spanish got tired of having their forts burned! The Castillo de San Marcos took 23 years to complete. This fortress has 12-foot-thick walls, a moat, a deep freshwater well, and a latrine flushed by the tide.

When the English attacked St. Augustine in 1702, the fort was besieged for 50 days. The citizens fled into the fort and refused to surrender. The British gave up the attack, but burned the village before leaving. Because of this burning, there are no buildings older than 1702 in St. Augustine today.

Standing at the high walls of the fort, I could see the boat anchorage and the Bridge of Lions. It was a pretty view.

Castillo de San Marcos has quite a history. The fort is the oldest masonry fort in the continental United States. In 1763, after the British gained control of Florida, St. Augustine became the capital of East Florida, and the fort was renamed Fort St. Mark until the Spanish regained control. In 1821, the fort became a United States Army base and was named Fort Marion after the Revolutionary War hero, Francis Marion. It wasn't until 1942, with an Act of Congress, that the fort's original name was restored.

I explored the fort and the City Gate, a gateway that used to be the only access to the city on the north side. My tour brought me to the Plaza and the Old Market. The Plaza was beautiful, with over a million white lights strung in the many trees. It was a magical place decorated for the Christmas season. People were strolling through the trees, taking pictures of each other and their kids with the beautiful holiday decorations as a backdrop.

As I was looking for a place to get a bite to eat, I bumped into Janet and her friend Dick. We sat on an outside patio, sharing cruising stories over a delicious meal, watching the horse-drawn carriages trot by. Janet and Dick are crewing for Richard and are waiting for engine parts for Richard's sailboat. They told me that they are impressed that I am solo sailing on such a small boat. I joked that my boat is too small to have a crew, so I *must* travel alone! I happened to mention that I was thinking of renting a car to drive to Sarasota for my brother and sister-in-law's big annual Christmas party. I invited Janet, and she and I made plans for our road trip tomorrow.

Before mentioning the Sarasota road trip to Janet, I was undecided about making the drive. I had no clothes to wear, I hated to leave my boat, and it would be an expense to rent a car and pay for dockage. Now I was committed. My brother Carl and his wife Bonnie have invited me to this annual gala for years, and I plan to surprise them with my presence. Unfortunately, I had to call brother Willy to retrieve my boat keys from him, but I asked him to keep my arrival a secret, which he did.

A Great Big Adventure on a Good Little Boat

December 17
St. Augustine to Sarasota via car

Janet and I met early and started our hunt for party clothes. We were both quick shoppers and in record time we had our fancy outfits in hand (fancy for boat people), we'd picked up the rental car, and we were headed to Sarasota.

Compared to sailing, our drive to Sarasota was simple, and Janet and I got to know each other. Remember, she and I had just met. She lives in Texas and is an avid sailor. I'd say that she is an attractive and an adventurous woman and I like her. She was a good companion.

I found out later that the night before we left, Janet was a little nervous about the impending trip. She voiced concerns to her crewmates about my family and me. "What if they are all ax murders?" Funny, she overcame her fears and rode with me to Sarasota. Sometimes you have to just jump in with two feet and experience life.

We stopped at brother Willy's house for wine and relaxation before the big party.

Bonnie and Carl's party was a huge success, and I was sorry that I had missed so many of their grand affairs. The food was delicious, the booze was plentiful, and the guests were stimulating and amusing.

My arrival was a surprise to my family. They all smiled and greeted me with open arms and made my new friend feel right at home. (There was not one ax in sight!) We were invited to stay one more day to partake of a dinner party the next night at Bambi and Steve's home. Bambi and Steve are long-time friends of my siblings, and Janet and I didn't need much arm-twisting!

I showed Janet around the Sarasota area and we enjoyed being tourists for the day. We walked around Marina Jacks and then we sat at the O'Leary's Tiki Bar on the water and sipped ice-cold beers. We relaxed and soaked in the warm Florida sunshine. I'm glad we stayed because that evening's gathering included just family and very close friends. I was able to spend more time visiting with these special people.

A Great Big Adventure on a Good Little Boat

Janet and I left with full tummies and happy hearts. We arrived back to St. Augustine and the marina around midnight. It was an enjoyable trip for both of us. I found Janet's company a nice change from my solitude. I liked talking with a person. I love talking to the birds and dolphins, but they never respond to my chatter.

Florida

December 19
St. Augustine

The next day, after I returned the rental car, Janet, Dick, and I met at the famous Flagler Museum. Flagler was a railroad pioneer, a land developer, and, with John D. Rockefeller, the founder of Standard Oil. Flagler built the Hotel Ponce de Leon, a huge and beautiful hotel for his rich friends. This gorgeous building is now a National Historic Landmark and is a near-perfect example of Spanish Renaissance architecture. The interior designer was Louis Comfort Tiffany, and his stained glass windows and murals are stunning. The Rotunda has a 68-foot dome, hand-carved columns, and an intricate mosaic tiled floor. The dining area seats

A Great Big Adventure on a Good Little Boat

800 and is ringed with Tiffany's stained glass windows. The parlor room's paintings and murals are spectacular. I could have stayed there all day. It was a real treat to see this beautifully maintained landmark.

I returned back to my boat and reviewed my charts, settled my dockage fees, and said my goodbyes to my friends here. I'll miss them, but we promised to keep in touch. I decided to walk through the city one more time before I leave in the morning. I did return to the Spanish restaurant to relish another dish of ceviche and wine. I met a cute young waitress who is learning to sail. She was so enthusiastic and I had a great time talking with her.

After dinner I strolled through the central plaza and reveled in the beauty of the Christmas lights. It's funny though, the beautifully decorated plaza didn't make me sad and long for the "good old days." I'm keeping those feelings at bay and the plaza is just another gorgeous sight on my voyage. One to enjoy and to recall.

I had a memorable time in this city. I've revisited some friends and I've made new friends. That's what ports are all about. Now I'm looking forward to traveling again.

Florida

December 20
St. Augustine to Daytona Beach
ICW mile 830
29° 14' / 81° 01'

I left the dock at 0730 and knew I was headed in the right direction because the wind and the tide were on the nose! The wind was strong, with twenty-five- to thirty-five-mile-per-hour gusts, making for a wet, rough, and cold day. There were whitecaps in even the narrow sections of the ICW. Another slog day. At least it's not raining! Today was a busy bridge day; fortunately, half of the eight bridges were high, fixed bridges that didn't have to open for me. I do love those fixed bridges. The terrain along the ICW was diverse and interesting, and I passed through winding rivers, a couple of small meandering creeks, and straight cuts that sliced through the sodden land of coastal Florida.

I got a Christmas e-mail from Ursula, my Annapolis friend. She wrote: "Good ships, and wood ships, the ships that sail the sea. But the best ships are friendships, and may they always be."

I anchored just north of the twin Seabreeze Bridges. It was an uncomfortable day, and I was happy to be at anchor enjoying some tummy-warming rum.

Florida

December 21
Daytona Beach to Indian River
ICW mile 876
28° 39' / 80 74'

After a calm and restful sleep, I raised my anchor at 0700 and motored on a pretty morning in the Halifax River. The marshes around me were alive with birds. The numbers and variety of birds were amazing. I saw lots of ospreys, as well as pelicans, both the brown and the white variety. The white pelicans stay in huge flocks and turn the marshy islands white. It reminds me of snow! There are always lots of herring gulls and I saw royal terns and many anhinga. Someone once said to me that they thought God must have been sleeping when he made the cormorant and the anhinga, because these water birds' feathers aren't water resistant and the birds must sit on land and dry their feathers before re-entering the water to feed. There were egrets and ibis and vultures and all kinds of ducks. I saw a huge flock of small black birds sitting on the water; there were so many of these birds that I thought it was an island until they flew away en masse. I don't know what they were, but there were a lot of them!

The dolphins have been my companions for weeks. I haven't seen any manatees; maybe the water is still too cold for them.

The jaw-dropping beauty of the marshes and mangroves in the Halifax River opened up into the Mosquito Lagoon, where I was exposed to stronger southwest winds with a chop and spray in my face again. At least it was too windy for mosquitoes! I came out of the wide Mosquito Lagoon and turned into the very indistinct, rock-surrounded, unmarked entrance of the Haulover Canal. I almost passed it!

Once in the little canal I found it filled with small boats. Everyone on the boats was fishing. There was a fairly strong current, and I was glad that it was against me because the Haulover Canal Bridge had to open to allow me clearance; it could have been an ugly scene if I had to circle or maneuver to wait for the bridge in such a tight and crowded area with a following tide. The bridge tender was responsive and he opened with perfect timing. This narrow and very short canal connects the Mosquito Lagoon and the Indian River.

The river was another open and choppy waterway. I did fly my jib for a while, until my direction changed and yet again the wind was on my nose.

I dealt with four low bridges today and had to wait for two of them because of their restricted opening times. There were also four high bridges that I passed under. I was weary when I anchored just north of a railroad bridge in the unrelenting current and wind. I needed to stop, and was too exhausted to find a better anchorage. It will be a sleepless night. I could continue a little further to the dock at Titusville, but I don't want to deal with docking, people, and the lack of privacy. I need to stop now. I need to get warm, and I need to sit and relax with my cup of rum in solitude.

As I tried to relax in my little cockpit in a strong current, after a tiring day, I thought about my family in Florida. I thought about how they welcomed me at Bonnie and Carl's party. There were no thoughts of past misunderstandings; there was only friendship and love. I realized that my family really loved

A Great Big Adventure on a Good Little Boat

me in spite of my many flaws. I understood that I could be a part of their world if I am able. The only restriction will come from me: I have a difficult time letting others into my inner me.

The death of my marriage was a major hurt and a huge failure. I refused to let but a couple of people know about my pain. I kept myself isolated until I could put on a strong front.

Until Don left and I started on my journey, defeat wasn't an option. Don and I were a team and I could depend on him to help me keep my equilibrium and face. Together we couldn't fail. When he left, I felt defenseless. I felt that I might fail. I couldn't let anyone see me in that horrible place. I hid. I hid from my friends, I hid from my parents, I hid from my siblings, and worst of all, I hid from my daughters.

During this voyage on my little boat I have realized that this reluctance to "let anybody in" during painful times is one of my biggest shortcomings. I have a need to never let anyone see my pain. Showing hurt has never been an option for me; even as a kid I remember not letting my parents see me cry when I was punished. I didn't want to let them know that they could hurt me.

I am not proud of myself. I became the tough guy. I isolated myself, and I pretended to need no one when I needed everyone the most. Thank God, I finally reached out for help. I asked for support and acceptance. I started to realize that I was strong. I was a strong person. I would not fail. I did not need Don. I have to think that I was too late in opening up my heart to my daughters. They are the most important people in my life, and I'm afraid that I have lost them. They are the ones who I need the most. Our relationship may never be totally mended, but there must be a way to somehow bridge the painful gap.

My voyage and my visit to Sarasota has made me feel confidant that I am capable of financially surviving and prospering there. I have many skills and I am an accomplished woodworker. My siblings and their families are loving and supportive. I could live in Sarasota, surrounded by family and new friends. I just don't know if that is what I want to do for the rest of my life. The scenario feels appealing. Very appealing, but now that I've tasted the independent travel bug, I have my doubts. I'll give Sarasota a try. If nothing else, I will have a wonderful time with my Florida family and friends.

A Great Big Adventure on a Good Little Boat

The great thing in this world is not so much where we are, but in what direction we are moving.

~Oliver Wendell Holmes

Florida

December 22
At anchor about 4 miles north of
Titusville to Dragon Point
ICW mile 914
28° 86' / 80° 36'

The event I've feared so long has finally happened! My anchor dragged overnight, but fortunately in this instance it wasn't a big deal because I had plenty of water and space around me and I didn't drag far. I didn't feel the drag during the night because there were no waves to jerk my boat, and I slept through the gentle pull of the anchor due to a mild current. I was lucky.

Crab traps surrounded my little boat. A crabber came by early to haul his traps and I tried to hail him, hoping to buy some crabs. He never acknowledged me, so I gave up and raised my anchor at about 0730 and left to begin my day's journey. The day was cloudy, but I did get to see the sunrise before the clouds filled the sky. The clouds were welcome today. The sun has been in my eyes for most of the day for quite a while now, and I find it very tiring. The glare of the sun makes it difficult to see the markers and it's almost impossible to distinguish their colors and shapes. I find myself switching from sunglasses as I try to distinguish the navigation marks, to reading glasses so that I can read the GPS, then back to sunglasses, then reading glasses. I *hate* glasses! I hate *needing* glasses!

It was a tranquil morning with a light wind, and I flew my jib for a long time today. I'm still in the Indian River; this section of the river is wide with no wind protection. I'm finding it difficult to find good places to anchor in the evening because the waterway is skinny and the water on either side of the ICW is very shallow. The 121-mile long Indian River was originally named Rio de Ais, after the Ais Indian tribe that lived along the east coast of Florida. I am getting tired of being in the wide and open Indian River. I prefer the quiet and meandering areas of the ICW.

Joyce's birthday was the 19th of this month. I miss her and think of her often. Joyce

Florida

—the whole family called her Joie—was my baby sister and she died about a year ago. She'd enjoy this trip. She would be content on this voyage and she would have gotten a lot of pleasure seeing the dolphins playing, following, and leading my little boat. She would have smiled, seeing the pelicans and cormorants dive into the water, struggling to swallow a big fish before a gull swooped down to try to steal it. She loved nature.

Joyce was the youngest of the Petrat clan. She was the only one of us who had dark hair, and she had long legs! The rest of us have what I call "hurricane legs": our legs are sturdy and close to the ground. A hurricane couldn't blow us down. Joyce loved books and worked in a bookstore for a few years until she became Mom and Dad's caregiver as they aged and needed help. Joie gave our parents loving care and we all appreciated our baby sister. Joie was so smart and had a quick humor. I love her and I miss her.

I anchored in a protected cove off the ICW, inside a place called Dragon Point, at the mouth of the Banana River. There used to be a 20-ton metal dragon on the point. A storm took it out and now it's just a collapsed pile of green metal lying on the rocks. It's sad to see the remains of this once huge creature. There is a house next to the poor dragon that calls to me to buy and restore it. The house and the dragon both call to me to help them. Maybe I should stop here and work here for a while. The house could be a worthy project. The dragon, I know, would be a labor of love. I've done those projects before! For the first time on my voyage I've been tempted to stay in one location and make a place for myself. To resist temptation, I decided to sail early the next morning.

The days passed happily with me whenever my ship sailed.

~Joshua Slocum

Florida

December 23
Dragon Point to an anchoring area about five miles north of Vero Beach, Florida
ICW mile 948
27° 43' / 80° 24'

At 0730, I left my anchorage, said goodbye to the sad, deflated green dragon, and continued south. A large ketch followed me out of the anchorage and she stayed behind me all day. This is highly unusual because everyone leaves me in their wake, and I know she could have passed me in a heartbeat.

I was getting a bit low on fuel, so I headed into a marina just off the waterway. The channel was poorly marked; I read the markers wrong and ran aground. I had been moving slowly and the current was running against me, so I managed to back off the sand bar easily; I gave up the fueling attempt and returned back to the ICW. Wow, the ketch was still behind me! Maybe she thinks I know where I'm going. That would be like the blind leading the blind! Would you believe, I am still sailing on the Indian River.

It was a very enjoyable day and the scenery was beautiful. I saw modest homes with small docks along most of the waterway. Cruising through the calm and placid sections of the ICW, I find myself singing or whistling. I remember that there is an old superstition among sailors: whistling calls up the wind. God knows I don't need more wind! After all the days of wild winds and rough seas, there is no way I want to influence the strong winds to join me today! So, after I found myself whistling, I tried to undo my bad omen by sucking in my whistle. I stood at the tiller un-whistling! Thank goodness I was alone.

Today there were lots of local boaters cruising on the water. Most of my travel today was in restricted wake zones. so I wasn't threatened by huge wakes. I love "No Wake" zones! Big wakes are nasty for a little boat like mine.

In the sections of the ICW where there are homes and docks along the waterway, boat speeds are restricted to eliminate wakes and their potential damage to docked boats, docks, and fragile shorelines. Even at my top speed, my wake is minimal! I fit right in here!

At one point during today's travel, I saw thousands of splashes all around me. I've seen schools of fish before as they jump out of the water, and they are grouped together; what I saw looked like individual fish jumping, but the splashes were about a foot apart. I never saw the fish, just the splash. It was strange. I still don't know what it was that I witnessed.

I enjoyed the company of a dolphin for a while. Usually the dolphins pass under me; this one swam with me for a long distance. We talked and we bonded! He was great fun to watch and I think we enjoyed each other's company, until he left me to jump and ride the larger wake of a faster boat. Ingrate!

I decided to quit early and I found a great little anchorage to pull up for the night between Pine Island and Hole in the Wall Island. It was a protected and quiet place with way too many mosquitoes! A little too quiet, I guess. After anchoring, while swatting mosquitoes and sipping my rum drink, I had the pleasure of watching four or five dolphins playing. I ignored the pesky bugs and fell into the trance of observing my favorite sea mammals and their antics. What a wonderful way to be entertained. I can't think of any better. I am so lucky and I am so content.

It was when I anchored in the lonely places that a feeling of awe came over me.

~Joshua Slocum

Florida

December 24
ICW mile 948 to ICW mile 966.2, just
north of Fort Pierce
27° 50' / 80° 18'

It's Christmas Eve morning. I made it a leisurely morning, relishing my time in my private cove. I heard, before I saw, a huge flock of birds. There were brown and white pelicans, cormorants, anhinga, and gulls. They flew into the cove and landed along the shore not far from my little boat. Shortly after landing, a feeding frenzy began! The noise they made was like nothing I'd ever heard before. So much for my peaceful anchorage! Thousands of birds flew in and landed, then flew and landed again, not far from their last spot. They moved along the shore only a few hundred feet from me, following the school of fish they were feeding on. The fish were thick in the water, leaping and swimming on the surface close to the shore. Those fish didn't have a chance! There were hundreds of birds!

Every once in a while, two birds would fight over the same fish. What a battle each bird fought to keep his catch! The squawking and screaming was unbelievable. What noise! It was quite a show, and I was thrilled to witness an amazing display of nature such as I'd never seen —or heard—before.

My journey today started late and it was an easy and enjoyable run. The wind and the tide were in my favor, and I flew the jib all day. Only two cruisers passed me and it was a beautiful and scenic day in the Indian River. Yes, I am *still* in this river!

I was afraid that gas for my outboard might be hard to buy over the holidays, so I stopped at Vero Beach to get fuel. The attendant said my boat was the smallest cruising boat he'd ever had at the dock.

The anchorage off the dock was crowded, with boats rafted two, three, and four abreast. It was too busy for me, and although I had a feeling that it would be a very happy and fun place to be for Christmas, I left. I wanted to be by myself and enjoy the first quiet and solo

Christmas I ever remember. I wanted to do what I wanted to do, not what I had to do and not what others expected of me. I wasn't sad and I wasn't happy; I was content and at peace. I was in a good place. I wished the gas attendant a very Happy Christmas and I continued on my merry way.

It was a short voyage today, only 20 miles. I anchored off Causeway Island and Fort Pierce. It wasn't a pretty place to spend the night, but my next good anchorage was over four hours away. Way too long to travel and drink that special bottle of wine I had been saving for Christmas Eve! I anchored and drank my special bottle of wine, and life was good and I was happy to be me.

December 25
Fort Pierce to Manatee Pocket
ICW mile 1
27° 09.' / 80° 11.58'

Upon finally leaving the Indian River and heading west into the St. Lucie River, ICW miles start at mile 1 again. There was no need to get up or leave early because I had planned just a 20-mile trip today, but I was up and making coffee at 0500.

I guess old habits are hard to break. As far back as I can remember, Christmas morning has meant getting up early to start cooking a huge turkey, a goose, and a ham, and preparing a vast array of vegetables and other food that accompanied a large family gathering and feast.

Florida

When my daughters got older and could help, it was a joy to plan and work together to make a memorable meal for all. We worked hard to make it a special day.

Christmas Day was always a fun day at our home and everyone was welcome. Even our dogs and birds participated in the festivities. Meg loved to open her gifts and it was so funny to watch Bart, my military macaw, try to nest in all of the spent wrappings.

Today is so different. I am who I want to be. I am a happy person. My future may be a little fuzzy, but that's fine. I am all right and I will be OK. Amazing how things work out. I am pleased with my life and with my choices. This is the first Christmas in my new skin and it is wonderful. I hope every future Christmas will be this brilliant.

If we are ever to enjoy life, now is the time. Today should always be our most wonderful day.

~Thomas Dreier

Today's goal is the Manatee Pocket off the ICW, which is close to the entrance of the St. Lucie River. Hooray, I'm finally off the Indian

A Great Big Adventure on a Good Little Boat

River! That river was just too long and choppy, and I'm glad to be out of it.

Unfortunately, today was another spray-in-my-face day. I had to deal with lots of wind and waves, wetting my cockpit, my charts, and wetting me all day. At least it wasn't raining. There wasn't much wildlife to see today, just a few dolphins and some birds—not much else. The sun was shining and there were a quite a few small pleasure boats on the water, many more than I would have expected on Christmas Day.

I was told that the Manatee Pocket was a nice place to anchor and that it was protected and a good place to go ashore. Well, I didn't have the option to go ashore, but it was a lovely spot to spend the rest of Christmas Day. I anchored and looked around. I was in a small area with the shore just yards from my boat. Most of the homes along the shore were decorated in the holiday spirit, and I heard Christmas music. People were outside their homes, sitting on their decks and calling Merry Christmas to their neighbors. Everyone was enjoying the holiday. I felt as though I was part of the celebration.

Shortly after anchoring, a large catamaran sailboat anchored near me. As they passed by me in their skiff, headed for shore, we wished each other a Merry Christmas. They were a cruising Mom and Dad with two young kids. The kids showed me the gifts that Santa had left them and they were quite pleased that the big jolly guy had found them aboard their sailing home.

I am happy to be here, safe and sound, on a great adventure and anchored in a comfortable place. I can hear Christmas carols from one of the nearby homes and they are lovely. This has been a very different Christmas for me, and I have enjoyed every minute of it. Just a few weeks ago, I was not looking forward to Christmas. Now I realize that I can be happy every day, and in every place. New beginnings can be a good thing.

Very little is needed to make a happy life. It is all within yourself.

~Marcus Aurelius

A Great Big Adventure on a Good Little Boat

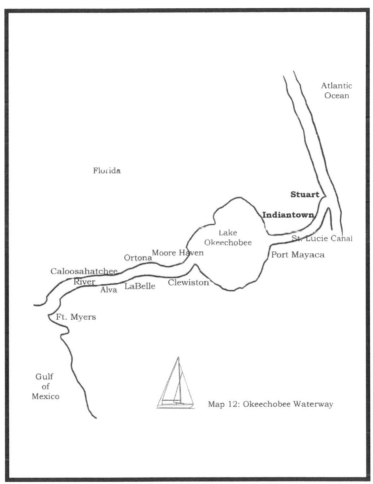

Map 12: Okeechobee Waterway

Atlantic
Ocean

Florida

Stuart

Indiantown

Lake
Okeechobee

St. Lucie Canal

Moore Haven

Port Mayaca

Ortona

Caloosahatchee
River

Alva LaBelle Clewiston

Ft. Myers

Gulf
of
Mexico

Okeechobee Waterway

431

December 26
Manatee Pocket to Indiantown on the
Okeechobee Canal
ICW mile 27
27° 00.74' / 80° 27.30'

At this point in my voyage I had a decision to make: I could either continue down the east coast of Florida, around the Florida Keys and back up the west coast to Sarasota, or I could take the shorter Okeechobee Waterway route through the middle of the state. My family in Sarasota is planning a big holiday boating trip on January 1st, and I want to join in the fun. I hate to miss a boating party!

There was no way I could reach Sarasota by the first of January, so I needed to find a home for my boat for about a week. My brother Willy said that he could drive to Indiantown and pick me up. There is a marina in Indiantown and I have heard that it wasn't too expensive. So, I am headed for Indiantown.

I left my charming Christmas anchorage at the Manatee Pocket and headed into the St. Lucie River. Inside the St. Lucie Inlet is the famous "Crossroads": the Atlantic Ocean, the Indian River, the St. Lucie River, and Jupiter Narrows all meet here. At the mouth of the St. Lucie River I cruised through another "Hell Gate." There were so many pleasure fishing boats headed toward the inlet that their wakes were rocking and rolling me every which way until I was able to pass through all the boat traffic and escape into the quiet river. It wasn't "hell," but it was uncomfortable for a while.

The dancing deck demanded acrobats rather than sailors...

~Edward H. Dodd Jr.

Just beyond the town of Stuart on the St. Lucie River there are two bridges. The first is high and was no issue. The second bridge needed to open for me, and I was concerned because the wind and tide were pushing me;

with a bend in the river and the closeness of the two bridges, I had no recourse if the bridge was slow in opening. The bridge tender was just slow enough to make me sweat!

It was a quiet and very peaceful trip through the St. Lucie Canal to Indiantown, and I enjoyed an easy transit through the St. Lucie Lock. I have to compliment these lockmasters. Every one of them that I've dealt with has been very helpful and pleasant. I did have to wait for a train to pass for the opening of the railroad bridge just east of Indiantown. It was a long train and a long wait. There was little current and no other boat traffic, so my wait was enjoyable. I floated in the canal and watched the many train cars pass over the bridge. I wondered what they were transporting, and where they were going.

I turned off the canal into the tiny Indiantown marina. Wow, every slip in the marina was full and the office was closed until tomorrow. I tied up at the fuel dock and spent the night there. I hope they can find dock space for my *Summer Wind*. After a refreshing hot shower, I walked around the marina and met a boating couple and joined them for dinner. I'm at yet another marina with fascinating and friendly people.

September 27
Docked at the Indiantown Marina

In the morning when the marina office opened, I
made arrangements to find a dock space. The
marina is so crowded that they had to raft me to
a large catamaran. My little boat now blocks
that cat and two other boats from leaving their
slips. I hate to abandon my boat like this, but
after meeting the staff here I am not too
concerned. She will be in good hands.

This is a weird marina. There aren't many
dock slips but there are over 450—yes, 450—
boats on the hard. I found out that Canadians
and other cold-weather people own most of
them, and many of these boats will be in the
water soon and heading for warm southern
climates. There is a big boat lift, and each day

that I've been here five to eight boats have been launched. Amazing for such a small place in the middle of nowhere.

The marina does have lots of amenities though. There is a common room with a fridge, microwave, sink, and dishes, and a screened-in porch off it. Outside is a pretty tree-covered patio area with a barbeque. Just beyond the restrooms and showers there is a washer and dryer. All this is available to the boat owners. You can even camp here while working on your boat. I was invited to a potluck dinner on Saturday, but I plan to be in Sarasota by then. Too bad, it would have been entertaining; these are exciting people. They have traveled to many places and they are planning to travel again.

While here, I did make the mile-long walk into Indiantown. There was a grocery store, a drug store, a gas station, a small restaurant, and not much else. I got a kick out of shopping in the food store. The Seminole Indians originally settled in the town, and the foods reflected that. I didn't recognize many of the fruits and vegetables. Some of the herbs and spices were unfamiliar to me also. It's fun to get a glimpse of other cultures.

December 28
Driving to Sarasota
27° 25' / 82° 35'

By noon I was on my way to Sarasota. I hated to leave my good little boat, but I know the marina staff will be careful if they have to move her. My brother's girlfriend Leona and her aunt Joy picked me up, and the drive to Sarasota afforded me a chance to get to know Leona better. Willy and Leona have been seeing each other for a while, and I do believe theirs is a serious relationship.

I'm excited about getting aboard the *Exuma Trader* again. I've lived aboard her since I moved to Sarasota last year, and I miss her. The *Trader* is a big boat. She is an 85-foot powered barge.

437

A Great Big Adventure on a Good Little Boat

She's not an open flat barge; she's got a cargo area and large cabin, with a main salon and a dining area, a large galley, a head with a shower, and a stateroom. Above the main cabin is the bridge, where the steering and the navigation take place. The bridge boasts a small stateroom and a head. Her interior areas are very finished and pretty for a working boat. She has large twin diesel engines, three generators, seven fuel tanks, watertight compartments, and systems and more systems.

My brother Willy built the barge—yes, he built it—from scratch, to eventually work and be a viable means of income. Willy hopes to move cargo, do salvage work, and whatever jobs may present themselves. Until then, we use her as our "mother ship" on the family's boating excursions. She is perfect for us. In the cargo area we carry kayaks, the Boston Whalers, my nephew's flat boat, and wave runners. We launch these small craft with the on-board crane when we've reached our destination.

Then, the other family and friends join us aboard their boats and raft to the *Exuma Trader,* and this mother ship supplies the other boats with electricity and the space that the smaller boats lack. We lower the forward ramp and swim and dive from it. Cocktails are enjoyed on the upper deck, where we can watch the sun set.

Okeechobee Waterway

She makes a great vacation boat. We will all miss her when she goes to work.

I've decided to take the Okeechobee Waterway when I get back. Last night I read up on the Okeechobee Waterway's history, which is fascinating. The Okeechobee Waterway is 152 miles long and connects the St. Lucie Canal (which connects the Florida's east coast to Lake Okeechobee) to the Caloosahatchee River, which in turn ends in the Gulf of Mexico. The waterway is operated and maintained by the U. S. Army Corps of Engineers.

Many towns along the Caloosahatchee are small and quite rural. Interestingly, Indiantown is the home of Payson Park, one of the nation's top Thoroughbred racing and training facilities. In New Hampshire I lived not far from the Runnymede Farm, which is the home of 45 stake-winning race horses, including 1968 Kentucky Derby winner Dancer's Image. By traveling the Caloosahatchee, I will see yet another side of Florida.

A Great Big Adventure on a Good Little Boat

December 29 through December 30
Aboard the *Exuma Trader,* Sarasota

I spent my time before our outing aboard Willy's big boat, readying her for the fun-filled voyage. Willy had been working on the boat, finalizing details and doing maintenance jobs. On a boat this size, there are always projects to do. Since I've been gone, the *Trader* hasn't had too much TLC and definitely not much cleaning has been done. I cleaned and helped to procure foodstuffs and booze until we were ready to go.

Fortunately, because I help to run the boat, I do not do the cooking. Our good friend Don and his wife Judy do most of the meal preparations. Don is an excellent cook and seems to enjoy feeding our large group.

Okeechobee Waterway

I am looking forward to a long weekend of fishing, kayaking, eating, and drinking with my family and a few good friends. After being alone, I hope I will be comfortable with people constantly around me.

December 31
Sarasota to Useppa Island
26° 40' / 82° 12.50'

We left the dock at 0530 on the high tide. (We need a high tide to navigate the *Exuma Trader* through the creek where she is docked.) Some members of the onboard group were unable to leave their jobs until later in the morning, so we anchored in Sarasota Bay, just off the creek, and waited. After our whole contingent of the ten of us was aboard, we headed out of Sarasota Bay and into the Gulf of Mexico, and then south toward the Boca Grande Pass.

The sun was shining and the seas were calm. The sun made the gulf waters sparkle. We called our brother Carl, who hadn't made the trip with us. We told him how gorgeous the day was and that he should catch a ride on one of the other boats headed for Boca Grande. We've usually been lucky and have had good weather during our cruises on the Gulf while heading toward our vacation spot. The weather usually cooperates during our stay, but many times we get hit with miserable weather as we head home.

We trolled for fish the whole way to Boca Grande without catching a thing. We were quite disappointed because a big fish feast our first night out is something we all look forward to. Oh well, we tried. It was a beautiful day and everyone enjoyed the trip.

We arrived at our anchoring spot behind Useppa Island after dark. Cindy and Tim and family, and Bambi and Steve were already on site aboard their boats and, after we anchored, they came alongside and tied up to us. We prepared prime rib with all the fixings. We set a long table for the crowd of us and served prime rib with all the fixings. The evening was gorgeous, with a sky full of stars. We ate heartily and drank fine wine.

We enjoyed our traditional card game of hearts. Then, at midnight, we opened the champagne and toasted each other. We toasted the New Year and toasted our family and friends.

A Great Big Adventure on a Good Little Boat

It was a long and fun day. We are very lucky people! It was a wonderful place to be and a wonderful group to be with on the eve of the New Year. It had been a beautiful day to travel on the Gulf, and we were warm and safe at our anchorage. I loved being with my friends and family.

That night I slept on the upper deck of the bridge. I cuddled in my sleeping bag and watched the amazing star-filled sky until my eyes closed.

January 1
Anchored off Useppa Island

The first day of the New Year was warm and sunny. My sister Cindy and I woke up early and enjoyed a private and traditional breakfast of mimosas and bagels with lox, cream cheese, onions, and capers. (This is the way to start a New Year: with someone special, champagne, and good food!)

After a leisurely morning and a huge breakfast, thanks to Don and Judy, we all headed in different directions. Steve took a group aboard his boat to go fishing in the Gulf. Cindy and I took off exploring in the kayaks. My nephew Marshal and a few others went fishing aboard his small flat boat. Willy and Leona left in the Boston Whaler to explore around the

445

islands. Others just relaxed aboard the *Exuma Trader.*

Cindy and I found several beds of oysters and we brought back enough oysters for all aboard the mother ship to enjoy a midday snack. It was a good thing because the fishermen came back with no fish. Later in the day we raised the crane boom and rigged it with a bosun's chair so we could swing off the boat and into the water. Great fun! We were kids again! Just another sunny day in paradise!

Happiness is enjoying the realities as well as the frivolities of life.

~Edward G. Bulwer-Lytton

January 2
The *Exuma Trader* trip back to Sarasota

As happens with all good things, our boat trip had to end. We started our journey back to Sarasota and were threatened with a massive cold front headed our way. This front carried big winds and heavy rain, so we decided to travel back to Sarasota in the more protected ICW rather than in the Gulf. This meant a slower and longer return voyage. It also meant no fishing. Too bad; we all love fresh fish.

I was at the helm in a restricted channel with the wind trying to blow me off course and I had to keep compensating by steering to port. At some point, the boat wasn't responding to my helm. I lost steering! I called to Willy just before we were pushed off the channel into shallow water. Fortunately, at this point we were in relatively protected waters and we were able to back off the shallow water and return to the channel.

We regained minimal steering and it was a bear to work the wheel. The waves and rain weren't too bad until we got into Sarasota Bay, where we were hit hard. The waves were spraying over the upper deck and the boat was pounding. It was very uncomfortable for the group onboard. The rain made it difficult to see the markers defining the creek, and I was glad when Willy took the helm again. We were safely docked and tied up by midnight. It had been another memorable and exhausting trip in paradise!

We had begun our vacation and traveled south in beautiful, sunny, and calm waters. The weather stayed warm and comfortable during our stay at anchor while we fished, kayaked, and relaxed. We were brought back to reality with threatening and difficult seas on our return voyage, but we all arrived home with great memories of our adventure. We are lucky to have such close friends who get along together and with whom we can share these good times.

Along with the steering issue, we ran out of water and we had a septic valve leak. Some landlubbers just don't know how to conserve water well enough. The next purchase for Willy is a water maker. The *Trader* is still in shake-down mode, and Willy is still in the building and refining process. All-in-all, it was a great trip and tons of fun! Willy figured out the steering issue and he and I fixed the valve problem before I headed back to Indiantown. I get all the fun jobs!

January 4
Indiantown to Boynton Beach
Florida's East Coast

I returned to Indiantown Marina and found my little boat safe and sound. The crew here took good care of her. It's amazing how much I missed traveling aboard my little boat. I missed sleeping in my cramped cabin and I think that I missed being alone.

Before I left Indiantown for Sarasota, I had made plans to go to Boynton Beach to visit friends; so my boat and I will have to wait before we start traveling together again.

Sue and Leo are long-time friends from New Hampshire who now winter in Boynton Beach. Sue owns the *Uncle Oscar,* and takes tours to the Isles of Shoals off the New Hampshire coast.

Sue also gives people a taste of lobstering with a demonstration of hauling lobster traps. People love that trip. Leo is the Harbor Master at the beautiful Rye Harbor and on occasion is called on to captain cruise boats out of the harbor. I had kept my boat in their yard in New Hampshire, and they were a big help to me while I was preparing my little boat for her trip. They are good people.

Sue picked me up in Indiantown, and we drove to their home in Boynton Beach. Vivian and Paul had driven down from New Hampshire to visit Sue and Leo, and I had a great reunion with my very special friends. If you remember, Paul helped me with the wiring on my boat and sailed on the first leg of my trip. Vivian treated me to delicious dinners and a comfy bed on many occasions.

These four people have been critical in my healing process and I've missed them. We had a wonderful time in the beautiful Boynton Beach area, and enjoyed each other's company touring, reminiscing, and birding together. Sue is an avid birder and she took us to a couple of bird sanctuaries, where we got to see just about every kind of bird there is in Florida. Sue and Leo are gracious hosts and it was a fun visit. I hated to leave, but I was ready to continue my

A Great Big Adventure on a Good Little Boat

trip by boat to Sarasota. Paul and Vivian drove me to Indiantown, since their next stop in Florida was Englewood, where another mutual friend, Linda, winters. I hope to get to Englewood and visit Linda while Paul and Vivian are there. It will be a much longer voyage for me!

Okeechobee Waterway

January 10
Indiantown to Torry Island Bridge
ICW mile 59.8
26° 54.88' / 80° 42.51'

I was so happy to be back on my boat. I had a blast in Sarasota with friends and family aboard the barge. My visit with friends in Boynton Beach was enjoyable and relaxing; however, I missed my days of adventure aboard the *Summer Wind.* My poor boat has been docked at the Indiantown Marina since December 27, and I can hardly wait to get underway again.

I have met some exciting people here at the marina, and it's always a little sad to say goodbye. I guess that's part of cruising. I remember one couple in particular: they were nice and friendly, and were planning an adventure together. They seemed to be fairly well off, but I felt that they skimped on the wrong things, like charts. She was proud of the fact that she found old and outdated charts at flea markets and yard sales. I believe that my charts are one of my most important investments and that I can't have too many current charts. Oh well, each to her own. I wish them well.

My trip in the Okeechobee Waterway to the Port Mayaca Lock was calm and uneventful, and I was able to fly my jib the whole distance to the lock. I wanted to wait until I got into Okeechobee Lake before deciding whether to sail the lake route or the rim route. The lake route takes you across the open waters of the lake. If the winds are strong—like any body of open water—it can get quite nasty. The rim route is longer but more protected. I basically had decided to go on the rim route, but if I found the winds favorable for sailing I would raise my mainsail and jib and sail on the lake.

The wind was on my nose when I entered the lake. They say the rim route is prettier. So, I would see the pretty route. And it *was* beautiful. I passed through miles of marshes and saw lots of birds and one huge alligator sitting on the shore. He was enormous and seemed as large as my boat!

It was getting late, so I anchored just east of the swing bridge at Torry Island. Shortly after anchoring, two old guys arrived aboard their small boat for an evening of fishing. They anchored not more than 50 feet from me. We waved to each other, I made dinner in my now very un-private cockpit, and they fished. I would have felt more comfortable if they had been further away but, oh well, they were two old guys having fun. Just before dark these guys started a very loud generator and turned on four six-foot fluorescent lights. Wow, I didn't appreciate the noise or the lights. They finally shut down their operation at 10 o'clock! So much for finding a quiet anchorage and enjoying a restful night of sleep. You can't pick your neighbors!

January 11
Torry Island Bridge to the "Lollypop"
ICW mile 93
26° 47'/ 81° 17'

I was up early and drank a leisurely cup of coffee while waiting for the Torry Bridge to open at 0730. The noisy old fishermen were gone! I saw more birds in the next part of the Okeechobee than I'd seen on any other part of my voyage. My gosh, I saw anhinga, lots of brown pelicans, herring gulls, terns, lots and lots of great blue herons, many tricolor herons, cattle egrets, strikes, great egrets, and other birds that I couldn't identify. I also saw lots of osprey. Many of the ospreys were carrying off a long skinny fish that looked like a snake but wasn't a snake. I don't know what that fish was.

Okeechobee Waterway

The amazing thing was that I saw all of these birds within a five-mile section of the waterway. I had a hard time steering for looking at birds. I talked to the birds and the cows along the shore. It was lots of fun. What an interesting section of the waterway. I was thrilled to be here.

I'd traveled through this area once before aboard a 36-foot sports fishermen. We raced past much of the waterway. We saw very little! We saw no birds, no alligators; we saw only a blur of marshes.

Those who travel fastest see the least, but he that would see, feel, and hear the most of life, nature, and God, let him go down to the sea in a small sailing vessel.

~L. Francis Herreshoff

I reached the Moore Haven Lock and Railroad Bridge. The lock was an easy passage, but I had to wait for a train to pass before the bridge could open. I'm getting better at holding position for 15 minutes, and I didn't lose my VHF radio this time! Beyond the lock, I entered the Caloosahatchee Canal, where cows grazed along the shores. I called to them and they raised their heads and watched as I sailed past.

A Great Big Adventure on a Good Little Boat

Thanks to my Skipper Bob book, I am anchored in an old quarry canal that the locals call the Lollipop. It does look like a lollipop, with a canal that opens up into a round, deep pool. I entered the very narrow canal, turned around in the deep pool, and anchored at the rim of the pool. This was a very quiet and isolated spot. The cows on the shore were my only companions. It was a quiet night.

January 12
The "Lollypop," just west of Franklin Lock
on the Caloosahatchee River, Florida
ICW mile 121
26° 43' / 81° 59'

This was a busy bridge and lock day. The Ortona Lock was my first lock today, and I was challenged with fog for most of the morning. My lock passage was easy, as was the bridge at LaBelle.

In my reading I found out that LaBelle began as a tiny settlement of cattlemen and trappers back in the late 1880s. Apparently, many historic buildings still stand in the town; I will have to return!

A Great Big Adventure on a Good Little Boat

My next bridge at Denaud was interesting. There were two cruisers about ten minutes ahead of me, and I heard them call the bridge tender for an opening. I called and asked the tender if he could hold the opening for ten minutes. There was no answer, and I assumed that the bridge tender wouldn't wait. (They don't usually wait.) I continued toward the bridge.

When I got close to the bridge, I called the tender. He said that he would wait the opening until the other two cruisers traveling with me got closer. I told him that I was alone and the cruisers had already cleared his bridge. Then he said, "I not see you." I told him that I am very small. He said, "You come close, I open." I said, "I *am* close!" Finally he replied, "I see you, I come now. You wait, I call you." Now I had to wait while he walked to the middle of the swing bridge. He opened the bridge and called me to pass through his bridge. I thanked him and continued on my way. The tender had a very thick French Canadian accent, and I think that maybe he did not understand my accent, and I didn't understand his accent.

All day I chuckled about this bridge opening and the two ghost cruisers.

My course under the other bridge and through the Franklin Lock paled in comparison to passage at the bridge at Denaud! The

Okeechobee Waterway

Franklin Lock marked my last lock passage on this voyage. There were two locks in the Dismal Swamp and five here in the Okeechobee Waterway. These locks allow boats to travel from one level of water to another, so a lock may bring your boat up or down. Some water level changes are very drastic and others are minimal.

As you approach the lock, it is recommended that you call the tender from about a half a mile away. I would call over my VHF radio something like "Franklin Lock, this is the sailing vessel *Summer Wind* approaching from the east, requesting a passage; do you copy?" Sometimes they don't answer, so I would continue motoring and make another call when I got closer. When they acknowledged my call, I would reply with "Good morning, Franklin Lock, this is the sailing vessel *Summer Wind* approaching from the east, requesting a passage." The lockmaster might come back with something like "*Summer Wind*, I have just closed the westbound gates and it will be a few minutes before I can give you the green light." (I found that a "few minutes" can mean 20 minutes or so.)

So I'd thank him and travel closer to the lock and stop to wait for the green light at the big Arrival Point sign. Some lockmasters will tell you which side you are to tie up to so that you can have your fenders prepared. (Lock walls are concrete and your boat rides up or down on these walls.)

The light turns green, the lock gates open, and upon entering the lock there are lines draped down the high walls. You must "tend" these lines as your boat rises or lowers in the lock. It is the boater's responsibility to take up the slack or let out line as your boat goes up or down. This is where it is handy to have a bowman and a stern man. Most times, I had to tie an extension on the lock's lines because my little boat lowered so much that I couldn't hold both the bow and the stern lines. My arms aren't long enough!

Then the gate behind your boat closes and the water enters or leaves the lock. At most of these locks, there is a peanut gallery of tourists and locals who enjoy watching the boats come and go. These people wave and you wave back. Sometimes they yell, "Where are you going?" After the water in the lock has raised or lowered and the gates in front of your boat have opened, the lockmaster will tell you that you can drop your lines and proceed out of the lock. You radio him a thank you and he responds with a "Have a nice day."

Okeechobee Waterway

The lockmasters I met were friendly and they seemed to enjoy their work. They made transiting the locks easy and I enjoyed each lock experience on my voyage.

I couldn't find the anchorage where I had planned to stop for the night. I traveled a few miles south and tried three different places. Each time I dropped my anchor, the water was either too shallow or I felt that I was too close to the waterway to be safe. I finally realized where my intended anchorage was: it was just to the south of the lock. I mean *just* after the lock! I had passed it. Finally I backtracked, determined to find my intended anchorage, and by the time I got the hook down for the fourth time it was almost dark and I was tired.

I was anchored off a small camping area and the smell of hamburgers cooking on the barbeques made my mouth water! I don't even eat hamburgers but they smelled so good! I made a rum drink and pretended that I was eating a big juicy steak and a big green salad. As I was sitting in my cockpit enjoying my rum drink, sans steak and salad, I saw a bald eagle! He was sitting atop a tree and he stayed there for quite a while. Maybe he wanted a hamburger too!

A Great Big Adventure on a Good Little Boat

It had been a long day of travel. Each day my destination gets closer. I want to get there, but I don't want to stay there. I want to continue this voyage and keep traveling south. I'll see what happens. I realize that I need to stay long enough to earn some money, enough to keep this trek financed. But really, I don't need much and I hope my stay will last just long enough to have a fun time with my Florida family and friends, earn some money, and continue my voyage toward more unknown and exotic ports. You never know, and I will keep my options open.

January 13
ICW mile146.8
The Franklin Lock to Glover Bight
Still on the Okeechobee Waterway
26° 32' / 81° 59'

After waiting for the opening and passing through the bridge off Beautiful Island, the Caloosahatchee River opened up into a wide and windy waterway. The wind was behind me, so I flew my jib as I sailed under five high fixed bridges, past Fort Myers, and then past Cape Coral. As I was cruising under the last high-rise bridge, I had my phone out in the cockpit because I had taken a picture. I noticed that it was getting sprayed. Where was that coming from? I was running downwind and I had no water in my face. The temperature is still cool enough that I was wearing my lightweight foul-weather jacket.

I looked around and realized that dolphins had come along my boat. They were playing on my starboard side and their breath was spraying me! I covered my phone, and I had a great time talking to my new companions. They glided so effortlessly through the water, keeping up with my little boat. We enjoyed each other's company for quite a while, until a boat with a better wake passed, and the dolphins deserted me. They gave my little boat an underwater goodbye nudge when they left, and I had fun watching them jump and play in the other boat's wake. I never tire of watching these graceful sea mammals, and they always put a smile on my face. They are such happy critters! I love their happy faces!

Joshua Slocum, who in 1895 was the first solo sailor to circumnavigate the world, claimed that during a storm while he was sailing off a rocky coast, dolphins guided his boat to safety. I don't doubt his story. It is also a well-known sailors' belief that a dolphin (or, better yet, a pod of them) swimming with a boat blesses it with good luck. I certainly have had good luck on my voyage. Yes, for the most part, the weather has been miserable, it's been cold, the winds have been strong and on my nose during most of my travels. Yet, I have had no disasters. My boat has endured everything thrown at her. I didn't blow out any sails. I haven't been injured. I *did* stub my toe once during the trip! It has been a lucky voyage.

Traveling on my little boat has taught me that one can overcome adversity and heartache with perseverance, determination, and the right attitude. Sometimes, just because everyone tells you that your ideas or plans can't work, "everyone" is not always right! Trust yourself, work hard, know that your pain will not last forever, and proceed with what is in your heart.

I have run beyond my edition of the Skipper Bob book. That means that I have no more insider information about hidden and small protected places to anchor, and am left with only my charts to guide me to comfortable nighttime hideaways. I did find Glover Bight on my chart. This anchorage is past Cape Coral and just east of the San Carlos Bay. I had to travel a bit out of my way to get here and I am anchored in a cove surrounded by marinas and hotels. Oh, well, I am in a protected spot and out of the increasing winds and seas. It looks like there is another storm approaching.

A Great Big Adventure on a Good Little Boat

I am determined to be cheerful and happy in whatever situation I may be. For I have also learned from experience that the greater part of our happiness or misery depends on our dispositions and not on our circumstances.

~Martha Washington

I have made it to the west coast of Florida and I am almost excited about completing my voyage. I have mixed feelings about finishing this trip. I don't want this adventure to end, but I am thrilled at the thought of being with my family again. And, it will feel good to be clean, dry, and warm.

Okeechobee Waterway

January 14
Stuck in Glover Bight

Today was cold and blustery. Wow, this is Florida? The wind is out of the north, and I have no desire to enter the open and rough San Carlos Bay with such strong headwinds. My little boat is protected and I am comfortable, so I'll stay here and try to keep warm. My *Summer Wind* is safe in this cove and, at this stage of my trip, I'm not in a real hurry to reach my destination. After three months of traveling, the thought of facing reality is too scary at times.

Reality is merely an illusion, albeit a very persistent one.

~Einstein

469

A Great Big Adventure on a Good Little Boat

I should find work when I reach Sarasota. I should become a productive human being again. Wow, I don't think I'm ready. I don't want to.

I buried my head in my books and studied my charts all day.

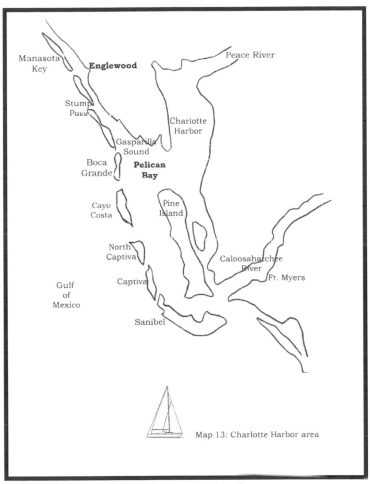

Map 13: Charlotte Harbor area

Labels on map:
Manasota Key
Englewood
Peace River
Stump Pass
Charlotte Harbor
Gasparilla Sound
Boca Grande
Pelican Bay
Cayo Costa
Pine Island
North Captiva
Caloosahatchee River
Captiva
Ft. Myers
Gulf of Mexico
Sanibel

Charlotte Harbor

A Great Big Adventure on a Good Little Boat

January 15
Glover Bight to Pelican Bay
ICW mile 25
26° 41' / 82° 14.25'

I have exited the Okeechobee Waterway and entered the West Coast Waterway with mile 0 at the mouth of the Caloosahatchee River. I've reached another milestone: Florida's West Coast. My *Summer Wind* and I have traveled for more than three months and covered over 2000 miles of ocean, bays, sounds, channels, cuts, swamps, and waterways. My little boat and I have done well. These next 80 miles to Sarasota will bring me into familiar waters. I've cruised much of this area with Willy aboard the *Exuma Trader* and on other family members' boats.

Charlotte Harbor

Overnight, the winds calmed and the water flattened. I am so glad that I waited to venture into the open San Carlos Bay; it made for a calm and peaceful journey. The sea was alive with dolphins this morning, and my trip through the bay was enjoyable, with the dolphins leading the way. It's like these amazing sea mammals are leading me home. Maybe these dolphins aren't guiding me like they guided Joshua Slocum, but they are fun to see and I appreciate their company!

I entered Pine Island Sound with Pine Island and then Sanibel to my east, and continued past Captiva and North Captiva islands to my west. I read—on the Internet—that Captiva Island got its name because the pirate Jose Gaspar held female hostages for ransom there. However, I do know for a fact that Sanibel is justly famous for its lovely shells.

It was a very pleasant day and it was fun to cruise past all the pretty beaches and mangroves. I anchored for the night in Pelican Bay, off Cayo Costa, and just north of Charlotte Harbor. Finally, I recognize my surroundings.

I did remember certain ports along my voyage, but I had been to these harbors and ports as a kid, not as skipper of my vessel. There is a huge difference! My Florida family and I have anchored in these waters many times

A Great Big Adventure on a Good Little Boat

during our "mother ship" weekends. I had intended to stop for lunch at the well-known Cabbage Key Grill. As I turned to enter the channel to the restaurant, I was almost swamped by seven or eight large go-fast boats. They turned into the channel and headed toward the grill. I decided that I didn't want to deal with their wakes, their noise, and now a lack of dock space.

It is rumored that Jimmy Buffett wrote his "Cheeseburger in Paradise" song after eating at the Cabbage Key Grill. With my mouth watering, I gave up the idea of eating a delicious, fresh fish sandwich, and I continued heading south to my anchorage here in Pelican Bay.

This beautiful bay is a favorite local anchorage and offers excellent protection. I'm here with about a dozen other boats. Pelican Bay is just south of Boca Grande Pass and nestled between Punta Blanca Island and Cayo Costa, where there is a state park. Next time that I travel like this I will have a little skiff or kayak or something so that I can go ashore.

Charlotte Harbor

January 16
Pelican Bay to Englewood Beach
ICW mile 43
26° 56' / 82° 21'

I was holed up in Pelican Bay for the morning. The wind had increased overnight, and I could see rough and nasty water in Charlotte Harbor. This harbor is large and open to the Gulf through the Boca Grande Pass, and with the right winds it can be quite rough. By late morning the winds had calmed a bit, and by noon I could see that the harbor was still sporting whitecaps, but I was anxious to get moving. I raised anchor and headed into a real rock-and-roll ride through the harbor. I had to tie everything down and it was all I could do to hold on to steer my little boat. At least it wasn't raining! It was cold though!

After dealing with the rough seas for about two hours, I reached the more protected and calm waters of Placida Harbor and Lemon Bay. As I approached the Tom Adams Bridge, I turned to the west and off the ICW to anchor for the night. I was just off Englewood, where I hoped to meet up with Vivian and Paul while they are visiting our mutual friend Linda. I anchored in an area close to shore and started to settle in for the evening. I heard my name being called. I looked around and saw my friends waving to me from shore! It was Vivian, Paul, and Linda. We talked by phone, and shortly after Paul and Steve—a friend of Linda's—met me at my anchorage in a small skiff.

Steve and his wife Joanne own a houseboat close by and offered to let me raft up to it while I'm visiting my friends here in Englewood. Paul joined me aboard the *Summer Wind,* and we followed Steve the short distance to his houseboat. I tied up, secured my boat, and Steve, Paul and I rode ashore and joined Linda, Vivian, and Joanne at Linda's winter home. Hooray—another reunion with my New Hampshire friends! We spent the night eating, drinking, laughing, and telling tall tales of adventures and misadventures. I ended up sleeping on the sofa, warm and dry.

January 17
Englewood to Crow's Nest Marina in Venice
ICW mile 57
27° 07.25' / 82° 27'

I hadn't planned to dock the *Summer Wind* in Venice, but the anchorage was quite full and I knew that the food was good at the Crow's Nest Marina restaurant, so I decided to pay the dockage fee and benefit from a shower and a delicious meal, sitting at a table, eating off a plate and using a napkin. What a treat! It never fails that I meet fascinating people at the marinas, and this dockage was no exception. I met Dave and joined him and his friends for dinner at the restaurant and then drinks after aboard his sailboat.

My voyage was enjoyable today, in spite of having four bridges to negotiate. Today's voyage was nothing but engine cruising through the skinny waterway of Lemon Bay and then a traverse through the tight quarters of the ICW just south of Venice, with one bridge after another that had to open for me. After docking, I took a stroll along the park at the Venice Inlet, watching the fishermen along the breakwater and just people watching. I continued my walk along the beautiful Venice Beach. I have never taken time to enjoy a leisurely walk along a beach before this trip. Really, I cannot remember ever taking the time to do such a frivolous thing, except on vacation. I guess I am on vacation!

This whole trip has been one novel experience after another. My eyes are opened up to a whole new world. I have a different outlook on life; I guess that this is what any voyage is supposed to be about. I'm afraid that when it ends, so will my newfound freedom and my fresh sense of me. I think that I will have to be very careful not to lose all that I have gained. I am sure that is why I have such mixed feelings about arriving at my destination. I want to enjoy freedom with no obligations. I own very little and owe nothing. This is a good feeling and I don't want it to end yet. For now, I will continue my journey, if only for one more day.

At sea I learned how little a person needs, not how much.

~Robin Lee Graham

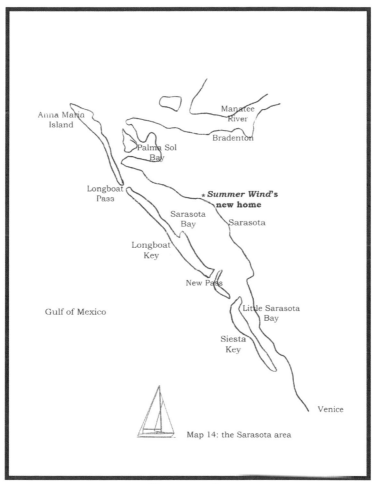

Map 14: the Sarasota area

Within the map:
Anna Maria Island
Manatee River
Bradenton
Palma Sol Bay
Longboat Pass
Summer Wind's new home
Sarasota Bay
Sarasota
Longboat Key
New Pass
Gulf of Mexico
Little Sarasota Bay
Siesta Key
Venice

Sarasota

January 18
Venice to the middle of Sarasota Bay and my Grand Homecoming!!!
Mile 77
27° 22' / 82° 35'

I left Venice late in the morning, after eating a large breakfast at a place in the park along the inlet. This morning the park was filled with people walking, fishing, and just enjoying life. Last night I had strolled to the beach to watch the sunset. I just sat there on the rocks and marveled at the view. I wasn't alone. Many people sat on the rocks, and others came by car and sat in their cars, watching the sun dip below the horizon.

Sarasota

Today's travel included navigating through five bridges to Sarasota Bay. At the last bridge, I told the bridge tender that his was the last bridge to open for me since my voyage's beginning in New England. He congratulated me and wished me many more safe journeys. Thank you, Mr. Bridge Tender.

I called my brother Willy to let him know that my ETA into Sarasota Bay would be just before noon. He told me that in no uncertain terms was I to pass the middle of Sarasota Bay until 3 p.m. Wow, at this point I wanted to get home, and I suddenly felt very tired. He said no, I must wait.

I anchored just north of the Ringling Bridge at the northern end of the bay, waiting for Willy's schedule. I knew that he and the family were planning something and I didn't want to spoil it for them, so I anchored, waited, and napped. Just before 3 p.m., I started my trusty engine and raised my jib. (I was too tired to raise the main.) I sailed under the high Ringling Bridge and headed north in the Sarasota Bay—toward home.

Sure enough, about in the middle of the bay I saw four fast boats headed straight toward me! I knew this must be Willy and my welcoming committee! My brother Carl and friends were aboard Willy's go-fast boat, and they sported a

A Great Big Adventure on a Good Little Boat

big fire hose and welcomed me like I was a tall ship entering Boston Harbor! The other boats carried my sister Cindy, her husband Tim, and other family members and friends. They toasted me with champagne and horns and yells and hoorays. What a fantastic homecoming! To top off this great welcome, Carl's wife Bonnie had made a huge paper banner, which they opened between two of the boats. Written on the banner was "MAINE TO FLORIDA—FINISH LINE"! I sailed through it, breaking it in half to hoots and screams and congratulations and sprays of champagne. Oh my God, what an amazing and unforgettable experience. I know now why I worked so hard to get here! My family is over the top, and I am looking forward to being with them, for a while at least.

Afterthoughts of my voyage

Many thoughts run through my head when I think about my adventure. Yes, I would like to repeat this trip. I would like to visit the many ports and anchorages that I missed on my first journey.

Sometimes I think that a bigger and more comfortable boat would be a good thing. I do love my little boat and she proved herself seaworthy in every situation she was put into.

It was always a bear to raise the main while solo sailing, and since then I've added slides to my mainsail, making raising the sail so much easier. I was disappointed at the lack of sailing that this trip afforded. I had to motor or at best motor-sail most of the time.

The cold weather was another issue. I should have left on the first of September and not the first of October. All the other cruisers who I talked to said that this was a very cold and windy year to travel south on the ICW. The lack of creature comforts was not too much of an issue for me, but better food would have been a very good thing!

I enjoyed the solitude and the challenge of navigating, sailing, docking, and anchoring alone. I would like to have a little tender (a small boat to get to shore with) aboard on the next trip. There were so many places I couldn't visit because I had no way to leave my boat. Docking gets very expensive, but it's at the docks and marinas that you meet lots of friendly and adventurous people, and where I have built some long and lasting relationships.

Initially, I dreaded waiting for bridges, and now it isn't too bad to wait and maneuver in narrow channels and pass through these obstacles. Lock passages were a lot easier than I had anticipated, and the lockmasters were pleasant and very helpful. Mostly, I enjoyed the quiet and peaceful little protected areas I found to anchor in at night, with a mug of rum in my hand and the sun setting on my day's journey.

The frigid temperatures and rough seas do stick in my memory. The uncomfortable weather plagued most of my voyage, but if every day was paradise, what would I be able to write about? The weather, the seas, and my little boat challenged me, and I think that's what my mind and heart needed. While battling the elements, I had no thoughts of the heartaches of the past. Yet, I was putting time and distance between my past and my now. I was giving my mind time to heal.

I will make another voyage, and it will probably be aboard my little *Summer Wind*. She's a good little boat and I am looking forward to our next adventure together.

I am a stronger person for making this trip. I have the confidence to go on with my life and I can do it with a big smile on my face. I am not a victim, and I never was—I am a victor!

May your joys be as deep as the ocean, your sorrows as light as its foam.

~Author unknown

Glossary

Backstay: A *backstay* is a part of the rigging that supports the mast, running from the masthead to the stern of the boat.

Bare poled: A *bare-poled* sailboat has no sails flying. Her masts are bare.

Barkentine: A *barkentine* is a three-masted ship having the foremast (the forward mast) square-rigged and the mainsail and mizzen fore- and aft-rigged.

Bascule bridge: A *bascule bridge* is sometimes called a drawbridge and is a movable bridge with a counterweight that balances the span, or leaf. *Bascule* is French for balance. The bascule is the most common type of movable bridge because it opens quickly and requires relatively little energy to operate. A bascule bridge may be single leaf or double leaf.

Bend: *Bend* means to prepare a sail for hoisting, to rig.

Bosun's chair: A *bosun's* chair is a seat used to hoist a person aloft to repair rigging.

Bowsprit: A *bowsprit* is a spar extending forward from the bow.

Cut: A *cut* is a waterway between two spits of land. On the ICW many rivers are connected by cuts, narrow and straight man-made waterways.

Dragging: *Dragging* means to drag the anchor along the bottom so that your boat is allowed to drift with the current or the wind.

Founder: To *founder* means to sink.

Freeboard: The *freeboard* of a boat is the distance from the deck to the water.

Jacklines: *Jacklines* are lines run on deck onto which a safety harness is clipped.

Jib: A *jib* is a triangular sail, set on the headstay at the front of the boat.

Jibe: To *jibe* is to change direction when sailing with the wind aft, so that the wind comes on a different quarter and the boom swings over to the opposite side; and accidental jibe can be dangerous.

Glossary

Halyard: A *halyard* is a line used to raise a sail.

Head: A *head* onboard a boat is the toilet.

Headstay: A *headstay* is a part of the rigging that supports the mast and the jib sail.

Launch: *Launch* has two meanings: *launch* means to move the boat into the water from land; a *launch* is a powerboat used as a ferry between land and a moored boat.

Lee or leeward: To *leeward* is the direction away from the wind.

Luffing: To *luff* a sail is to bring the sailboat into the wind so that the sail trembles, or luffs.

Mainsail: A *mainsail* is the sail hoisted on the back side of the mainmast and is pronounced "mains'l."

Markers/Day markers: *Markers* and *day markers* are aids to navigation. They mark navigable channels and waterways.

On the hard: A boat *on the hard* is a boat on land and not on the water.

Pot warp: A *pot warp* is the line attached to a crab or lobster trap.

Pooped: A boat that is *pooped* is filled with a huge amount of sea water and is under the threat of sinking.

PFD: A *PFD* is a personal flotation device.

Rafting or Rafted: *Rafting* is a mooring procedure when two or more boats are tied up side-by-side at a dock or on an anchor.

Ranges: *Ranges* are a pair of aids to navigation placed a distance apart, with the far marker mounted higher than the near one. When the range marks are in line, the vessel is in the channel.

Reefed: A *reefed* sail is one that's area is reduced. Sails are reefed in strong and gusty winds.

Roller furler: A *roller furler* is a method of stowing sails by rolling them up.

Rode: *Rode* is the anchor line which may be line (fiber rope), chain, or wire rope.

Schooner: A *schooner* is a sailing vessel with two or more masts, with the foremast shorter than the mainmast.

Scope: *Scope* is the ratio of anchor rode let out and the depth of the water.

Sea cock: A *sea cock* is a through-hull fitting with a valve that can shut off the flow of water between the boat's interior and exterior.

Shake-down cruise: A *shake-down cruise* is a short cruise or a series of short cruises to work out any small problems that might occur on a longer cruise.

Sloop: A *sloop* is a sailboat that has a single mast and flies a mainsail and a single jib.

Tender: A *tender* is a small boat accompanying a yacht or other pleasure boat used to transport people, gear, and supplies. Also, a vessel is deemed *tender* if she is unstable.

Transom: A boat's *transom* is the stern (back) of a boat.

VHF-FM Radio: VHF communications are basically limited to line-of-sight between the transmitting and receiving antennas, which means that the average ship-to-ship range is 10 to 15 miles. Mine is a hand-held unit and I used it to radio the bridge tenders, lockmasters, and other boats.

Wing-by-wing: *Wing-by-wing* means to sail before the wind with the sails set on both sides of the boat.

A short description of the numbers in the heading of each day's travel:

A Great Big Adventure on a Good Little Boat

The numbers at the heading of my day's travel represent the latitude and longitude of my position at the end of each day. Lines of latitude and longitude provide a precise means of defining a position on the surface of the earth. Latitude lines encircle the earth in an east-west direction and measure distances north and south of the equator, with the equator at 0°. These lines are measured in degrees, thus the symbol °. Each degree is divided into 60 minutes (60') and each minute is divided into 60 seconds. Every degree change is 60 miles. One minute of latitude is equal to one nautical mile. A nautical mile equals 1.15 statute mile. A knot is a speed of one nautical mile per hour.

The longitude lines or meridians run from north to south through the earth's poles. Distances to east or west of the prime meridian, which passes through Greenwich, England, is designated as 0° longitude. As with degrees of latitude, degrees of longitude are divided onto 60 minutes and each minute is divided into 60 seconds. The left and right margins on charts indicate latitude scales, while those on the top and bottom of the chart are longitude scales; you can pinpoint any position on a chart by using these scales.

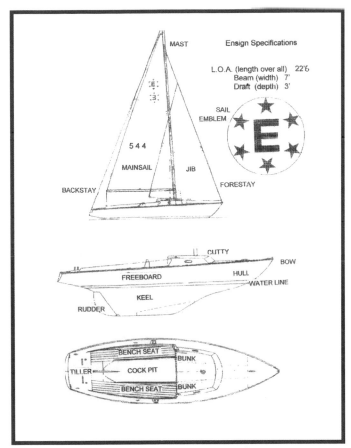

Ensign Specifications

L.O.A. (length over all) 22'6
Beam (width) 7'
Draft (depth) 3'

Ensign Specifications

A Great Big Adventure on a Good Little Boat

To read more about Linda Petrat and to follow her on her next adventure, please visit AGoodLittleBoat.com.